Hearing a Different Drummer

To My Dear Friend Ronda with affection

Hearing a Different Drummer

A Holocaust Survivor's Search for Identity

By Benjamin Hirsch

Mercer University Press
Macon, Georgia
2000

ISBN 0-86554-688-6
MUP/H508

© Benjamin Hirsch
Published by Mercer University Press
6316 Peake Road
Macon, Georgia 31210-3960
All rights reserved
2000

First Edition.

∞The paper used in this publication meets the minimum requirements
of American National Standard for Information Sciences—Permanence
of Paper for Printed Library Materials, ANSI Z39.48-1984.

Library of Congress Cataloging-in-Publication Data

CIP data are available from the Library of Congress

If a man does not keep pace with his companions,

perhaps it is because he hears a different drummer.

Let him step to the music he hears,

however measured or far away.

Henry David Thoreau, 1854

Walden

This book is dedicated to the memory of my beloved mother, Mathilda Auerbach Hirsch, whose courage and foresight made it possible for my four siblings and me to survive the Holocaust and to make meaningful lives for ourselves;

my dear father, Dr. Hermann Hirsch, who left me a legacy of community responsibility, concern for my fellow man, and a belief in God;

and my dear brother and sister, Werner and Roselene Hirsch, whose wanton murder I still cannot and never will accept;

and the million and a half other innocent Jewish children who were victims of the Holocaust.

—Benjamin Hirsch
Atlanta, Georgia

CONTENTS

FOREWORD

I CANNOT PROVE THIS, BUT I AM convinced that most survivors of the Holocaust, whether they experienced the horrors of the Death Camps, the Concentration Camps and/or Labor Camps, or survived in hiding, have felt, at one time or another, that the reason they survived is to tell their story, thereby bearing witness to the systematic, bureaucratic annihilation of six million Jews by the Nazis. I include myself in this generalization.

By the time I was nine years old, I had lived in six countries on two continents. I arrived in New York Harbor in September, 1941 with my two older sisters. My two older brothers were already in Atlanta, Georgia, and within three weeks after our arrival in the U.S., we were also in Atlanta. The war in Europe was in full force, but America had not yet entered what came to be known as World War II. The other war in Europe, the War Against the Jews, which later became known as the Holocaust, had been grinding along since before Kristallnacht.

I am a child survivor, who along with my two older sisters and two older brothers, was sent away from home in Frankfurt am Main, Germany, by our mother who tried to shield us from harm. We were in hiding for 2 1/2 years in France and ultimately escaped to the United States of America. Our parents, as well as our younger brother and sister who were infants at the time we were sent away, perished in the Nazi Death Camps. Even though I did not personally suffer through the Camp experience, just being torn away from home and family, being shuttled from place to place in an attempt to escape the Nazi onslaught, and ultimately being confronted with the death of my loved ones, carries its own form of permanent suffering. The pain of the murder of my family, among six million of my people, is as real as if I had suffered through all of the horrors that I have felt compelled to read, study, and speak about all these years.

For over twenty-five years, my way of bearing witness has been to accept any opportunity to address schools, churches or civic groups to relate personal Holocaust experiences, to enlighten them on the history of the War Against the Jews, and to discuss with them the implications of the Holocaust as it relates to today's society. My first opportunity to speak on this subject came when I was asked to be a keynote speaker for a BBYO (B'nai B'rith Youth Organization) weekend, entitled "Lest We Forget." I argued with the BBYO director, when he asked me to speak, saying that I had not been in a Concentration Camp or Death Camp, and therefore I would not be considered to be a Survivor. He insisted, persuasively, that I had a story to tell and a message to give. I spoke and realized that he, Yoni Werzberger, was correct.

A good procrastinator never does today what can be put off until tomorrow. One drizzly day in 1983, I was on my way to an appointment, when my car hydroplaned off a rain slicked clover leaf intersection between two highways. In the few seconds that my car was soaring in flight, I thought of all the things I had not done, including leaving my story. The car plopped down in the soft ground of a marshy area around the newly built clover leaf ramp, and I just sat there, buckled in my seat belt, making a mental check of all my body parts to make sure that everything was there, accounted for and functioning. I breathed a sigh of relief and looked around. There was no one there that had witnessed the miracle. I had survived, unscathed, a mishap that by all logic should have killed me or at least left me severely hurt and totaled my car.

After forcing the door open, I stepped out of the car into calf deep mud. I positioned myself to flag down any on coming motorist. I reflected on the flight pattern of the car, the unlikelihood of surviving such a stunt and the realization that my time just hadn't come yet. I figured that there must still be more for me to do, but what? A kind motorist took me to a service station that was known to have a wrecker. I thought along the way that this was not the first time that I had survived against the odds and resolved to make plans to write my story. I was thirty minutes late for my meeting.

Eight years and many speaking engagements later, in May of 1991, a conference entitled "The Hidden Child" was held in New York City. I was among the over 1,500 Child Survivors that showed up at this conference. Some had been in the Camps, the majority had been in hiding. The term Child Survivor was coined at that conference. After years of being told that we had been too young at the time to remember or to have been affected by what was going on, we were finally being seen and heard. All of us were exhorted to write our stories and I promised some of my newly found friends that some day soon I would.

My first attempt at writing was a short story about a particularly moving event. That came easily. Starting on more detailed memoirs of the early years in my life, however, was a much more difficult task. The fact is, I couldn't get it to flow. I have much selective memory, considering the fact that I was four months old when Hitler came to power, and only six years of age when I left Germany.

Long before I thought about writing my childhood experiences during the Holocaust, I had the idea to write about my experiences in the military, during the time of the Korean Conflict. My 21 months, 12 days, 4 hours and 23 minutes tour of duty in the U.S. Army not only helped me see the world as it is, but taught me that humor can be found anywhere, under almost any conditions, and that life can be so much more livable when we can learn to appreciate the humor of it.

So I put aside the memoirs of my earlier life and started on my army stories. The army stories began to flow in spite of the forty years that had lapsed. Writing should be fun. I wasn't having fun in my earlier attempts at writing memoirs, at least not until I started to tackle a segment of my life that had humor, even though it had been no bed of roses. Most importantly, I began to realize that, as in my life growing up in Atlanta, Georgia, whatever I did, whether as soldier, student or professional, I did as a survivor of the Holocaust. My actions and reactions were influenced by that reality. I have never tried to escape what I am, never wanted to, and couldn't if I tried.

As a teenager growing up in Atlanta, I tried so hard to fit in to the world around me that I started slowly giving up the essence of what made me what I am, a Jew and survivor of the Holocaust. I had long since given up wearing a kippa, except to pray. I was working on the Sabbath and was no longer restricting my dietary intake to Kosher food. It was while I was in the army that non-

Jewish soldiers, with a thirst for knowledge about Jewish practices, started asking me questions that I could not answer. They helped me come to the realization that I was turning my back on the religion for which my mother, father, brother and sister had been killed. I was doing it without full knowledge of what I was giving up. This realization turned my life around. It made me resolve to delve sufficiently into traditional observant Judaism, so that if I ever decided to give it up, I would be doing it with full knowledge of what was being given away. In the process, I became much more committed to bearing witness.

This book, therefore, relates my trials and tribulations as an orphaned child survivor of the Holocaust, as I went through service in the United States Army, an experience that turned out to be an important segment of my life and one which I found that I had little or no control over. In that respect, at least to some degree, it was not too different from the first nine years of my life. The major difference is that there was a light at the end of the tunnel, a given date on which the ordeal would be over, and even though there was a relatively small amount of suffering, there was humor at almost every step along the way.

AUTHOR'S NOTE: In telling my story of my Army experience some of the names have been changed to protect the privacy of the individuals.

ACKNOWLEDGEMENTS

FEW WORTHWHILE ENDEAVORS CAN BE ACHIEVED WITHOUT the encouragement of others. When I decided to write my story, I was blessed with interested and caring friends who encouraged me even during my periods of self doubt.

My brother Jack, when just the mechanics of committing my thoughts to writing seemed insurmountable, provided me with a computer. He and my sister-in-law Gladys were a source of strength every step along the way.

My sister Sarah (Shartar) inspired me early on to chronicle my army experiences, about which I had been writing her during my military service. After my discharge from the U.S. Army, she elicited a promise from me to write the stories down before I might forget them. While I am sorry I didn't heed her suggestion while she was alive, I never forgot that promise and her suggestion was a catalyst for this book.

I want to thank my wife Jacqueline, our children Shoshanah, Adina, Michal and Raphael and our grandchildren for bearing with me while I took time away from them to work on this manuscript.

Special thanks go to Ida Selavan Schwartz who is my oldest daughter's mother-in-law, Jane Leavey the director of the Breman Jewish Heritage Museum in Atlanta, and my niece Sue Ann Pliner for their review of the manuscript at its various stages and the encouragement they gave me to continue.

I owe a debt of gratitude to my agent, Alan Garner, who after reading the manuscript, encouraged and guided me in preparing the manuscript for publication. His dedication to getting my story published went beyond encouragement.

Many thanks to my dear cousin Helen Auerbach Rosenthal for clarifying her story, providing her father's Holocaust memoirs, contributing photos and for being there when I needed her; to my brother Asher for the pictures of his and Henny's wedding.

I want to recognize and thank the professionals who helped me:

Michael Lenarz, Archivist of the Jewish Museum in Frankfurt A/Main, Germany for his assistance with my research and for finding the deportation list which included my mother, brother and sister. The lady archivist at Sachsenhausen (whose name I did not get), for helping me research the final days of my father's life; Dr. Kruger, Zehlendorf Branch Director of the Federal Archives in Berlin, for his clarification of the data in the *Gedenkbuch*; Jan Parcer, Archivist and Teresa Swoboka, Exhibits Curator at Auschwitz for assisting me in researching the murders of my father, mother, brother, and sister in Auschwitz; Ann Weiss of "Eyes From The Ashes" for finding the photographs in Auschwitz that included the one of my siblings, Werner and Roselene; Adaire Klein, Research Librarian at the Wiesenthal Center in Los Angeles, for making the entire Ann Weiss collection of 2400 photographs available to me and for providing a clear blow-up of the photo of Werner and Roselene; and Dr. William Helmreich for his insightful editorial comments and suggestions.

Most of all, I thank God Almighty for allowing me to live long enough to document these stories. May it be His will that this book be only the beginning.

Benjamin Hirsch
Atlanta, Georgia

Mathilda Auerbach Hirsch & Hermann
Hirsch. My mother and father at either
their engagement or after their wedding
(c. 1924).

My mother and father holding their first child Blimel
(Flora) Hirsch Speigel
(c. 1926).

Hirsch children playing on a sled. Left to right: Gustl
(Sarah), Anselm (Asher), and Blimel (Flora).

Hirsch family portrait, late 1937. Ben on father's lap, Dr.
Hermann Hirsch, Gustl (Sarah) standing, Werner on
mother's lap, Mathilda Hirsch, Blimel (Flora) standing,
Jack sitting, and Anselm (Asher) standing. Roselene was
born March 1938.

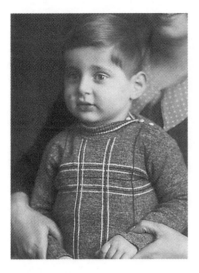

Werner (Shmuel Moshe) Hirsch. My brother as I last saw him.

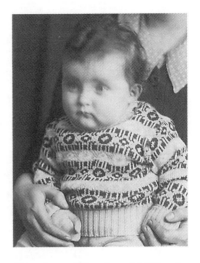

Roselene (Shoshanah) Hirsch. My sister as I last saw her.

Mathilda Auerbach Hirsch, mid 1930s. She is the hero of our survival story.

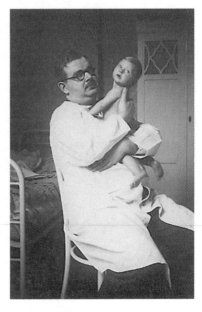

Uncle Philipp Auerbach holding Helen as a baby, around January 1934, in Brussels, Belgium.

Werner and Roselene with caretaker (c. 1939).

The Friedberger—Anlage Synagogue. I stood across the street with my cousin Arno on 10 November 1938, along with scores of onlookers, as destruction of the synagogue was in progresss.

COMPANHIA COLONIAL DE NAVEGAÇÃO

Paquete «Mousinho»   Tonelagem bruta 8.374

S. S. Mouzinho, the Portugese liner that Ben, Sarah, and Flora boarded in August 1941. Asher and Jack boarded same ship in June 1941. Both voyages traveled from Lisbon, Portugal, to New York Harbor.

Helen Auerbach in Cuba (c. 1941). (Photo courtesy of Helen Auerbach Rosenthal.)

Aunt Martha Auerbach (Helen's mother) in Cuba (c. 1941). (Photo courtesy of Helen Auerbach Rosenthal.)

AFFIDAVIT IN LIEU OF PASSPORT

REPUBLIC OF FRANCE
DEPARTMENT OF BOUCHES DU RHONE
CITY OF MARSEILLE
CONSULATE OF THE UNITED STATES
OF AMERICA
} SS.

Before me, G. McMurtrie Godley Vice Consul of the United States of America, in and for the district of Marseille, France, duly commissioned and qualified, personally appeared Benjamin HIRSCH who, being duly sworn, deposes and says :

That this full name is Benjamin HIRSCH and resides at Marseille, France.

That he was born on Sept.19, 1932 at Francfort s.M., Germany

That he is single, married to

That he is the bearer of no valid passport or other document for travel to the United States because the French authorities stated that they were unable to provide him with an official travel document prior to the date on which he must depart for the United States as arranged by U.S. Committee for the Protection of European Children.

That this affidavit has been executed to serve in lieu of a passport to allow him to proceed to the United States.

DESCRIPTION :

Height : 4' 2"
Weight : 44 lbs
Hair : fair
Eyes : grey
Marks : none
Complexion : medium

Hirsch Benj.

Subscribed and sworn to before me this 8th day of August - 1941.

G. McMurtrie Godley
Vice Consul of the United States
of America.

Service No 7439
No Fee Prescribed

Benajmin Hirsch, August 1941.

Hoke Smith High School Class picture (c. 1949). Ben on top row hearing a different drummer.

Uncle Philipp (2nd from right) at Henry and Asher's wedding dinner, Basel, Switzerland, 1949.

Private E-2 Benjamin Hirsch in Class
A Army uniform (c. 1954).

Ben in fatigues, shaving during war
games in Yakama Desert, Washington
(June 1954).

Philipp Auerbach in New York on business (c. 1950).

Dr. Philipp Auerbach, paramedic for Red Cross in Dusseldorf, 1945. (Photo courtesy of Helen Auerbach Rosenthal.)

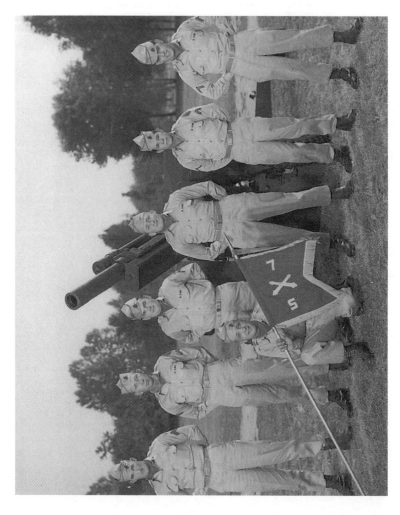

Ben's platoon, Svc. Battery, 7th Field Artillery Battery. Ben is third from right. Germany, July 1955.

Cast photo of Ben for the play "Time of Your Life," by William Saroyan. The photo was displayed in the marquis sign of Atlanta Women's Club Theater, c. 1956. Kirk Douglas's "Lust for Life" was playing at the 13th Street Theater across the street. (Photo by Helen Burke Studios)

Helen Auerbach Rosenthal and Ben at a family reception in New York, March 1965. (Photo courtesy of Helen Auerbach Rosenthal.)

Family picture at Raphael Hirsch's (Ben's son) Bar Mitzvah, Atlanta, Georgia, 1982. L to R: Jack Hirsch, Flora Hirsch Spiegel, Claire Heyman (who stayed at our parents' house from 1939-1941), Ben Hirsch, and Asher Hirsch.

This picture, which was among the 2,500 snapshots discovered by Ann Weiss at Auschwitz in the 1980s, is believed to be Werner (left) and Roselene Hirsch (c. 1942).

L to R: Helen Samuels, Ben Hirsch, and Nathan Samuels, Jerusalem, December 1998. The Samuels' had taken into their home in Paris, France, six-year-old Ben, sixty years earlier in December 1938.

Ben Hirsch, architect of the Holocaust Gallery at the William Bremen Jewish Heritage Museum.

Ben Hirsch's sketch of Zugspitze, 7 June 1955.

Ben Hirsch's sketch of Bavarian Inn, Garmisch, 7 June 1955.

Man in Bavarian clothing waited for Ben to finish the sketch before leaving in a huff.

Memorial to the Six Million. Built in 1965. Next to Memorial is buried "the four bars of soap."

1

WOULD A SANE PERSON VOLUNTEER?

YOU HAVE TO WONDER IF ANYONE IN his right mind would volunteer for the draft in the midst of the Korean Conflict, when all he had to do to avoid being drafted was continue his college education and stay in the upper 15% of his class. The fact is, I needed a change. I mean, "How many years straight can you go to school without a break?" And then there was the money. It was getting harder and harder to hold down a job in the afternoon and evening while taking a full load of courses in the Architectural School of Georgia Tech. If I volunteered for the draft, I would be eligible for the G.I. Bill to help support me while I finished college after my tour of duty—and, was architecture really the field I wanted to be in? After all, I had started out as an Art major at the Atlanta Division of the University of Georgia and switched to Georgia Tech at the suggestion of one of my friends.

All these things went through my mind before I visited the draft board in September of 1953, just after completing a tedious summer quarter to finish my sophomore year at Tech. Of course, there was one more thing, the nagging feeling that I'd had since the news came in 1945 that the war in Europe was over. Over—before I was old enough to volunteer for the armed services so I could go over there and fight those bastards who were murdering my people. It really wasn't fair. I had dreamed and dreamed of getting revenge and now it was over, without me.

The people at the draft board were very accommodating. They gave me a choice of dates for reporting to be inducted and I chose October 22nd. It was too late to help win World War II, but with luck I could get sent to Germany and try to find Werner and Rosalene, my younger brother and sister.

I had been informed, in 1947, when I was fifteen years old, that in the fall of 1943 my younger brother and sister had been seen going into the "showers," along with my mother, in the notorious death camp called Auschwitz. I had been told that my uncle, Philipp Auerbach, witnessed the procession and that my loved ones, as well as the other naked prisoners waiting in line to be deloused, had no idea that lethal gas would be emitted from the showerheads. When I last saw them, I was six years old. Werner was eighteen months and Roselene was about six months old. My father had been arrested a month earlier on Kristallnacht and taken to Buchenwald. Kristallnacht, "The Night of Broken Glass," occurred on 9-10 November 1938. It was a state sponsored and coordinated attack on the Jews and Jewish establishments of Germany and Austria. As a result, my mother decided to send the five oldest of her seven children to France for safety.

The details of my father's demise in the Oranienburg/ Sachsenhausen Concentration Camp in 1942 were also given to me on that day in 1947 when my oldest brother, Asher, told us what he had found out from the International Red Cross, during his search for our family while he was serving as a U.S. soldier in Germany. For some reason, I could accept the fact that my mother and father were dead, but I could not accept the thought that little Werner and Roselene were no longer alive. Who could kill such adorable baby children? After all, there was no real proof that they were dead, and isn't it possible that someone made a mistake and Werner and Roselene were wandering aimlessly around Europe trying to find where they belong? I had to try, or die trying.

October 22, 1953 came quickly. I was ordered to report for induction at the army base in Chamblee, Georgia, and did so without a great deal of enthusiasm, but with a resolve to try and make the best of the two years I had obligated myself to serve. It was a hot fall day, a perfect day to get indoctrinated into the essence of army life—"hurry up and wait." For someone who cannot stand waiting in line, the army should be avoided like a plague. I had brought reading material along, but the noise of my fellow inductees and the stifling heat was not conducive to reading, or relaxation for that matter.

There were only a small handful of us from the Atlanta area, and most seemed to be from South Georgia. I started talking to one guy from Cairo, Georgia, who informed me that he was the champion grapefruit picker of his county. What he lacked in education he made up for in resourcefulness. It was about 11:00 A.M. and he was hungry. Demanding to be fed, he was told that lunch would not be until noon. To get around that problem, he climbed up on a chair, changed the clock to read 12:00 and again demanded to be fed. His vociferous outbursts convinced the army personnel that this man had no doubt that changing a clock actually changed the time of day. Before the day was over, he was deemed unfit to serve and was sent home to Cairo. They had questioned his IQ. Many of us considered him to be brilliant.

Michael Hobgood and I agreed that this guy knew what he was doing all along. I had met Hobgood early on that day. He had been checking out the list and pointed out that he and I were the only ones that had completed high school. Our grapefruit picker illustrated to us that intelligence is not an exclusive attribute acquired by graduating from high school. With all the paperwork, procedures and waiting in various lines, it was good to have Hobgood to talk to. Among the things we had in common was a propensity for pulling tricks and playing practical jokes on unsuspecting victims. One of those tricks ended up haunting me, off and on, until my discharge from the army in August 1955, and even beyond.

I was standing in a line, reading a magazine, when a young recruit came up to me and asked, "Is it true that Kirk Douglas is your brother?" I looked up, startled, and noticed Hobgood, about twenty feet away, motioning to me to go along with the gag. Picking up on the chance to pull a fast one, I threw my magazine to the floor feigning disgust and muttering loudly "Damn! I told him not to tell anyone!" That little stunt had the desired effect, at least the effect that Hobgood had been hoping for to pull off this caper. All of the recruits and some of the permanent personnel at the Chamblee base were convinced of my "true secret identity."

My new celebrity status did not exempt me from the indignities of the pre-induction physical. At the onset, I informed the medics that I had been classified 4F (physically unfit) by Air Force ROTC at Georgia Tech. In reality, the instructors at Tech didn't know what to do with a candidate for advanced ROTC who was not yet a citizen of the U.S., and was born in a foreign country that had recently been at war with ours. Therefore, they searched for ways to disqualify me even though I had done well in my freshman ROTC courses. I was asked why I had been disqualified. When I responded that I had flat feet and chronic bronchitis, they said, "No problem, we'll cure you." I had to doubt the sincerity of that response, but what recourse does an army inductee have? I was volunteering, and to this day I don't know why I seemed to be unvolunteering. After the infamous spreading of the cheeks, I was told to go down a hallway and then someone yelled "Hey you!" I turned around and he said, "You just passed your hearing test." I was beginning to feel this was not the Mayo Clinic.

Before taking the eye test, I informed them that my glasses had been broken a few days before and that my optometrist had suggested that I wait and have the army issue me a new pair of glasses. "No problem, just read the chart." I cautioned them that I was far sighted and thus could read the chart as if I had 20/20 vision, when in fact, I was blind as a bat at close range. "No problem, we'll just mark it down on your chart, and you can report for sick call at your assigned base and then ask to be fitted for glasses." They were so reassuring that I actually believed them.

It turns out that Chamblee was just pre-induction. Fort Jackson, South Carolina, was our induction base and our first real taste of what it was like to be army property. Glasses were out of the question. I was told to wait until Basic Training. In the meantime, we were subjected to a series of written tests to presumably evaluate our intelligence quotient and skills potential. We were herded from one formation to another, with sergeants competing to see who could be the cruelest and most debasing. The idea, I was told, was to take away our illusions of being independent thinkers. The hair-cutting scenario helped bring that point home. The barber sat me down and calmly asked how I would like my hair to be cut. Naively, I requested that he take a little off the top, trim the sideburns and leave the sides alone. As he said, "OK," he proceeded to practice his sheep shearing techniques on my head. The last time I had looked like that was when our heads were shaved in the children's home in France, because of lice.

IN THE MIDST OF THIS PLANNED CHAOS, we were fitted for uniforms and shoes. A master sergeant measured my feet and proceeded to give me size nine shoes and boots. I explained that while my feet measured for a size nine, I actually needed a 10-C because of a long vamp. I added that I had been a shoe salesman for about four years and that this unusual requirement in my shoe size had been determined by a shoe expert. This was yet another lesson in my crash course on how to survive in the army. A lowly private never corrects or offers information to a noncommissioned officer. He insisted that I wear a size nine, and to support this decision, allowed that he had been fitting shoes for seventeen years, as if it mattered. I responded that I had been wearing shoes for almost twenty-one years and that my intimate knowledge of my feet, backed by the expertise I had sought to resolve my shoe size problem, qualified me to offer an opinion on my shoe size. The sergeant was not impressed or amused. He called in the ranking officer, a colonel, to hear me out. The officer appeared to listen to my concerns about my feet and then threatened to have me court-martialed if I did not accept and wear the boots and dress shoes issued by the sergeant. I thought about these two people often, especially during long marches as my feet cramped, my corns and calluses hurt and my calves ached, and I had unkind thoughts and questions regarding their ancestry.

Fort Jackson was unique in many aspects, but the water supply to the bathrooms in the induction area took the prize. There were signs in the latrine warning users of the toilets to stand before flushing because the water used to flush the toilets was scalding hot. I can only surmise that this was done to weed out those soldiers with poor reading skills. The occasional blood curdling screams that were heard during our several days' stay in Fort Jackson bore that theory out. My guess is that the hospital treated two to three cases of scalded testicles for each group of recruits that went through this induction center. I wondered if they had a quota for this type of injury.

Sleep was never plentiful during my entire stint in the army, but at Fort Jackson it was virtually nonexistent. By the time we got to lie down, it must have been almost two in the morning. Reveille was at about 4:30 A.M. My body wasn't used to this type of rigor and I woke up in the morning with my face in a pool of blood. I was startled and concerned at the amount of blood that had come from my nose and asked our barracks sergeant if I could go on sick call to have my nose checked out. He reluctantly agreed to the sick call, but insisted that I pay for the pillow and pillow case since it was against army regulations to bleed on army equipment. I asked if that meant that I got to take the pillow and case with me since I had paid for it. Yet another lesson, logic is irrelevant in the army. He responded that questions like that are invitations to KP (Kitchen Patrol) and that I was welcome to take the pillow and case if I wished to be court-martialed. I was very happy to leave Fort Jackson in one piece and with only a cauterized nose and a bruised sense of my individual worth to show for my experiences.

So far, I seemed to be doing okay in my new occupation as an U.S. soldier. However, when I laid down at night I found myself thinking about those soldiers that I dreaded seeing as a young boy in Germany, those goose-stepping SS bastards who wouldn't think twice about killing an unarmed civilian without provocation. What kind of training did they and their Gestapo cohorts go through to become such instruments of evil? I anticipated that my basic training was going to be a rough and degrading experience, but I took heart in knowing that no matter how bad it might get, I would never allow myself to lose my humanity.

2

WOMAN OF VALOR

IT WAS ON KRISTALLNACHT, NOVEMBER 9–10, 1938, that I, a six-year-old German Jewish child, watched as our synagogue, the Friedberger Anlage Shule, was being destroyed. It was also on that day that the Nazis came to our house to arrest our father, Dr. Hermann Hirsch, a lay leader of the Frankfurt a/M Jewish community. They came in with uniformed S.S. men, plainclothes men and German police dogs. They confronted my mother, Mathilda Auerbach Hirsch, who was holding Rosalene, my six months old baby sister, and told her to have my father come to the door. When she told them that Dr. Hirsch was not home, a plain clothed Gestapo soldier quickly grabbed Rosalene and threw the baby to the floor. He then pulled out a pistol and pointed it at Roselene and matter-of-factly told my mother that if my Dad did not appear within 30 seconds, he would first shoot Rosalene, then shoot each of my mother's other children, one at a time, by age, so she would watch her children die before he would shoot her. Within seconds, my father appeared from his hiding place, was arrested, and taken to Buchenwald. I never saw my father again.

Many Jews had already fled Germany, some when Hitler came to power in 1933, others left after the Nuremberg Laws took effect in September 1935, while others left as the quality of life for Jews in Germany continued to deteriorate. My father felt that the threat to Jews in Germany and Austria, at that time, was no different than during the purges of European Jews over the last seven centuries, and that, as in other times, these bad times would pass. He was also one of the last, if not the last, Jewish dentist still practicing in and around Frankfurt. This not only played on his heightened sense of duty; it also improved his dental practice, which had been suffering from the government-sponsored boycott of Jewish businesses. Counter to my mother's thoughts of sending some of the children out of Germany for safety, he felt strongly that our family should stay together, until all of this mess was over.

It was after Dad's incarceration on Kristallnacht that Mom decided to go against his wishes and seek a way to send her children to safety, at least the children in the family who were old enough to travel alone. She found out about a KinderTransport that was leaving for Paris in early December, just a few weeks after Dad's arrest. The KinderTransports were part of an exchange student system that had been in place for some years. It was for Jewish school children, up to age thirteen, and went to places like London and Paris. She was able to book the five oldest children, including Flora, who was already thirteen. Ordinarily, a thirteen year old would not have been allowed to be a part of this program, but since I was only six and there were other equally young children signed up, Flora was allowed to go as a helper for the younger children.

We left for Paris on the KinderTransport on December 5, 1938. I still remember seeing Mom cry at the Banhof (train station), as she put us on the train and waved goodbye. My older brothers and sisters cried too, but I was so excited with the anticipation of a trip to Paris that I could not fathom everyone's sadness. That was the last time I saw my mother, my baby brother and my baby sister. That may not have been Mom's plan, but that's the way it turned out. If I had understood, I would have cried too.

When we arrived in Paris, I was immediately separated from my brothers and sisters. Flora and Gustl (Sarah) went to stay with Uncle Gusti, Dad's brother, while Anselm (Asher) and Bob (Jack) were put in a religious boarding school that was run by cousins of my father. I was supposed to be placed with Uncle Yacqui, Dad's youngest brother, but something fell through and I was taken in by people not related to us, Helen and Nathan Samuels, a very kind family with a three year old daughter, Fannie.

Our stay in Paris was short lived. The word was out that the Germans would be attacking France any day and that they would head straight for Paris. French Jews were aware that Jews would not be safe in German occupied areas, so plans were made to evacuate them from areas vulnerable to German occupation. An organization was founded to create a network of children's homes for Jewish children made parentless by the Nazis' "War against the Jews." In the section of France that included Paris, Dr. Ernst Papanek was put in charge of this effort and the organization, Oeuvre des Secours aux Enfants (O.S.E.), started operating almost immediately. I was sent to Villa Helvetia in Montmorency while the Samuels went into hiding somewhere in the French countryside.

Montmorency is just north of Paris, so our stay there was temporary at best. From there I was sent to Chateau de Magillier, another children's home under the jurisdiction of O.S.E. Magillier was in Creuse, a rural town in the south central region of France. It was there that I developed a healthy appreciation of air raid shelters and an aversion to oatmeal or farina. I gag at the thought of lumpy cold cereal that was intended to be hot and smooth. I also learned to eat everything on my plate, no matter how repulsive it might be, but with the exception of oatmeal and farina. I learned to eat stale bread because it's better than none at all. I learned to catch 20 flies in one swoop of the hand, and to walk in the snow in sabots, (wooden shoes). I learned to not cry at night. I never did learn how to stop worrying about my family, and where they were.

In May of 1941, I was told to pack my few belongings and board a bus for Marseilles where I was to meet my two brothers and participate in an escape route out of Europe. After almost two and a half years, it felt good being with my brothers again. Just before we were to board a train for Spain, I came down with severe stomach cramps. I was diagnosed as having appendicitis and I was left behind. I was very upset. I couldn't stay in Marseilles, so they sent me to Chateau de Morrelles at Brout Vernet, the O.S.E. home where my two sisters were staying.

Brout Vernet was just outside of Vichy, the capital of "Free France," the collaborationist government of Marshall Henri

Petain. I stayed in Morrelles less than three months, long enough to get a taste of having motherly authoritative figures in my life again. In August, my sisters and I were told to board a bus for Marseilles to be part of the second group that would attempt the same escape route out of Europe. We boarded the train for Spain that traveled through the Pyrenees Mountains and through the Spanish countryside to Madrid.

We arrived in Madrid after dark to avoid detection by German espionage agents, and were taken to a Catholic Convent to spend the night. We were awakened very early the next morning, so that the train could leave before the sun was up. Our next destination was Lisbon, Portugal, where we stayed at some sort of religious institution for about two weeks until the boat was ready to sail. The S. S. Mouzinho was a Portuguese liner, the same boat that was used for the first escape voyage. As it turned out, our voyage would be the last escape using the route we took. Somehow the Nazis had found out about the route and closed it off.

I had wondered why we were chosen to participate in this escape when so many others were left behind. Somewhere I heard or read that Dr. Ernst Papanek had escaped to America and soon after his arrival in New York, placed a full page ad in a New York newspaper listing the names of the over 300 children in the O.S.E. homes in France. The ad purportedly exhorted readers that if they could recognize any of the children as relatives, they should work through a local welfare organization to sponsor that child's entrance into the United States. It appears that there was a small window in the steel wall that blocked the immigration of European Jews to the U.S. If a Jewish European child, under the age of 16, was the relative of an American citizen and his or her support had been vouched for to guarantee that the child would not be on welfare, that Jewish child would be allowed to enter the United States of America.

A first cousin of my mother's, Rabbi Selig Auerbach, had a pulpit in Rome, Georgia. I was told that he read an ad in a New York newspaper, recognized our names and went to Atlanta to seek assistance in finding a support system for the five children of his cousin. The Atlanta Jewish community had an agency called the Hebrew Orphans' Home, which actually had been an orphanage until 1930. The name was retained until 1948 when it was changed to the Jewish Children's Service. In 1941, it already had been an organization that placed orphaned Jewish children into Jewish foster homes and monitored their progress. Rabbi Auerbach spoke to the director, Mrs. Armand Wyle, about us, and she agreed to have her agency sponsor the five Hirsch children. Those were the circumstances, I believed for many years that brought us to Atlanta, Georgia.

3

THERE'S NOTHING BASIC IN BASIC TRAINING

We arrived at Camp Gordon in Augusta, Georgia, for eight weeks of Infantry Basic Training and were assigned to a company that would be starting its eight-week cycle in fourteen days. This gave us two weeks of what was called "pre-basic" to get used to our new environment. Actually it was two weeks of getting the place ready by pulling all sorts of work details to fix up the company grounds, doing menial work for other areas of the base that needed manual labor, and getting used to being under the total domination of our company commander, a first lieutenant, and his staff of non-coms (a non-commissioned officer) who had recently returned from the front in Korea.

Hobgood and I were assigned to the same barracks and often went on details together. Most of the assignments were janitorial in nature or cleaning up grounds or K.P. Everywhere we went we had to line up in formation and march, even for latrine duty. After about a week of laborious details, formations, and getting used to taking orders for the sake of taking orders, a small group of us, five or six guys, were assigned to clean an Intelligence Office. It was a small wooden structure and the department was manned by a sergeant, a draftsman who had the most advanced drafting equipment I had ever seen and his superior officer, a second lieutenant named Zimmerman.

I was really fascinated with the array of drafting equipment. I had been to Architectural and engineering offices, but never had I seen such a well-equipped drafting room. He had every imaginable piece of equipment available to draftsmen, and I wanted to see it being used. While sweeping the floors, I fantasized about being able to spend my two-year stint as a draftsman with equipment like that. My co-flunkies had seen me doodle and sketch and decided to tell the sergeant that they had a major talent in their midst. Unlike the other details we had been on, the army personnel here were quite casual and had no qualms about talking to us as if we were human beings. The sergeant began talking about what he did and what his department was all about. He seemed interested in what my friends had said about me and asked if I could draw likenesses of people's faces. I told him that, as it turned out, one of my hobbies since I was a teenager was to sketch people every chance I had. He asked if I would be willing to make a sketch of him to back up my story.

When I sat down with pencil and paper, the sergeant was sitting across from me posing for his portrait and the other guys were looking over my shoulder, then the phone rang. The sergeant was wide eyed as he handed me the phone and said that the Post Commander, a Full Bird Colonel, wanted to speak with me. I picked up the receiver, thinking this was some kind of a joke, and I jumped to attention when Colonel Wade introduced himself. "I just want to welcome you to the base, and I want you to know that I think Kirk Douglas is one of the finest character actors in Hollywood." He added that the next time I speak to "my brother," aside from giving him regards, I should convince him to seek a script that would have him play the role of an infantry general. I didn't know whether to laugh or cry. I almost soiled my pants. I had almost forgotten about our harmless prank in Chamblee and the few times I was confronted with questions about "my brother" Kirk, I had just walked away saying I didn't want to talk about it. I thanked the colonel for his kind words and told him I would try to bring pride to the family by my performance in basic training. I hung up in a sweat and thought, "What a dumb thing to say!" This thing had gotten out of hand. I would have to get together with Hobgood to find a way to get out of this mess. Responding to the question in the sergeant's eyes, I told him that it probably was the commanding officer's policy to pick a recruit at random to welcome him to the base. Who knows if he bought that? At least I got us off the subject.

I started back on my sketching assignment as if nothing else was on my mind. About twenty minutes later, I handed the skeptical sergeant the finished sketch and I could tell that he was pleasantly surprised. He said he would hold on to it and told us to go back to our chores. Within the hour, Lt. Zimmerman came in and told the sergeant that he had heard that a celebrity was in their office. Fortunately, the sergeant was so anxious to show him the sketch that he ignored what the lieutenant had said. "I think we've found the portrait sketch artist we've been looking for, Sir," he blurted out as he shoved the sketch into Lt. Zimmerman's hand.

The lieutenant looked at the sketch. "Where did you find him? Get him back here, I want to talk to him right away."

"He's right there, Sir, sweeping your floor. Shall I bring him in?"

Lt. Zimmerman's enthusiasm was contagious. He wanted to know what outfit I was with and how long I had left to serve. When I told him that my outfit was in pre-basic, he said that if I didn't mind, he would get me out of basic training because his high priority need for a sketch artist was critical. I tried to stay calm and not show my excitement at the prospect of getting out of basic training, and having the job description of a sketch artist for an intelligence unit during my two-year stint in the army. All the other guys on the detail were so excited for me; it was hard for me to stay cool. What I was also excited about was getting away from my unit before this celebrity sham blew up in my face.

Lt. Zimmerman took my Company Commander's name and said he would take care of everything through channels. He assured me that approval for my transfer was just a formality and that I should be assigned to Intelligence within a few days. The march back to our barracks was more lively than the usual end of the day march. Like all good gossip, word got around fast about my impending good fortune, and a couple of guys even expressed sorrow that I wouldn't be around for Basic. Hobgood was happy for me and a little envious, but mostly he wondered who he could talk to and join forces with in his practical jokes.

After chow, I had a message that our C.O., Lt. Bonnette, wanted to see me. "Wow!" I thought, "Lt. Zimmerman works fast." I walked into the C.O.'s office, saluted him as I announced myself. "Private E-1 Hirsch reporting, Sir!"

"At Ease, Hirsch." He looked at me with steely eyes; "Lt. Zimmerman tells me you're an artist. Why didn't you tell me that you're an artist?"

"Sir, I do like to draw and I was an architectural student when I volunteered, but I'm not a professional artist, and I was never asked if I could draw."

"Well," he said as he stroked his chin, " Lt. Zimmerman needs an artist with your particular talents, but then I also need an artist." He paused for effect. "Zimmerman is a 2nd Lieutenant." He paused again, "I, on the other hand, am your Commanding Officer and a 1st Lieutenant." Yet another pause. He was really enjoying this. "Both of us have a pressing need for an artist. Now, who do you think is going to get the artist?"

I was afraid to answer, particularly since nothing I might have said would have mattered and I might make matters worse if I opened my mouth.

"We understand each other then. You will report to me on your free time, after all your other duties are taken care of, and I will show you the important artwork I need which is so essential to the operation of this outfit. Dismissed!"

I felt like all the air had been let out of my tires as I walked back to my barracks. Hobgood couldn't help but wonder what kind of artwork would be so essential to this unit. I, on the other hand, felt that the C.O. had a cynical streak and enjoyed pulling rank on Lt. Zimmerman, while I was just a pawn in this little game.

Unfortunately, I was right. While everyone else was relaxing after a hard day, I reported to the Company Office to receive my extra curricular assignment from the C.O. He gave me a roll of 1" wide masking tape, a paintbrush, a can of black paint and a roster of every soldier in the Company. "Now, Mr. Artist, I want the name of each dogface in this Company painted on this masking tape to put on their helmet liners. When you finish that, I'll need another set for the helmets and then another set for each bed. You'll spend two hours every evening on this art work until it's done."

Before I reported for induction, I had been cautioned by veterans to never volunteer for anything and try to remain inconspicuous. I guess I didn't try hard enough. I later pleaded with my platoon to never volunteer me for anything; that if something came up that I thought I had special abilities for, I could raise my hand without any of their help.

BASIC TRAINING PROMISED TO BE ALL IT was cracked up to be: Hell. Our first forced march was on a Saturday morning. Though I wasn't sure whether I would be working on my art assignment or would be participating in the march, I covered all bases by packing my field pack for the march. Two hours before the march was to begin, I was summoned to my artwork. I left my neatly packed field pack on my bed figuring that there was no way that the C.O. would let me get out of the march. I wasn't wrong. While everyone else had plenty of time to prepare for and even rest before the hike, I was told less than ten minutes before we had to fall in for the march, that I was to join the formation, in full hiking gear. Fortunately I had prepared for this eventuality, or so I thought. I ran back to my barracks, straight to my bunk, only to find that someone had taken my field pack. It was too late to confront anyone, as most of the men were already in formation.

I noticed one soldier's field pack that was very haphazardly packed and sitting by his bunk. He had just gotten off KP and was told that I wouldn't need mine. My second thought was to quickly repack it, my first thought is not printable. The Platoon Sergeant ran in and insisted that I put the field pack on my back immediately and fall into formation. I tried to explain that the mess kit was improperly packed and would stick into my back and that I had nothing to do with the lousy packing job. Platoon sergeants are not known for their compassion and have no patience for excuses. I fell into formation and started the five-mile march with a mess kit digging into my back and a pair of boots at least one full size too small. That's when I started counting the days until discharge. Only 702 days left.

I naively complained to the drill sergeant marching beside us about the excruciating pain I was experiencing. His response was one that I would hear over and over again. "Good training, Hirsch," he said with a grin, "good training!" That had to be the longest five miles I ever walked. It only took two weeks for the pain in my back to subside. My feet were another matter.

I had previously attempted to go on sick call to get a pair of glasses. The C.O. checked my chart, saw the 20/20 designation, and put me on K.P. This time I had a legitimate reason to go on sick call. My feet were a compilation of sores and blisters. The medic felt bad for me but could do nothing to get me a better fitting pair of boots. To do so would have implied that I had not been properly fitted in the first place and that isn't done in this man's army. The best he could offer for the short term was a pair of arch supports. After Basic Training, I could buy a new pair of properly fitting army regulation boots at my own expense. I mentioned my need for glasses. He looked at my chart. Strike two. Only 701 days left.

THE FIRST FRIDAY NIGHT OF BASIC WAS our first weekly "G. I. Party." That's when we all get on our hands and knees and scrub the barracks floors until they're clean. This was part of the preparation for the regular Saturday morning inspection. Our Platoon Sergeant came in and called out my name. I snapped to attention and he came over to me and suggested that, since it was Friday night and I was Jewish, I should go to chapel. I explained that as much as I would like to go to Friday night services, I was uncomfortable with the idea of going to services while the rest of my platoon was scrubbing floors. I told him that I didn't want to get out of doing my share of work, thereby, inviting feelings of resentment and hostility from the other guys in the barracks. After all, I had experienced enough resentment for being Jewish without receiving special treatment. I was afraid that getting out of the G. I. party to go to Chapel would be asking for trouble.

After a few exchanges, he ordered me to put on my class A's, (dress uniform), and go pray. I felt very guilty as I got dressed. For the most part, the guys in the barracks understood that I had no choice. I came back in less than two hours and found that there was still quite a bit of work to do. Changing my clothes and getting right to work kept the snide remarks to a minimum. We finished about 2 a.m. The place was spotless and we were as proud as we were tired as we all jumped into the sack.

We weren't in bed fifteen minutes when the Drill Sergeant threw the doors open and yelled, "All right, everyone fall in with your footlockers at port arms! You have two minutes!" We all shook the cobwebs out of our heads, jumped into our O.D's (olive drab work uniform) and boots, and fell into formation on the muddy ground in front of our barracks. The Drill Sergeant went up and down the formation scrutinizing the tired, motley crew of recruits as if he was actually looking for something. Within moments, he dismissed the formation and ordered us to fall in next to our footlockers, at the foot of our beds, for an inspection in thirty seconds. In the mad scramble, no one had time to wipe off the mud from their boots, or, for that matter, to even think about it.

As we stood at attention, he walked in, took one look at the floor and screamed at the top of his lungs, "I thought you s--- heads had a 'G.I. Party!' This floor looks like a pigsty! This floor better be spotless for inspection tomorrow or the C.O. is going to want to know why it ain't! Any questions?" I had heard that the cadre for basic training would go to any length to put the recruits in their place, but this was ridiculous. We stayed up all night scrubbing the mud off the wooden floor and stood for inspection in the morning like a bunch of zombies.

Rumor had it that our Cadre (Drill Instructors) had recently returned from Korea where they saw a bunch of improperly trained soldiers get killed. Therefore, they were committed to giving us the most rigorous training that we could live through, in order to save our lives, of course.

I couldn't make the Kirk Douglas thing go away. By this time, in spite of my efforts to ignore the situation, a small fan club had developed. I was relieved not to hear from the Base Commander again, but things were getting sticky in our platoon and it was spreading to other platoons in the company. Although I tried to avoid all conversation about my "movie star brother," people would not let it alone. The company was split between those that believed and those who thought I was full of it. The corporal in charge of the kitchen was a major skeptic and didn't hide his feelings whenever I had KP. His skepticism turned into a strong dislike for me, which resulted in my getting to wash pots and pans—a two-man job—by myself once a week. He would not even allow others on KP to help me when they had finished their assignments. It would take at least three showers to get rid of the smell of bacon grease after each stint of KP duty.

I was at my wits end. Hobgood was no help. He was actually getting enjoyment out of seeing how far a little prank could go, at my expense of course. There was only one thing to do. Write to Kirk Douglas, explain the situation and get his advice on how to make it go away without getting me into more trouble. I had read that he was in Rome, Italy, filming *Ulysses*. I got the address of the studio and frantically wrote him a letter, pleading for his help. I really never expected to hear from him, but I so badly wanted to share this dilemma with someone who might appreciate the humor in this sticky situation.

The redheaded corporal in charge of the kitchen was also in charge of mail call. Even though he had mellowed a little and eventually allowed others on KP with me to help with the pots and pans when they had finished their chores, he still had no kind words for me. That is, until mail call one day during the fourth week of our Basic Training.

Mail call was always a highlight of the day. The anticipation of getting mail from a loved one, or a friend, and the hope that there was someone out there that cared enough to be in touch was enough to create anxiousness in all of us waiting to hear the mail clerk shout our names. As names were called out, arms and hands reached out in excited anticipation. The redheaded corporal called out, "Hirsch!" As I reached out in excitement to see who had written to me, he held the envelope back and scanned it carefully. It was the letter I had sent to Kirk Douglas, returned to sender. The filming of *Ulysses* was completed and there had been no forwarding address. I found out later that he had gone to Paris for the premier of his new film, *Act of Love*. I never could have anticipated the effect this returned letter would have. For some reason, all doubts that the red head had about Kirk and me were erased and Red became my number one fan. All because I wrote a letter and it was returned. I thought that things could not get more bizarre. I was wrong.

A few days later, someone bought a movie magazine that featured an in depth story on none other than Kirk Douglas and brought it to Red. Hobgood had also seen it and showed it to me. According to the article, Kirk's real name is Isor Danielovich, he has six sisters, he is Jewish, and he has no brothers. Talk about timing. I saw Red running over to my barracks and I thought it was the grease pit for me, for sure. " Hey, Hirsch," he yelled at me almost out of breath, "Did you see the lies they printed about your brother?"

Hobgood looked at me in disbelief. "You can't get upset at this kind of stuff, Red. When you're a star you have to go along with whatever the publicists want to print. I promise you I'm not upset or hurt in the least." I said all this as calmly as I could to ease Red's obvious agitation. I discouraged him from writing a nasty letter to the publication or to Kirk, explaining that he and I had an understanding about matters of publicity. Red walked away somewhat mollified and I let out a deep sigh. How long could I go on dodging bullets like this? Somehow this thing had to end, but how? There was always the hope that after Basic I would be sent to a totally new outfit, maybe to the Antarctic.

THE SIXTH WEEK OF BASIC WAS BIVOUAC. An entire week of playing soldier in the woods, sleeping in pup tents, fighting the elements while being grossly under-equipped. If that couldn't divert everyone's minds from the inanities of movie magazines, nothing could. I'm convinced that the weather in these bivouac areas is controlled by the officers who schedule the exercises. It had rained the whole week before and there was no sign of the rain letting up for us. The foxholes that had been dug by the previous bivouackers could not be filled back in, as they normally would have been, because they were full of water. The Cadre advised us of how lucky we were that we did not have to dig our own foxholes. All we had to do was pitch our puptents next to the existing foxholes and we had a ready-made protective foxhole in which to stand guard, for every other four-hour stretch, alternating with our tentmates. The fact that the holes were full of water and that, while the rain had finally stopped, the temperature was approaching freezing, was incidental and came under the category of "good training."

It was cold. So cold that when the chow truck came by for breakfast with hot S.O.S.,(the accepted name for chipped beef on toast was "S--- On a Shingle"), we fought to get in line for seconds. For whatever reason, we were not issued liners for our field jackets. The Cadre had them, but we didn't. That also went under the category of good training, and was the cause for what nearly was a mutiny on our last night of bivouac.

On the fourth day we were treated to a very special exercise, the opportunity of being run over by a tank. Holes had been dug for this exercise by one of the preceding bivouacs. The plan was for individual soldiers to jump into a hole, slightly larger than a foxhole, as a tank approaches. The soldier, holding his rifle above his head to protect it from the mud in the bottom half of the hole, would duck as the tank treads straddled the hole and the tank turned around over the hole and proceeded in the direction it had come from. Every recruit got his turn to be awed at the experience. There were several holes and I had the honor of being the first to jump in a hole that was waist deep in mud. I was exhorted by the Cadre to hold my weapon over my head so that it wouldn't get muddy. As the tank rode over, the hole collapsed before he could try the turning maneuver and the tank driver quickly moved forward, away from the hole. As I stood there, like a mud statue of a soldier holding his mud rifle over his head, the Cadre frantically ran over to the edge of the hole, blew his whistle and pointed down at me as he yelled, "This hole is out of order." It was a shame that no one had brought a camera.

After they made sure that I was alive, I was allowed to go clean up, change clothes and, most important of all, take my rifle apart and clean out all of the mud. I felt fortunate not to be threatened with a court martial for allowing mud to get into my weapon. By this time we had learned to disassemble and reassemble our M-1s in the dark, so cleaning our weapons was not a major problem. One thing they taught us, and taught us well, was a healthy respect for the M-1 rifle, the weapon we were issued that might one day save our lives. I salute them for that.

On the final day of bivouac, after all of our other gear was packed on trucks, we went on our final exercise with full backpack and were told to meet at central point that evening to board busses for the trip back to camp. I never thought I would be looking forward to sleeping in those barracks again. It had just gotten dark when the various platoons began to appear at the pick-up point, and the temperature was dropping rapidly. We could see the busses in the distance, so we figured it wouldn't be long before we were on our way. Each small group had its area to wait in while the Cadre, with their field jacket liners and long johns on were near the busses, standing around a fire they had built to keep their hands warm. After about an hour and a half of waiting without any explanation, one of the recruits ran over to the fire to warm his body. He was severely reprimanded and told to get into the position of a push-up, with his arms stiff. He was not allowed to actually do any push-ups. We were all told that we could not do calisthenics to keep warm, but that we could light up if we had cigarettes, and be sure to field strip them when we were done.

It was 9° above zero, the wind was blowing, and I had never been so cold before, not even going to school in rural France, in sabots (wooden shoes) without socks, in snow that was over a foot deep. The combination of the cold weather, our forced inactivity and seeing our well-insulated Cadre joking and laughing by a fire, brought us to the brink of mutiny. If they were trying to instill the killer instinct in us, they succeeded. To vent my frustration, in lieu of trying to kill someone, I smashed my rifle, that weapon that I had learned to respect and protect, against a tree. We must have been out there for at least three hours when groups started to gather to plan an attack on our instructors. As they saw an angry horde approaching, the First

Sergeant wisely blew his whistle and yelled out for us to fall in and prepare to board the busses.

I never quite understood the meaning of this exercise in frustration. It must have been planned that way to get us to the brink of violence, or maybe they just wanted to see how far they could go with us before we turned into animals. I decided not to ask, knowing that I would be told that it was "good training," but I will never forget that evening. We boarded the heated busses and in very little time things were back to normal.

BACK AT THE BASE, WE WERE BEGINNING to feel like soldiers. There was even a hint of weekend passes in the near future. Hobgood had been hanging around with a guy named Hollins and one of the Cadres, a corporal who definitely was not Regular Army. I had been friendly with them, but it was hard to get close to people as long as this Kirk Douglas sham was still an unresolved issue. I was feeling like a spy with a secret identity and I had no idea if Hobgood had confided in anyone about this. So you can imagine my surprise when Hollins pulled me aside to confide in me the problems he was having with his wife.

Hollins had not been married that long when he was drafted, and his wife tried to get him to seek a hardship exemption from the army because of her unique circumstances. Both her father and her uncle had been killed in action during World War II and her only brother had been killed in the early part of the Korean Conflict. The thought of her husband being sent to do battle after what happened to the other men in her immediate family was too much for her to cope with. As much as she professed she loved him, she was seriously considering divorce, since he apparently was unable to get a hardship discharge. He had been in daily telephone conversations with her for the last two weeks and things did not look good. In their conversations, he would tell of the happenings of interest at Company C in Camp Gordon.

Among the topics of conversation was the tidbit that Kirk Douglas's brother was in his barracks. He knew that she was a movie buff and constantly read movie magazines, but he didn't realize how excited she would get at this news. During the last few telephone conversations, all she could talk about was wanting to meet me. In a desperate effort to save his marriage, he asked me if I would meet with her and try to talk her out of the divorce. He truly felt that she would listen to anything I said and follow any advice I would give. This definitely was no time to come clean. I figured if they really loved each other and I could play a role in keeping the marriage together, maybe that's why this farce came to be in the first place. Her father and uncle died doing what I had wanted to do anyway, fight and kill Nazis. I agreed to meet with her, he thanked me profusely and ran to the phone.

It was all set up. She would drive in on Sunday and we would spend some time together in the afternoon. I was feeling a little nervous at the prospect of having that much power over someone's decision-making process. Looking back though, I remembered that some of my peers had often come to me to listen to their problems and to advise them on what course to take. This time was different, though. I was only being sought out because of a lie. I felt that I had no choice. This was an opportunity to try to make something good out of this stupid mess.

Sunday came quickly. Strangely enough I wasn't nervous. I was just going about my business when Hollins came over to my bunk, after lunch, to take me to meet his wife. She was a beautiful girl with long wavy blond hair who could have passed for a movie star herself. Hollins suggested that she take me for a drive in their white Chevrolet convertible, although I had the distinct impression that this was her idea. I felt kind of funny being alone with her at her husband's behest. I'd be lying if I said that the thought of seducing or being seduced by this lovely lady didn't at least enter my mind, but I fought those basic instincts and thought of trying to do something worthwhile for two troubled people. I amazed myself. We chatted at length about Hollywood, movies in general and Kirk's movies in particular. She was really at ease and seemed to be enjoying herself.

After a while she got to the topic of her marriage. She cried almost uncontrollably when she spoke about the fate of her father, uncle and brother. I listened and tried to comfort her by telling her that I too had lost loved ones in WWII and understood her grief. She put her head on my shoulder and I gently caressed her until she was able to stop crying. I told her that while I understood her motivations, divorcing the man she loved would just be another way of losing a man that was an important part of her life. Only this time, she would be responsible for forcing the separation. I told her that if she loved him, she should stick with him through this ordeal because I knew that he loved her very much.

She looked at me and said that I could never imagine what our conversation had done for her, that she had been so confused and now she knew that staying with her husband was right for her. It all seemed so easy. Even though I meant everything I had said to her, it was amazing to me that it took so little conversation, knowing how close she had been to filing the divorce papers. She drove me back and we chatted some more about movie stars and Hollywood. We arrived back at the Company about an hour and a half after we had left. I told Hollins, "She's all yours now," said my good-byes and went for a 3.2 beer with Hobgood who only wanted to know if I had made out with her. I playfully slapped him across the head and told him to get his mind out of the gutter.

That evening, Hollins came over to me and gave me a big hug. "You're a good friend," he said. "I don't know what you said or did, but I'm very grateful." I tried to be nonchalant, but a little tear sneaked out of my eye. I was actually pretty proud of myself. After all, I could have had more selfish motives and even a possible conquest to feel guilty about later.

After eight weeks of Infantry Basic Training, we all wondered where each one of us would be sent for the second eight weeks of specialized training. Possible assignments came down to the unit and officers along with the cadre would evaluate each soldier's performance in Basic, his "Area 1" test scores and any other talents that he displayed, to ideally match up the assignment with the right personnel. That's the theory. However, the Army way is to send PhD's to the infantry and high school drop-outs to apprentice for brain surgeons or nuclear physicists.

Among the assignments sent to our unit was one for a recruit with unusual mathematical ability and background to be assigned to Guided Missile school at Fort Sill. Hobgood heard about it from his corporal friend in the office and congratulated me on the plum.

I asked what made him think that I would be awarded this special opportunity. I wasn't being humble. I knew that my "Area 1" scores were the highest in the Company and that my math proficiency score was the highest in the Battalion, but I had also learned, the hard way, that being qualified for a job is the best way not to get it in this man's army. In my heart, I was hoping to get that assignment, but my skepticism proved to be well-founded. The assignment went to the sharpest soldier, according to the Drill Sergeant, a squad leader who was proficient at drilling his squad, was sharp at responding to all the commands, and was a high school drop-out. The reward was a feather in his cap, even though he lasted less than two weeks in Guided Missile school.

Most of the rest of us either went on to more infantry training or to artillery training. One guy, who was so fat that he couldn't do one chin-up, was sent to the M.P.s. Rumor had it that he was going to be a road block. He was one of at least two in our Company who never should have passed the induction physical. There was a chinning bar at the entrance to the mess hall and the Cadre, at random, would order any of us waiting in line to enter to do five chin-ups before going in to eat. Almost every time this weight-challenged recruit approached the mess hall entrance, he was challenged to do at least one chin-up, which would be like pressing over 300 pounds. When it was evident that he could not achieve even one chin-up, he would be challenged to try a push-up. After everyone else had been served, they finally let him go through the chow line even though he couldn't perform. After eight weeks of Basic Training he was actually able to perform one push-up. Chin-ups were out of the question.

The other unfortunate fellow had insisted during his induction physical that he had a sleeping sickness, but he was never tested for Narcolepsy. He was a country boy who had never had his sleeping problem diagnosed by a doctor and the skeptical medics were not about to give him that much credibility. Within a week it was obvious that if this guy was faking, he was the best actor in the world. There was the night that we had to crawl under barbed wire with our rifles cradled in our arms, and with live machine gun fire over our heads. When we finished the exercise, we were told we may have set a new record for time of completion, but when heads were counted, one man was missing. The lights were turned on and there was our missing recruit, sleeping under the barbed wire with machine gun bullets whizzing over his head.

Then there was the time that we were lined up for inspection. Responding to the order "Inspection Arms," each man in the formation held his rifle in front of him with the breach cocked open so that the inspecting officer could look inside to see that the rifle had been properly cleaned. Our man was in the middle of the formation and by the time the inspecting officer and the drill sergeant reached him, he was fast asleep in the "Inspection Arms" position. The sergeant, not believing what he was seeing, put his thumb in the breach, pressing the spring to shut it. The force of the bolt flying shut woke him up with a jolt. He was written up for the infraction, even though this was far from the first time that this man was found asleep in bizarre situations. The officer also recommended that he be given a medical discharge. Who said there was no justice in the army?

As for me, I had had my shot at being an artist/draftsman and at attending Guided Missile School, without success, so I really didn't care much where the second eight weeks of Basic would be as long as it would not be advanced infantry training. The word came that a group of us were headed for artillery training at Camp Chaffee near Fort Smith, Arkansas.

4

WE RESPECT EDUCATION IN THIS MAN'S ARMY

ARTILLERY TRAINING AT CAMP CHAFFEE, ARKANSAS WAS broken down into two totally separate specializations, cannoneering and Fire Direction Center (FDC). There were skills involved in cannoneering that were acquirable through training, but did not necessarily require a particular level of education. The cannoneers were part of a ten-man field artillery gun section that included a Chief of Section, a Gunner seven cannoneers and a truck driver. The Chief of Section was an instructor and all the others, except the truck driver, were being trained to man every position on a 105mm Howitzer cannoneer crew. These positions ranged from Gunner, which required considerable skill, to the handler of powder charges, which required alertness and the ability to count to seven and to read the numbers. The ammunition for a 105mm came in two pieces, a projectile and a cartridge case, the latter of which contained seven numbered bags of explosive powder attached by strings. The maximum number of powder bag charges that could be ordered by the FDC was seven. If, for example, the order was for a three charge, the handler would cut the string between the three and four bag, place bags one through three in the cartridge case, put it with the projectile to be loaded into the gun for firing, and throw away bags four through seven.

On the other hand, FDC required a working knowledge of geometry, trigonometry and basic algebra to properly calculate the trajectory and explosive charge required for the shell to hit its target. In battle, the FDC would take coordinates by radio from

Forward Observers who would locate the targets for the artillery guns, and transpose that information into firing directions for the Gunner. The Gunner, as head of the cannoneering crew, would then transmit the directions to the members of his crew.

We arrived at Camp Chaffee and were split up according to education levels. Though this was never told to us in any way, it was very apparent. Those from Camp Gordon, who had a tenth grade education or less were assigned to Charlie Battery (C-47) and, as it turned out, all of those assigned to Dog Battery (D-47) had at least two years of college under their belts. It came as no surprise that C-Battery was training for FDC while D-Battery would be training to be cannoneers. Dog 47 had several men with doctorate degrees and even more with masters' degrees. The best part of this split was that most of the soldiers in Dog 47 had more intellectual pursuits than movie magazines. With the exception of occasional visitors from Charlie Battery, who remembered me from Gordon and felt the need to introduce me to their new friends, or take pictures with me to send home, the Kirk Douglas issue was, for the most part, played down.

Infantry Basic had been physically grueling. Artillery training was going to entail a lot more classroom work. Though we marched in formation to all classes and programs and did our share of PT—physical training— exercises, I felt like we weren't being challenged enough physically. The ravenous appetite resulting from the grueling work in Basic was still there, but we weren't burning as many calories in this new training schedule. It wasn't long before we all started putting on noticeable weight.

It was a very full and busy schedule, with a lot of studying and a lot of exercise, but unlike Basic Training, it all fit within a ten hour day. We had a lot more free time on our hands. We weren't so exhausted when we had free time that we went right to sleep. We had time for poker games, going to the Beer X, and occasionally going into town. I got into a regular poker game with two guys who had flunked out of Ranger school and a couple of other "pigeons." I was not what you would call a card shark, but I had earned some tuition for my sophomore year at Georgia Tech by playing Gin Rummy.

I was a fairly good poker player and that was all that was needed with these guys. I was doubling my paycheck every month and having a good time doing it. Then came the bad news. My two Ranger "pigeons" had decided they would apply for Airborne school and were accepted. They convinced me that parachuting out of airplanes would be fun, not to mention an extra $50 per month for jump pay. I can't believe that I actually took the physical to apply for Airborne. I breathed a sigh of relief when they told me that my ankles were too weak for me to become a paratrooper. I was sad over the loss of potential revenue, but relieved that I would not be going through the rigors of Airborne training.

Offers for alternate training seemed to be abounding. One of our drill sergeants came running to me with the "good news." Someone high in the chain of command had been reviewing the files of all the personnel in Dog Battery, and based on my Area-1 scores and who knows what else, I qualified for O.C.S., Officers Candidate School. After excitedly relating what a high honor this was, he proceeded to tell me what the school was all about, mainly that after an intense ninety days of schooling and rigorous training, I could be a 2nd Lieutenant.

It all actually sounded very tempting, but there was one piece of information missing. I asked him if I would have to increase the length of my tour of duty in order to take advantage of this offer. I was told that the Army would require that I re-enlist for a three year term from the date of acceptance of the appointment to O.C.S., and the remainder of my two year stint as a volunteer would be wiped off the books. He figured that no one in his right mind would pass up such a deal and maybe he was right, but, over the past twelve weeks I had had my fill of the confinement of army life, and I was looking forward to getting on with pursuing my career. I said that I was honored to be asked, but I could not commit to extending my tour of duty.

I had no idea that it would be a slap in this career non-com's face for me to turn my back on an opportunity to become an officer, an opportunity that he would have given his right arm for. As it was, he really took it as an insult and did everything within his power to make sure that I would regret this insult to him and to the United States Army. All of the Cadre were notified to look out for this soldier who thought he was too good to become an officer, and before long I started hearing the oft repeated phrase, "You think you're smarter than me because you have two years of college!" K.P. became a more regular assignment and it wasn't long before our unit was introduced to Guard Duty.

IN THE LATER WEEKS OF OUR TRAINING, it came as no surprise when we were told that we were now qualified to be on guard duty with live ammunition, and that I would be among the first for this new assignment. Up to this point, everything we were involved with was basically on a Battery level and all of our superiors were known to us. Guard duty was for the entire camp, and our Battery sent only a small contingent to be part of an overall security system.

There were about sixty of us charged with guarding one section of the camp and we were divided into three shifts. Our Officer of the Day was a Chinese 2nd Lieutenant and a couple of the non-coms were from our outfit. The officer was told that we were new at this game and he proceeded to instruct us on our duties and on the chain of command. He explained that while he was the Officer in charge of this area, there was also an Officer of the Day in charge of the Guard Duty of the entire camp. This officer's name was Marvel, Captain Marvin Marvel.

My duty was to guard the ammunition dump in four hour stretches. In between, we all were exhorted to sleep so that we would be wide awake for our shifts. The Sergeant of the Guard would show me the area for which I was responsible, and I was to march back and forth for four hours with a loaded M-1 rifle on my shoulder. We were told emphatically that if *anyone*, no exceptions, came along, the guard had to stop, take the rifle from his shoulder, hold it in front of him with both hands, and shout "Halt, who goes there?" The Intruder had to state his name, rank and serial number, had to be able to show identification and had to tell the guard what business he had at this off-limits area.

Hearing all the instructions made me feel that I was really a soldier with a mission for the first time since induction. After two hours of walking the shift, I wasn't that enamored with the duty. Even though it was pretty awesome protecting the ammo dump, it was pretty dull walking back and forth in the moonlight with no one to talk to, trying to find ways to fight the boredom.

With about an hour left on the shift, the boredom was interrupted. I actually heard someone coming my way and could barely see a silhouette of this fairly large person. "Halt! Who goes there?," I dutifully screamed, with my weapon at the ready.

"It's only me, Captain Marvel," the figure responded as he kept walking toward me.

"I don't give a s--- if you're Batman, and if you don't stop, I'm gonna shoot!" I shouted, trembling with every word.

He stopped, but then he started laughing uproariously. When he regained his composure, he said "Soldier, you're doing your job, I should have been more specific, I'm the Officer of the Day, Captain Marvin Marvel." He then proceeded to show me his I.D.

I really felt stupid. Of course, I should have recognized that name. I hoped that this encounter would be between me and the Captain, as the last thing I needed was a reprimand. He went about his rounds and I continued my shift until I was replaced. When I walked into the guard room to sack out, I was greeted by the lieutenant, "Hey Batman, how was your first shift of guard duty?" It went down hill from there. I took at least an hour of ribbing before they finally let me go to sleep. Of course, the word got out to the Cadre in our Battery, and everyone had some good laughs at my expense.

SOME OF THE CLASSES WERE INTERESTING, OTHERS were a colossal bore. The classes having to do with artillery equipment and the components of that equipment fascinated me the most. Ever since I was in grade school, I used to sketch in classes to keep from getting bored. In these classes, instead of sketching people, I did sketches, with annotated parts, of the equipment that was being presented. Corporal Vanderschnik, who marched us from place to place, would look over my shoulder and actually was pleased with my graphic way of taking notes. I wasn't always on his good side. The non-technical lectures were usually somewhat banal, and occasionally I would have an irresistible urge to make a funny remark. On one such occasion, Cpl. Vanderschnik was standing during the lecture monitoring his troops when I slipped out with a quip that caused some laughter.

"All right, wise guy, stand up and let's all have a good laugh," he said in a very annoyed tone of voice. He continued, "Let me have a good look at you, I never forget a face. What's your name?! I'll deal with you when we get back to the barracks."

"Hirsch!" I shouted jumping to attention, and as he wrote it down, I quietly took my seat in the bleachers.

There was another soldier, from North Carolina, in our group. He was about my height and weight and his name was Hurst. He had a unique talent of which he was very proud. He could sleep with his eyes wide open. About a week earlier, Hurst made the mistake of sitting on the end of an upper row of bleachers during a boring lecture. To keep us awake, Vanderschnik would motion to the lecturer to stop, then he would yell "Jab!" At this command every one was supposed to jab an elbow at the neighbor to his left, rudely awakening him if he were asleep. Not suspecting that the wide eyed soldier at the end of his row was asleep, the Corporal yelled "Jab!" and Hurst fell about four feet to the floor. He bruised a few bones as well as his ego, but the only lesson he learned from this experience was to not sit at the end of a row again.

The evening after my unfortunate wise crack, as we marched back to Cpl. Vanderschnik's cadence count, Hurst was bragging to me about how he had slept through most of the classes without getting caught. We reached the Mess Hall and I hoped that Vanderschnik had forgotten the whole incident of that morning. Before he dismissed the formation, he yelled out as he looked at a piece of paper, "Hirsch! front and center!"

Before I could make a move, Hurst jumped out of formation and stood at attention in front of the Corporal who looked at him and said, "I told you I never forget a face. Get in the kitchen, you're on K.P. tonight." Hurst didn't know what hit him. He figured he must have been caught sleeping.

OUR DRILL SERGEANT WAS A REAL SOLDIER. He was a tall, trim black man, sort of a cross between Lou Gosset and Robert Parish. He knew what he was doing and he exuded confidence in his ability to lead his men. Unlike most Non-coms, he had that ounce of compassion, though sparingly and selectively displayed, that set him apart from other Drill Sergeants.

On our long marches or hikes for example, I would inevitably complain to him about my aching feet and cramping calf muscles caused by the poor-fitting boots I was forced to wear. He would listen intently until I finished, then smile gently and respond, "Good Training, Soldier. Good Training." His response was not unlike that of his counterparts in Camp Gordon but it was easier to take because he made you feel he cared about you.

With my epileptic friend Cannady, however, he really rose above the crowd. On our first long march, Cannady fell out of formation and was lying on the ground convulsing from over-exertion. In the past, particularly at Camp Gordon, the Cadre would accuse him of faking an epileptic fit and put him on KP without allowing him to go on sick call. This sergeant listened intently to Cannady as he explained his illness and how it could be controlled with medication as long as he did not overly exert himself. You could see in Cannady's eyes that he was just waiting for the accusations and threats of punishment to fly, but our Drill Sergeant believed him. Cannady was sent back to Base by Jeep, allowed to go on Sick Call and was assigned to light duty in either an office or supply room for the remainder of his tour of duty.

ONE OF THE LEAST PLEASANT BUT ESSENTIAL pastimes was polishing boots. To make sure that we changed boots every day, the Cadre devised a different shoe lace pattern for each alternate day. This meant polishing at least one pair of boots every night in case an unannounced inspection was in the offing. One evening, I was sitting on my foot locker polishing a pair of boots, when I felt eyes burning a hole through me. I looked up and there were three guys from another barracks standing there staring at me as if they were dumbfounded.

I tried to look them straight in the eyes. "Is there something I can do for you?"

"Watson, two barracks down, said you're a Jew," they said, expecting me to deny the absurd allegation.

"Well, I don't even know who Watson is, but he sure has his facts right, I am a Jew. Is that a problem?"

They kept staring, maybe looking for the horns or the tail. Finally, one of them broke the silence, "You can't be a Jew," he protested.

"Why not?"

"We know you, and you're a regular guy, and your brother's a movie star." With that remark, they turned and walked away.

"I guess you realize that he is Jewish too." I couldn't resist adding that as a parting shot. I sat there kind of dazed and very sad. These guys had never even seen a Jew before, but they had been taught some horrible things about the Jewish people, and never taught anything about who we are. I wondered how they felt about the Holocaust, or if they had even heard of it. My mind floated back to Germany. Was this kind of ignorance part of the cause for the Nazis' "War Against the Jews"?

The PX had a liquid shoe wax that could make old boots shine like patent leather. The only problem with this product was that the finish would crack when the boots were worn. Necessity being the mother of invention, I coated one pair of boots with this liquid wax and proceeded to change the shoe lace pattern every night. It was so simple that I was sure to get caught, but it was worth the try. To my surprise, no one ever snitched on me and none of the inspectors ever caught on. In fact, I always got high marks for the shined boots I displayed and the inspecting officers used to bring in other officers to show them this exemplary job of shining boots on a daily basis. They would look at the boots and remark that I had the makings of a good soldier, while my barracks mates stood at attention, trying to keep from cracking up with laughter.

I NEVER THOUGHT THAT I WOULD BE gung-ho about anything in the army, but I really enjoyed being a Gunner on a 105mm Howitzer. Maybe it was because I was good at it. Our Field Artillery Section was always among the top in performance exercises and I took great pride being part of a Section that was among the best. One of our section members, however, was a bit disgruntled. Even though we excelled as a group, he felt his job of grabbing the projectile from the truck and handing it to the next Section member, who then handed it to the ammo loader, was too menial a job for a man with two Masters degrees from Mississippi Southern University. He really coveted my job as a Gunner, but he couldn't display the necessary proficiency with the Panoramic Telescope, Gunner's Quadrant, or any of the other technical equipment used by the Gunner, to even think of making a realistic challenge. He continually complained to the Section Leader that he was getting a raw deal and finally wore the man down.

The Chief of Section reluctantly decided to give the Mississippi Southern scholar a chance at cutting the powder charges. What could go wrong? Obviously, a man with two Master's degrees would know how to count and read numbers and should have little trouble responding to orders given on the number of powder charge bags to place in the cartridge case before it was put together with the projectile, shoved into the breach, and fired.

The firing range for the Howitzer Sections was limited simply because Camp Chaffee had finite boundaries and abutted local farm land. Therefore, we had been advised that orders from FDC regarding the ammunition charge would never exceed a four and would generally range from one to three. Our maiden exercise with our new powder charge man could not come soon enough for him. He was very excited and equally nervous. No one dared look over his shoulder, knowing how paranoid he was about no one trusting his ability to do any job properly. Every man in the Section had his own assignment anyway, and was really too busy to check him out.

The "Fire" commands came: Pieces to follow, special corrections, charge, fuse, pieces to fire, method of fire, direction, site, time setting, and elevation. The one command that was relevant to our man was "charge-3," all he had to do was cut the string between the charge bag marked 3 and the one marked 4, place bags 1, 2, & 3 in the cartridge case and put the case together with the projectile. Everything went like clockwork. The settings were perfect and the piece was fired in the time allotted. As we congratulated our new charge man on a job well done, the clean up crew members asked where the remaining four charge bags were. They were nowhere to be found. As the Chief of Section questioned him, I silently prayed that he had not placed all seven bags in the cartridge case. It was an obvious question and he vociferously denied having done anything as stupid as that.

We continued our firing exercises with the line-up as it had been before. Somehow, our would-be charge bag-man failed to fill the Chief with confidence in his ability to think or follow orders. Before we left the field for home base, we got word that we had made a direct hit on a farmer's barn outside of Camp Chaffee. We were thankful that no people or animals were either injured or killed, and were reassured with our choice of replacing this man after he had screwed up his one big chance. Our "scholar-in- residence" insisted that his was an honest mistake and could not see why everyone was making such a big deal out of it. The whole incident left serious questions in my mind about our educational system in this country, in particular, about the requirements for earning a Master's Degree from an accredited University.

AT CAMP CHAFFEE, THE SOLDIERS WERE NOT divided along racial lines. The major split had to do with taste in music. Each barracks had at least one country music buff with a phonograph continually playing Hank Williams or Hank Snow records, to the revulsion of those with an appreciation for either classical music or popular music and soft jazz. I loved to sing. I knew the words to all the Joni James songs, not to mention most of the popular songs of the time, and I enjoyed participating in impromptu songfests. One of my friends was a black man from Alabama who was also musically inclined. He sang great harmony, knew every song I knew, and had a great ear for Jazz. He suggested that we enter a weekly talent contest at the servicemen's club. He would accompany me at the piano and I would sing.

I had never done anything like that before, but he said we had to start somewhere if we were going to make it into show biz. He signed us up for the following Sunday. I asked him when we would rehearse and what song or songs we would be presenting. It was scary to hear that everything was going to be impromptu. There was no time to rehearse and we would have to pick a song from the music sheets available at the Center. We were really glad that a few of the guys from my barracks came along, because without them, we would have felt like a couple of Indians at a Cowboy Jamboree. One performer after another plucked at and made twangy sounds with his guitar, while giving a nasal rendition of a country song to a wildly receptive crowd. By the time our turn came, I wanted to sneak out of the back door but my buddy wouldn't let me. Musical scores for non-country songs were scarce. I think we did "September Song" and "Rags to Riches" to polite applause, and were followed by the emcee singing "Bimbo" and jumping around the stage like a jack rabbit to a crowd gone mad.

The guys that went with us said we sounded fine, although a soloist singing with his hands in his pockets and standing still at the microphone, was a little out of place in this satellite of the Grand Old Opry. I wish my piano playing buddy and I had not been split up after artillery training. It might have been fun performing to audiences more appreciative of popular music after having had the opportunity to practice and refine our presentation.

THE RIFLE RANGE WAS BEYOND NORMAL MARCHING distance, so we boarded busses for what would be a full day's activity. After eight weeks of Basic, I had finally developed confidence in my ability to handle and fire the M-1 infantry rifle. Naturally, that proficiency became obsolete. Artillery men were issued M-1 Carbines, which were smaller and lighter.

From the moment we arrived, something seemed strange at the firing range. Up to this time, wherever we had gone as a training unit, we were treated with anything but respect. Here, of all places, at a rifle range, the instructors were treating us with kid gloves. No obscenities were shouted at us, not even cute little denigrating adjectives to describe our low status in the order of creation. We all wondered what was going on as we went about trying to develop our skills with the Carbine. This weapon was so light, I found it hard to hold steady when firing in the standard prone position. Surprisingly, I could shoot more accurately from the waist, while standing, than from any other position. I guess that's one of the reasons I never made marksman.

After we boarded the busses, we glanced back at the rifle range instructors and noticed them breathe sighs of relief. We were well on our way when our Cadre decided to fill us in. It seems that, six to eight weeks before, there had been another Dog 47, a Battery of incorrigible misfits from the slums of New York City. They had been part of an experiment to see if putting incorrigible young men into the army instead of jail would help straighten them out. The story went that when this group was at the rifle range, one of the instructors used the normal abusive language, commonly used by instructors in the army, at a soldier improperly holding his weapon while in the prone position. Apparently, the soldier did not take kindly to being addressed in that fashion, swung his weapon around, pointed it at the instructor and squeezed the trigger, to the applause of others among his group. The instructor was shot between the eyes and died instantly. Although the firing range instructors knew that we were not the same Dog 47, and that the shooter had been prosecuted for murder, they apparently were psyched out and did not want to take any chances with any group bearing the designation of Dog 47.

THERE WAS NO BIVOUAC PER SE IN our artillery training, at least not as far as sleeping in pup tents was concerned. We did camp out in the woods for a week, but we slept in large tents that held over twenty men. Between the dampness, the chill, and the constant smoking in the area, my chronic bronchitis really started acting up. It was bad enough that I couldn't fall asleep because of my coughing, which was so deep and loud that it kept the entire tent awake. It was so bad that Corporal Vanderschnik insisted that I go on sick call the next morning. On sick call, after waiting in line for almost two hours, I was finally examined by a master sergeant in the medical corps who was not a doctor, and, I would wager, had no formal medical training. He gave me some APC pills and a bottle of GI gin, a clear liquid cough medicine with codeine, and told me to report back to my unit.

I reported back and joined up with my squad, taking the medicine as prescribed, hoping that it would do some good. That night the cough got even worse. If the guys weren't feeling so sorry for me they might have killed me. Cpl. Vanderschnik insisted that I go on sick call again the next morning. It was well known that no matter what symptoms one had when going on Sick Call, the prescribed medicine would always be APCs and GI gin. I reminded him of that, but he was not impressed. His men couldn't sleep because of me, therefore, I should be put in the infirmary. I was sent on sick call again with explicit instructions to let the medic know that over twenty soldiers were not sleeping because of my coughing. I was again examined by the same sergeant and given more APCs and GI gin. I tried to explain to him the concerns of my Corporal and all of my tentmates, but he had no sympathy or interest in these matters. My orders were to return to my unit and to continue to take my medicine.

That night was no improvement over the previous two nights. I was weak and frustrated. Cpl. Vanderschnik was, understandably, highly agitated as were the guys in my tent. He ordered me to go on sick call and to not come back until I was cured. I felt like I was between a rock and a hard place. I got to sick bay and there was my friend, the master sergeant with the crew cut. I relayed to him what the corporal said to me, and he was quick to remind me that he outranked the corporal.

He gave me another bottle of GI gin, some more APCs and ordered me back to my unit. I didn't move. I just stood there at attention. He screamed "What are you waiting for, Soldier, I told you to report back to your unit!"

"Sergeant, with all due respect, I'm not going anywhere until I get to see a real doctor."

He wasn't used to having his authority challenged. "If you don't turn around and go back to your unit this instant, I'm going to have you court-martialed!" As he was screaming, a crowd began to gather, but I continued to stand there at attention. Finally a Captain with a white jacket on and a stethoscope around his neck, appeared out of his office.

He looked around trying to size up the situation, "What the Hell is going on here, Sergeant? This is a sick bay, not a drill field!"

The sergeant was beside himself. "Sir, this soldier is a goof-off. This is his third time here and he refuses to follow my orders to go back to his unit."

The Captain looked at me, still standing at attention, and approached me. "What do you have to say for yourself soldier? And it had better be good. You are refusing to obey the orders of one of my best medics, a master sergeant. That could get you court-martialed."

"Sir, I'm sick. I realize I don't have a fever, but I have chronic bronchitis, and I hardly ever run a fever until it gets to pneumonia. I was ordered by my corporal to not return until my cough is cured, because I've kept everyone up for three nights now. I'm sure the sergeant is a good medic, but I need to see a doctor who understands that someone can be sick without running a high fever." I was surprised that he let me finish all of that.

"Soldier, it took a lot of guts to do what you've just done. I'm going to examine you shortly, but I warn you, if you're faking, you may be in big trouble." He turned around to go into his office and ordered me to go to an examining room and wait.

"I'll take my chances, Sir." I felt so weak that I probably couldn't have made it back to the unit anyway. "Thank you, Sir!"

I didn't dare look at the sergeant, whose veins were popping out of his neck the last time I looked at him.

The examination didn't take long. The doctor had me admitted into the field hospital. After three days, I was ready to go back to the unit just in time to pack up and go back to the barracks. While at the field hospital I ran into a recruit who had been in the army for less than two weeks, and after hearing his story, I realized how lucky I had been.

He had passed his induction physical even though his trigger finger was missing and he had a hernia. He went on sick call before Basic because the hernia caused him great pain. The medics recognized the severity of the hernia and sent him to the hospital. At the hospital, a doctor looked at him and was appalled that this man was allowed to pass the induction physical. The soldier asked if that meant that he would get a medical discharge. The doctor told him that he should never have been allowed into the army in the first place, but now that he was in, his hernia would have to be operated on. He asked the doctor what would happen if he did not consent to the operation. The doctor replied that he would be court-martialed for disobeying the order of a commissioned officer. As far as the finger was concerned, after basic training, he would be given non-combat duty.

I had been concerned about not having glasses, or boots that fit and now I was worried about my bronchial condition, but after listening to him, I decided to count my blessings.

AMONG THE EVENTS OF OUR LAST WEEK at Camp Chaffee was a Battery-wide PT test, the scores of which would go on our permanent records. I was good at everything except running, and I couldn't even blame that on the bad fitting boots. I had always been a slow runner, maybe due to flat feet, but I had the stamina to run long distances. I was able to do about thirty push-ups, which was in the top ten percent of my outfit. I was tied for first place in sit-ups and held my own with chin-ups. The last exercise was running about sixty yards five times, there and back twice, and there one more time. There was a crowd of guys at each end and several candidates would start together. I started the run there and back and was so far behind the others, that I stopped to take a breath. By the time I caught my breath, the leader of the pack was coming toward me. No one seemed to notice that I had missed two laps, so as he came within inches of me, I took off and sprinted to the finish line. I fully expected to get caught, but it was fun making the speedsters think that I could outrun them.

When they announced the scores, I realized that I wasn't caught cheating and I was too petrified to admit what I had done. Every bad deed has its own reward. I was called in to the first sergeant, who told me that he was going to request that I get to stay at Camp Chaffee as a PT instructor, instead of going to Ft. Lewis, Washington, with half of the guys in my Battery. I expressed my excitement over this opportunity. I continued that he should be aware, however, that my chronic bronchitis did not fare well at Camp Chaffee due to the climate, and that if I were given the choice, I would respectfully decline for health reasons. I was incredibly relieved when he seemed to agree, and prayed, to no avail, that those ill gotten PT scores would get lost.

We said our good-byes, some of us promised to write to each other, and we boarded our military planes, half of us to Fort Lewis and the other half to Fort Leonard Wood, Missouri.

I picked a window seat for the flight, and Calvin Watson, who I had heard was bucking for a Section 8 discharge by claiming that he was homosexual, sat down next to me. He reminded me that he was the one who had told those Midwesterners that I was Jewish. He apologized for any embarrassment that incident may have caused me, and explained that his intent was just to illustrate that Jews were like anyone else. Calvin, or Cuddles as he preferred to be called, was really quite the conversationalist. We talked about everything from soup to nuts, until, at one point in the conversation, he put his hand on my knee.

I looked up at his grinning face and told him that if he didn't move his hand, pronto, he would be needing it to pick up his teeth. After he quickly moved his hand, I told him that I liked him as a person, and if he could be satisfied with that, we could be friends. He agreed, and at the risk of being branded a queer, I became friends with Cuddles.

5

MY FIRST CAR

WHEN WE ARRIVED AT FT. LEWIS, WASHINGTON, it wasn't clear whether we were going to be permanent personnel or be shipped to the battlefront in Korea. We were placed in the North Fort that was the point of debarkation for SEACOM, the Southeast Asian Command. North Fort was obviously a transient place. We had the opportunity to check out the main base, and even though the billets were the same wood frame barracks, the surrounding landscape, walkways, fields and ancillary facilities were in such good shape that one could sense the obvious feeling of pride that the "permanent personnel" had in their quarters. North Fort was also in good shape, and we had our share of duties to make sure that it stayed that way, but it lacked the finishing touches that set the Main Post apart.

We had a fair amount of free time on our hands which made for the pursuit of extra curricular activities, one of which was poker. A game was formed that included players from our games in Camp Chaffee. The other participants were soldiers waiting to be shipped to SEACOM who had time on their hands, a love for the game, and money burning a hole in their pockets. Fortunately, my luck from the games at Chaffee had not run out. Before the first week at North Fort was out, one of the soldiers bound for Korea was in to me for ninety-five dollars, which was approximately a month's pay for me. No one was allowed to play on credit in these games, unless they put up some collateral. This fellow had put up a 1942 Nash sedan that he couldn't have taken overseas anyway. So, by the first weekend at Ft. Lewis, I was the proud owner of my first car, a four door, green sedan with the Battery under the driver's seat. It had coil springs and no shock absorbers. It also burned one quart of oil for every gallon of gasoline used.

None of these drawbacks bothered me very much. I had never owned a bicycle or roller skates, much less a car. My brother Jack had talked me into taking driving lessons when I was eighteen, and on rare occasions had let me use his car, but my fantasies of owning my own car were focussed on the time that I would have graduated from college and had a full time, decent paying job. For my remaining days at North Fort, before being assigned to an Artillery Battalion at the Main Base, I took great joy in driving my new toy all over Fort Lewis with new found "friends," who had come out of the woodwork. The car was quickly dubbed "The Ramblin Wreck," partly because the coil springs without shock absorbers made the rear bounce like a carnival ride, and partly because I had been a student at Georgia Tech.

I SHOULD NOT HAVE BEEN SURPRISED WHEN I was assigned to a Service Battery. In Artillery Battalions, the Service Battery had the responsibility of supplying ammunition for the Cannoneering Batteries in the field. Actually, I was more disappointed than surprised that the fact that I had been the best Gunner to come out of Dog 47 was not a factor in my assignment within this Artillery Battalion. Then again, I surmised that this was par for the course in the Army's unstated policy of matching the highest level of ability to the lowest level of challenge. I consoled myself with the thought that if I had been given the opportunity to further develop my skills as a Gunner, I would have been in combat in Korea within six months, thereby missing any chance to get to Europe. The other point to consider was that this was a 155 Howitzer Battalion and I had been trained on the smaller 105 Howitzer. I tried to ignore the reports that virtually all the cannoneers in Able, Baker and Charlie Batteries had been trained on 105s. I chalked up the disappointment to "good training" and promised myself that I would try to behave and stay out of trouble while serving out the rest of my tour of duty.

The first guy to greet me after I was assigned a bunk, was a short red-headed corporal from New York who was quick to let me know that he too was Jewish, and that he would take me under his wing and show me the ropes. Of course, he strongly suggested that I should entrust him with the keys to my car. He reasoned that I would have very little free time as an Ammo Handler, while he, who worked as a clerk in the office, would have the time to keep my car in good shape by driving it daily. I got the feeling that this guy was a Number One User and a Goldbrick, but I felt sorry for him, for some reason, and I didn't have the inclination to tell him to bug off.

I was told to report to the Supply Room, where it looked like I was going to have a cushy job compared to my compatriots from Camp Chaffee, who were already going to the field for their first day as Ammo handlers. I kept very busy in the Supply Room and it didn't take that much brains to get the hang of the system. The Supply Sergeant seemed to like having me on duty there, but at the end of each day when I saw my buddies coming back to the Base, all tuckered out, I would feel guilty about having it so much easier than them. I heard more than one guy complain that it was unfair that they should have to work so hard while I was just keeping busy doing the work of a stock clerk.

I took what was being said to heart, even though most of my friends told me to pay no attention to the complainers and enjoy my good fortune. After about two weeks in the Supply Room, I did something that I would later deeply regret. I asked to be transferred out of the Supply Room to an Ammo Handling unit so I could be one of the guys. A handful of the guys appreciated the sacrifice I had made to be with them. Everyone else just laughed at the stupidity of my gesture. In less than a week, I vowed that if I would ever get another opportunity for a relatively cushy job, I would grab it, relax, and enjoy it.

AMMO HANDLING WAS AS PHYSICALLY TAXING AS everyone made it out to be. The 155mm projectiles were so big and heavy that a large eyelet was screwed in at the cone so that it could be grabbed by a steel hook, and swung from one location to another. At the end of the day, you knew that a good day's work had been done. I kicked myself more than once about my transfer request, and the Supply Room personnel never missed an opportunity to tease me about it, particularly the jerk that took my place.

One saving grace was that we didn't have to handle ammo every day. One of the more inane alternate activities was Motor Pool duty. We would go as a group to the Motor Pool to wash the trucks, clean the insides, and touch up the paint on the bodies. Hollis had been made Squad Leader while I was still in the Supply Room, and was promoted to PFC right away, with the promise of making Corporal if he did a good job as Squad Leader. He reminded me that had I stayed in the Supply Room, I probably would have made PFC right away, as well.

Forgetting his rank, he started horsing around with me at the Motor Pool as we used to do at Chaffee. First, while we were washing trucks, he sprayed some water on me, and I, in turn, sprayed him back. This monkeying around went on intermittently and continued as we started touching up the paint on the vehicle bodies. First, a little dab of red paint on me, then some black paint on him, then it was back and forth with O.D.(olive drab) paint. As a final thrust, I dabbed some O.D. on his forehead, he threw down his brush and hurled the contents of a gallon can of O.D. in my face. I was so startled that my eyes did not close. I then started screaming when I realized that my eyeballs were covered with paint and I couldn't see a thing.

I could hear a lot of commotion. Noncoms wanting to know what the hell was going on and a lot of people, including myself, wanting to know how someone could do such a stupid thing, or why the hell I didn't blink before the paint hit my eyes. Someone had the good sense to suggest that all the questions could be answered later, and that I should be taken for medical attention. Hollis promised me that he would explain that he was at fault, and told me to just take care of my eyes and not to worry about the Motor Pool. Two people were assigned to take me to the medics at Sick Bay even though the hours for Sick Call had long been over. It was amazing how I could tell what was going on around me, even though I couldn't see. I was escorted into Sick

Bay with one guy on each side of me holding on to my arms. As the door opened, I could hear the gasps of the Medics who, I was told later, had thought they had seen a "monster from the deep lagoon." The Medic in charge took a quick look at me and decided that they were not equipped to handle this type of emergency. He quickly called the hospital and asked them to send a vehicle to pick up an emergency patient.

Fortunately for me, Madigen Hospital was one of the top military hospitals in the country. Even more fortunate was the news that a world famous Swedish eye surgeon was on temporary duty at Madigen Hospital, giving lectures and demonstrations to the surgical staff of that hospital as well as other hospitals in the area. I was taken to a section appropriate for dealing with my problem and was examined briefly by an army ophthalmologist who decided that the Swedish guest doctor might want to look at this unusual case. The Swedish doctor came in, looked at my truck paint covered eyes, and agreed that it would be a great challenge to find a chemical that would cut the paint and not damage my eyes permanently.

He gently escorted me into another room and sat me into what seemed like a dental chair, and proceeded to work on me. The man had a way of keeping me calm and relaxing me with conversation and jokes. I was glad that it was only he and I in the room. He seemed to exude so much confidence in what he was doing, that I was totally at ease with him as he tried one solution after another. I didn't know how long it was that he worked on me, but I'm sure that it was at least an hour and a half. I didn't have time to dwell on what was going on, because he kept me laughing at his witty repartee for almost the entire time.

His manner had engendered unqualified faith in his ability to help me, and as it turned out, my faith was not misplaced. In the midst of his repartee I finally heard an exuberant, "Voila!," as he had finally mixed the solution that he felt sure would allow me to see again. He gently applied the solution to my eyes with Q-tips and before long I was beginning to get some vision back.

As I sat up to look around, I noticed what seemed like a hundred people, who it was later confirmed, were doctors standing in their white coats around the perimeter of the room.

They had been in there with us all that time, without making enough noise to let me realize that we weren't alone, watching the master perform his craft. As I looked around they started to applaud in unison. I was totally shocked and somewhat overwhelmed at being in the midst of what appeared to be a medical happening. That feeling quickly gave way to the emotions that had been welling up inside of me, fear that I might never see again, and then the amazing realization that my eyesight had been restored by this doctor, a specialist who just happened to be on the scene. I was so full of mixed emotions that I started to cry. I instinctively embraced the wonderful doctor and the applause around the room got louder.

I took a good look at the man responsible for saving my eyesight. He was tall, blond headed, and very Nordic looking. He shook my hand, wished me well, and left the room with his entourage of doctors following behind him. As I was basking in the euphoria of the moment, an army medic reminded me that I was still in the army, and that I would have to stay in the hospital overnight for observation, and then report back to my unit in the morning. In a few days, I was told, I should report to the base ophthalmologist to get my eyes checked for glasses.

I raced back to my unit the next morning, fully expecting to get a hero's welcome. I was welcomed by the First Sergeant who told me that the "incident" had been dealt with. Hollis had been restricted to the barracks for the remainder of that day, and I, as the instigator, was restricted to the barracks for fourteen days. He added in passing that I could forget making PFC for a while. "Oh, by the way," he almost forgot to say, "I'm glad you didn't lose your eyesight, you had us scared for a while." When Hollis came back with the squad that evening, he explained that if he had taken the blame as he had promised, he would have lost his position as Squad Leader and his opportunity to make Corporal, not to mention losing his PFC stripe. He felt that I would surely understand and promised to make it up to me. I decided I had enough of his promises, but kept it in mind anyway.

I was allowed to break my restriction to visit the ophthalmologist. He was a Major, who happened to be Jewish and he was very interested in my story. After examining my eyes, he told me that the paint had done no damage to my eyesight, but that I should have been wearing glasses all along. Even though I explained the helplessness of my situation in trying to get glasses since induction, he called me a "shmuck" for not pursuing the matter more vigorously. "Ain't that one Hell of a note," I thought to myself. "In the future," he advised me, "when something important is at stake, such as your health, you should insist on seeing the I.G. (Inspector General), if the system is keeping you from getting what you need to survive." Up until that time, I had never even heard of the I.G., or had any idea that there was a form of help for soldiers who were getting shafted. I kept that piece of advice in mind for future reference. His next piece of advice was in form of an order. "Start going to Chapel on a regular basis," he said, "We need you at the Friday night services and a little spirituality wouldn't hurt you either." After what had just happened, I didn't need much of a push.

THE NEXT FRIDAY EVENING I DECIDED TO go to Chapel. I don't remember going to Chapel at all at Camp Chaffee, and I had only gone three or four times at Camp Gordon. I had been brought up to go to services regularly, at least every Friday evening and Saturday morning for Shabbat, but since graduating from high school, I had been slacking off. I had actually thought about starting to attend services since arriving at Ft. Lewis, so the Majors urging did not fall on unreceptive ears.

The Chapel was not overcrowded. In fact, there were barely ten men for a Minyan when the scheduled time came to start the services. The Chaplain's Assistant asked if anyone had cantorial experience or was proficient at leading a service. When no one volunteered, the Assistant was forced to lead the services himself and didn't do that bad of a job. At the end of the services, some punch and cookies were served and everybody made a point of trying to find out who everyone else was, and where they were from. We call it "Jewish geography." When it came out that I was from Atlanta, Georgia, everyone's interest was piqued. "They have Jews in Atlanta?" Some New Yorkers actually thought that Jews were not allowed below the Mason-Dixon Line.

For the next thirty minutes, the focus of conversation was on Judaism in the South. When I told them that I had gone to Hebrew school and that I had led part of the service for my Bar Mitzvah, they pleaded with me to lead the services the next Friday evening so they could hear Hebrew with a Southern accent. I got a kick out of that. I warned them that they might be disappointed with the accent, since I was born in Germany and had lived in France before settling down in Atlanta. Nevertheless, I agreed to be the Cantor for one week.

I don't know how the word got out to the Jewish soldiers, but the question came up regarding the validity of my being the brother of Kirk Douglas. As much as I wanted to tell everyone that it was a joke that had gotten out of hand, I was afraid that this revelation might get back to some of the soldiers that had sent photos of themselves with me back home to their loved ones, and the result may not be easy to live with. Therefore, I made quick disposal of the question. I told them that I had no desire to discuss the matter, that if anyone wishes to befriend me, he should do it on the basis of who I am and not some speculation as to who my brother might be. To my surprise, the matter was put to rest, at least for the moment.

Back at my unit, the word got out that I had gone to Chapel and therefore I must be a practicing, religious Jew, even though I obviously had not been keeping Kosher at the time, or putting on Tephilin (phylacteries) and saying my prayers every morning. All the questions that anyone had ever wanted to know about Judaism, but were afraid to ask, were now being posed to me. I had enough background to answer many of the questions, and just enough knowledge to fake the answers for the rest of the questions.

The questioners were satisfied, but I was not. I had been a top student in afternoon Hebrew School and had even taught Sunday School for a while. Until my late teens, I had always kept Kosher and observed the Sabbath, and I was even offered an opportunity to go to a Yeshiva, in New York, to train to be a Cantor after my Bar Mitzvah. However, I had worked too hard at becoming the typical American boy and had given up a lot of my Jewish practices in the process. It was at this point, that I realized that my knowledge of Judaism left much to be desired and that what I had been doing was turning my back on the religious practices with which I had been brought up. This was the religion that my mother, father, little brother and sister were born into, and for which they were summarily condemned to death.

Some time during this process, I made up my mind that I would gradually return to practicing Judaism and eventually keep Kosher and be a Sabbath observant again, in order to delve more deeply into the Judaism and Jewish practices that I had been learning and practicing only superficially prior to diminishing my level of involvement. I knew that I wouldn't get far with this quest while I was in the Army, but I felt I could at least start with small steps, such as attending and participating in weekly Sabbath Services, as well as periodic Holy Day Services.

The two or three devout Christians that had been asking most of the questions inspired me to go regularly to Chapel and even asked to come along on occasion. They were particularly eager to go when I would be leading the services. These men probably have no idea how their interest in the Jewish religion ended up affecting my life. They made me realize that it was wrong to be giving up what so many of my people had died for, without at least being fully knowledgeable of what it was that I was abandoning.

For Passover, we were allowed to go into Seattle and sign up, through the U.S.O., to get invited to a Seder at the home of one of several families willing to have Jewish G.I.s join them and participate in their Passover Seder. I signed up to be considered by an Orthodox family, feeling that I would be more comfortable with a traditional Seder. To my surprise and disappointment, there were no Orthodox families, at least through the U.S.O., who had offered to host Jewish soldiers as their guests for the first or second Seders.

I was one of three Jewish soldiers who went to the home of a very gracious Jewish family who had stated they kept Kosher although they happened to belong to a Reform Temple. The father of this family inquired if any of us could read Hebrew or were proficient in the reading of the Haggadah, which recounts the story of the slavery of the Jewish People and exodus from Egypt. Reading the Haggadah is one of the major Mitzvot (Commandments) of the Passover Seder. I told him that both my Hebrew and my familiarity with the Haggadah were a bit rusty, but that I would be happy to help with the Seder in any way he wished.

The Seder went well. Most of the reading of the Haggadah was in English and when Hebrew was desired, I helped out as best I could. I thought about some of the traditional Seders I had been to, where the Haggadah had been read in the traditional Hebrew and Aramaic. Those Seders, however, did not have the feeling of reverence that permeated the Seder I had attended that evening. This family seemed to have had a desire to perform the ritual with the intention of following the Torah Commandments to the best of their limited knowledge and ability. I admit that I had been apprehensive about attending a non-Orthodox Seder, but I was not sorry for this experience. It is traditional to invite strangers to participate in the Seder ritual and meal. This was the first time that I had been one of the strangers and I felt good about it. There were no second Seders available to the Jewish soldiers. No offers had come from Orthodox or Conservative homes, and Reform Jews normally do not celebrate a second Seder. We went back to Fort Lewis to participate in the Seder at the Chapel. Matzos and Kosher-for-Passover canned goods were made available to us for the entire week of Passover by Jewish organizations through the Chaplain's office. The Rokeach canned chicken made us the envy of the barracks. It was much more appetizing than C-Rations, which had been on the menu in the Mess Hall for at least once a week. My first Passover in the Army came and went without much incident.

FIFTY DAYS AFTER THE FIRST DAY OF Passover is the Festival of Shavuot, which is traditionally celebrated for two days outside of the Land of Israel, in the Diaspora. This festival celebrates the giving of the Torah to the Jewish people by the Almighty. On the second day of Shavuot, as on the last day of Passover, and two other times in the Jewish calendar year, the Yizkor memorial prayer for departed loved ones is recited, primarily by those who have lost immediate family, as an integral part of the Holiday Service. My planning to attend the Services for this Holiday would probably not have been a problem any other time. However, that morning happened to be the day that the Battalion wide P.T. test was scheduled.

I had not given any thought to not being allowed to go to these Services. Shavouth (Pentecost), is one of the three major Jewish festivals of the year, and I had figured on making up any duty or responsibility that I would be missing, by going to Chapel. I was dressed up in my Class A uniform, walking to my car, when the First Sergeant stopped me as I was passing his office, and asked where I thought I was going. When I told him where I was going and why. He told me that I couldn't go because of the P.T. test. I hoped that his was not the final word and I asked to see the Captain, who had walked out when he heard the rather loud discussion going on.

In response to his inquiry, I explained to Captain Englehart the importance of the Yizkor Service in Judaism and to me, in particular, since this was one of only four times during a year that I would be able to say these prayers to honor the memory of my loved ones who perished in the Holocaust. While he wanted to be understanding, he couldn't comprehend why this service would be so important to me when the other Jewish soldiers in the outfit had made no request to go. That was a frustrating position for me to be put in. Accounting for the lack of need, or concern for saying Yizkor, of the two other Jewish soldiers in our unit, was not something that I felt I should have the burden of doing.

I told the Captain that I knew him to be a fair man, and I could understand that his lack of knowledge of Jewish festivals might have made it appear to him that my motive in wanting to go to Chapel was to get out of the rigor of this P.T. test. I told him, in an agitated voice, although I had made an effort at remaining calm, that he would have to trust me on this one; that when I came back from Chapel, I would do all of the P.T. exercises with the instructor of his choice, until one of us dropped; that if in checking out the legitimacy of my request to attend Chapel, he found that any of what I had told him was incorrect, I would be willing to be subjected to court-martial proceedings; and, because I did not wish to be delayed to the point that I would miss the Yizkor Service, that I would insist on going now and talking to the I.G. later, if the Captain felt that this step was necessary.

I had said the magic words that had been suggested to me by my army ophthalmologist. The Captain let me go, but not without an admonition that I had better be telling the truth about my reason for going, because he was going to check it all out before I got back. I couldn't believe that I had actually raised my voice and spoke back to an officer in that way. I did not like doing that. Yizkor was very important to me, but the idea that my integrity was being questioned because two other Jewish soldiers couldn't care less about attending Chapel for a holiday really set me off.

I returned to the unit ready for the worst. Talking back to an officer was inexcusable, even if I happened to be right. I immediately reported to Captain Englehart. He asked me to come into his office and close the door. He then inquired if I had been aware that talking back to him was a court martial offense. I responded that I did and that I had no excuse that had not already been stated. He paused for a while, with his hands clasped together, looking me straight in the eye. "I checked you out with the Chaplain," he said, "and, if you will pardon the pun, everything you told me is Kosher. On the other hand, the Chaplain could not justify the disrespectful way in which you addressed a superior officer."

I had no idea where this was leading, but it didn't appear to be good. The Captain was a short wiry man. He stared at me a while longer. If he was looking for contrition, he found it in me. He finally said that as much as he faulted me for my actions, he admired the way that I stood up for what I believe in. He hastened to add that this was not a trait that was conducive to succeeding in the Army, and admitted that the timing of the circumstances and his lack of knowledge of my religion had left me little choice other than to miss the Yizkor service, that was so important to me, a sacrifice which, I could only assume, a good soldier would have made. He informed me that my punishment would be seven days of restriction to the Battery area, and I breathed a sigh of relief. He then added that he was glad to have me under his command. I felt like somebody was watching over me. "Life can't get much better than this," I thought to myself.

I insisted on performing all of the P.T. exercises, even though it had not been made mandatory, and I invited the First Sergeant to do them with me. He opted to watch me do them to make sure that I didn't cheat.

THE MOST TIME-CONSUMING CHORE IN GETTING ready for weekly inspections of the barracks had always been cleaning the windows, so that the panes do not show streaks. That is until someone came up with the idea of using toilet paper to wipe the window panes, instead of using rags, which left lint on the windows. We started doing this on our barracks with great success, and before long, the entire Battery was using this window cleaning technique. The only problem was that before each month was half-way over, the supply room had run out of toilet paper.

Our First Sergeant retired after thirty years of service and was replaced by a Master Sergeant from the hills of North Carolina. I think he may have been from Hurst's home town or at least the same basic area. Our new First Sergeant was a well decorated soldier with a chest full of medals. He also had the reputation, so we were told, of being a problem solver. Hurst had been working in the supply room and he posed to his friend, the new First Sergeant, the on-going problem of the toilet paper shortage toward the middle of each month.

The Sergeant took this problem very seriously. He compared our monthly allotment and consumption of toilet paper with that of other batteries, and concluded that we simply were not economical enough in the way that we used toilet paper to wipe our posteriors. Being a man of action, he assembled the entire Battery in a lecture hall, and proceeded to give us a lecture he had prepared on the proper way to economically use toilet paper, so that we would not run out of the commodity by the second or third week of each month. We had all thought that Hurst knew why every barracks was using an inordinate amount of toilet paper. Now we knew that he didn't have a clue, and apparently the Sergeant, with all of his research, didn't have a clue either.

The technique we were being taught was very simple. He instructed us to take a piece of toilet paper, the length of two perforated squares, and wipe, then fold it in half and wipe again. If necessary, fold it in half again and wipe. By this time, any normal excursion to the bathroom would have been wiped clean with the one doubled piece of paper. He proceeded to explain that an especially loose movement might take as much as two or three doubled pieces. Hollis and I had been gripping each other's forearms as hard as we could to keep from bursting out laughing. By the time he started demonstrating his revolutionary system of toilet paper usage, which included inspecting the paper after each step, I lost it. I fell over in the aisle and was convulsed with uncontrollable laughter. I had worked so hard at trying to contain myself that I must have exploded.

Laughter is contagious. The whole place fell apart and there I was rolling in the aisle unable to control my laughter, that is until I looked up and saw the Sergeant standing over me, hands on his hips and red as a beet. "That does it, Hirsch!, You will report to Fireman's School at 15:00 hours." The place quieted down rather quickly. I surmised that no one wanted to share Fireman's School with me although I had no idea what that was. I was instructed to leave the session and reminded that I had approximately one hour before the deadline of reporting to Fireman's School. Failure to report on time, I was told, would be disobeying a direct order that was an offense that could be subject to court martial.

I exited the lecture hall with mixed feelings. I was glad to be out of that asinine lecture, but felt that I might be missing some more hilarious stuff. The scary thing was that I had no idea what was in store for me at Fireman's School. If it was a punishment, it had to be bad.

I reported to Fireman's School at least fifteen minutes early to avoid any chance of being late and to find out what it was all about. To my surprise, this was a four hour course on how to be a "Fireman," not the kind that puts out fires, but the kind that keeps them going. We were being taught to tend the furnaces that heat the barracks. We were instructed on how to start a fire in a furnace, feed coal, stoke the fire, clean the furnace, and, most importantly, how to bank the coal on cold nights so that the fire would last longer between coal feedings, allowing the Fireman a longer stretch of sleep. The most exciting thing I learned was that a Fireman's duty hours were 24 hours on and 24 hours off, during the week. Weekends were alternated, one 72 hour weekend on duty, the next one off. This was particularly exciting news in light of the fact that Service Battery had only two barracks with one coal bin in between the two. After completing the course in less than two hours, I speculated that the 24 hour duty might only entail four or five one hour spurts of actual work. Of course, all this was based on the assumption that the First Sergeant actually intended to assign me to the post of Fireman for Service Battery.

The First Sergeant was waiting for me when I returned to the barracks. An apology for my conduct was probably in order, but I was afraid that if I had made any reference to that afternoon's lecture, I would start laughing again. He asked me how I liked Fireman's School and I nonchalantly responded that it wasn't so bad. He took great joy in advising me, in front of my barracks mates, that he had officially assigned me to the position of Fireman for Service Battery, especially since it was common knowledge that the position of Fireman was usually assigned to an individual with very low intellectual capacity, or someone who lacked the ability or desire to perform more essential tasks. In the Sergeant's eyes, this was the ultimate punishment for my laughing at his lecture and I actually felt a little debased inside, but I didn't want to give him the satisfaction of seeing me unhappy about this.

As it turned out, this assignment couldn't have been better. It took me one 24 hour shift to get the hang of banking the coals in the furnaces so that I would only have to get up once in the middle of the night. While all other Firemen in our Battalion, except for the one I alternated with in Service Battery, were responsible for at least three furnaces, I was responsible for only two. So once I got the hang of things, my work on a twenty-four hour shift consisted of about 45 minutes to an hour every six to eight hours. This meant that on the days that I was on duty, I had all kinds of free time, not to mention that I was off every second day and every second weekend.

All this time I had been dreaming of becoming a Chaplain's assistant or getting an office or supply room job, and of all things, I fell into the cushiest job on the base by screwing up. All this time off and a car to take me away from the Unit whenever it suited my fancy. Life was good, I thought to myself, or as good as it could be in the Army.

The First Sergeant was satisfied that I had gotten my just desserts, but Captain Englehart could see that I had too much free time on my hands, compared to everyone else in the Battalion. He called me in to discuss how my talents could be utilized on my time off. He was aware that I had some art background and wanted me to paint charts and signs for the Battalion on my days off. I realized that I was in a unique bargaining position. There was no way that the Captain would override his First Sergeant and take me off Fireman's duty. On the other hand, the Captain needed someone with reasonable talent to paint charts, which would be required for an I.G. inspection that was scheduled down the road, and he needed someone to paint various and sundry signs.

I had the time and ability to do what the Captain needed, but I was not inclined to give up my days off. I made a counter offer to accept the unofficial position of Battalion Sign Painter with the provision that I would only paint on the days that I was on duty as Fireman, and would never be required to paint signs, charts or anything else on my off duty days. I assured the Captain that I could get all of his work done with this arrangement, and to my surprise, he agreed to the deal without much argument. We shook hands, I stepped back and saluted him, and we began what was to be a very amicable working relationship.

6

CUDDLES

THE FIRST SERGEANT WAS AS PROUD AS Hurst was of his home state of North Carolina. He was as equally embarrassed at the fact that Cuddles was also a North Carolinian. Cuddles had been working almost full time at trying to get a Section 8 discharge for being homosexual, but the more he acted out the part, the more his superiors, from squad leader up to the Captain, resisted taking him seriously. The fact that Cuddles was so open about his sexual orientation probably did not work in his favor, considering that he did not want to be in the Army. I actually believed that they didn't doubt his homosexuality. I felt, and Cuddles agreed, that they just didn't want to kick out a man who wanted out, particularly one who made it a point to act obnoxiously queer.

We had gotten word that a sergeant from North Fort, who had only two years left before he would retire with full pay as a thirty year man, was found out to be homosexual by being caught in the act and summarily kicked out of the Army. How ironic that this sergeant had been trying to hide his sexual preference so he could stay in the Army for at least another two years, while Cuddles couldn't even get a hearing on his illegal sexual orientation.

Cuddles and I talked a great deal and there were quite a few guys in the Battalion who insisted that I was queer, because I befriended him. I had never heard of same-sex marriages until Cuddles showed me his wedding band and told me about the man he had married a short time before being drafted. I wondered why that wasn't enough evidence of his homosexuality. He responded that he had not been given the opportunity to present this evidence. I suggested that he should request to see the I.G., and present this evidence to him. If he ever got to see the I.G., it was after I was long gone from Fort Lewis.

Cuddles was the repository of all the scuttlebutt on the base. He was a real "yenta" with a nose for gossip and rumors. After the Sergeant from North Fort was dishonorably discharged, I expressed my surprise that a homosexual person could stay in the Army for twenty-eight years, and reach the rank of Master Sergeant, without his homosexuality being discovered. Cuddles couldn't believe that I was so naive. He asked me if I thought that there were any other homosexuals in our Battalion.

I thought for a while and could only come up with one soldier whose manner was somewhat effeminate, but whom I knew to be a happily married man, as well as one of the most accomplished sketch artists I had ever come across. He was the only person I had ever seen sketch portraits with a ball point pen. He insisted that once you started erasing and altering a drawing that it was no longer a sketch. It wasn't long before I took up sketching with ball point pens, with the goal of getting to be as good at it as this soldier was.

I told Cuddles that, to my knowledge, he was the only homosexual in the Battalion. Cuddles looked at me with a smug smile. "You really believe that, don't you?" I nodded my head in the affirmative. "Well..." he paused for a moment, "I'm gonna just tell you about the people in this Battalion that you come in contact with daily. There's no point in you knowing about anyone else." I figured he was pulling my leg, and after he listed the non-coms and then PFCs and Private E-2s, I was convinced he was full of it. He promised me that it was all true and that he was only telling me about them so that I should not be surprised if any of them came on to me, because of my friendship with him. I still had my doubts. Cuddles was usually correct about all the scuttlebutt that he passed on to me, but these guys were so macho, such gung-ho soldiers, that I found it hard to take him seriously. Still, I started observing these soldiers more carefully. If Cuddles was right, all of these guys were in the closet. Before I left Fort Lewis, I was convinced that Cuddles was right to a man.

THE "RAMBLIN WRECK" WAS ONE OF A kind, but it got me where I wanted to go. About a month after I received the car, its wiring system developed a short and the mechanics in the motor pool couldn't seem to find it. At that point, I came to appreciate having the battery under the driver's seat. Whenever I would reach a destination, I would lift up the seat and remove the battery cable. When I was ready to drive again, I would again lift the seat and reconnect the battery cable. This became the method of operation for keeping the "Ramblin Wreck" in driving condition and continued to be until we finally found the short, about a month before I left Fort Lewis.

Having a car at my disposal, and a good amount of free time, gave me an opportunity to see some of the state of Washington. I developed a nucleus of buddies that went with me at different times to various localities. Tacoma was the closest town of any size and we went there often on week nights. Olympia, though it is the capitol of the State, was a sleepy little town with very little to attract young soldiers on their days off. Climbing Mount Rainier was something we all wanted to do, especially since it was the most beautiful view we had from Ft. Lewis, but climbing a snow capped mountain was something that few people would want to do more than once. Seattle, on the other hand, was a neat city. It was only sixty miles away and it became our most frequent destination on weekends.

My closest friend was Steve Groff. He was a really cool guy from Sheepshead Bay in Brooklyn, New York, whom I had met at Friday night Services. Steve was easy to get along with and we seemed to have a lot of interests in common. He was one of the least gullible guys I had met, sort of a Jewish Hobgood. I was convinced that he did not believe the Kirk Douglas's brother bit, but he never pressed me on the issue, after I initially told him that I preferred not to discuss it. Almost every time I drove to Seattle, Steve went along. Most of the time there would be three or four guys, but some times it was just Steve and me. Being a seasoned New York driver, he taught me how to drive defensively, and how to pull forward into a parallel parking space when traffic didn't allow me to back into one.

On our first trip to Seattle, after looking around, we ended up at the Stewart Hotel and rented a room as a base of operation. One of the guys on this trip suggested that we go out and buy a fifth of gin, a bottle of grape juice, and some Tom Collins Mix and make a concoction that he called Purple Jesus. We ran out and picked up the ingredients and soon realized that we had no bowl to mix up the P.J. I looked up at the ceiling and noticed that our room had a surface mounted ceiling light fixture with a glass, bowl shaped, lens that was easy to take down. I got the bright idea to take down the fixture lens, wash it out, and use it as a mixing bowl. It worked like a charm and to my surprise, the purple concoction was very good. So good in fact, that making this concoction became a ritual. Every trip to Seattle, we would rent a room in the Stewart Hotel, make sure that our room had the proper light fixture, and proceed with procuring the ingredients and mixing the P.J., generally before any thought was given to our agenda for the weekend.

Seattle must have been built on mountains. I was sure that its long, steeply sloping streets had been featured in many car chase scenes from Class B movies. More than once, the brakes on the "Ramblin Wreck" failed as we were driving down one of those steep streets. Steve taught me about pumping the brakes, which worked on occasion. Other times, we depended on blowing the horn and hoping that drivers on the side streets would be alert enough to listen for it. We also relied heavily on luck and prayers. Between these frightening scenarios, the short in the wiring system, and the fact that the car burned one quart of oil each way for every trip to Seattle, I was almost ready to junk the car. I told Steve that if it had been a horse, I would have been forced to shoot it long before, but he would remind me that without the car we would not be able to afford the frequent trips to Seattle and Tacoma. I realized that I was quite fortunate to have a car at all, and counted my blessings.

IF THERE COULD HAVE BEEN A PROBLEM with having every second day off as part of my job description of Fireman, it was that there hardly ever was anyone to share the time off with. I didn't know the Firemen of the other Batteries, and from the few times we ran into each other, I sensed that we had very little in common. It was a good thing that I had the car, otherwise I might have gone batty trying to find things to amuse myself with around the Battalion post. Steve had a buddy who ran the miniature golf concession. Luckily, Steve also had a fair amount of time that he could get away from his post.

On several of those occasions, Steve borrowed two putters and some golf balls from the miniature golf place, and we sneaked onto the last nine holes of the officers' golf course. Aside from the fact that I had very little experience or expertise with the game of golf (miniature golf was about my speed), it was absurd to the point of being fun to play nine holes of golf with only a putter. After a while we sort of got the hang of it, considering the limitations of our equipment. Putting was a breeze. Getting the ball to the green was another matter. The real challenge, however, was to keep from getting caught. Finishing nine holes on a golf course we had no authorization to be on, leaving with our putters and golf balls in hand, and the risk of getting caught, kind of got the adrenaline flowing.

Another place we occasionally went to was the beach on a lake that was on the Ft. Lewis grounds. While I loved to swim, I always made it a point to not over expose my skin to the sun, because I burn very easily. This was not a major problem, because it rained almost every day that we were at Fort Lewis, except for sometime in July and August.

On one of my days off, I had tried to get Steve to go to the beach with me, but he had to work. It was an overcast day, but warm enough to make the water seem inviting. I had the whole beach to myself and kind of enjoyed the solitude. I swam until I was thoroughly exhausted, got out of the water and lay down on the beach, on my stomach, to relax. About two hours later, I woke up. The sky was still overcast and it looked like the rain was going to come down any minute. I was fine until I tried to put my shirt and pants on. My back and the back of my legs were so burned that I couldn't bear to touch them with anything. I had not intended to fall asleep. I had heard that the sun's rays get magnified through cloud cover and had meant only to lie on the beach for a few minutes.

Driving back to the barracks was a weird scene. I couldn't lean back on the car seat and I couldn't allow the back of my legs to touch anything. It was amazing that I didn't get stopped by the M.P.s for indecent exposure, or at least, attire. Driving on the post in just a bathing suit was not allowed. I sneaked back into the barracks before the rest of the guys returned from their duties, without being seen by anyone. I was sitting on my bunk, wondering whether to go on sick call, when everyone came in from their day's work. Those who noticed me gasped as they stared at their Fireman who looked like a lobster. I sat there bewildered as a discussion on army regulations ensued. Everyone agreed that I could not go on Sick Call without risking a court-martial. I was told about a soldier that was court-martialed a year before for allowing himself to get so severely sunburned that he had to miss over a week of duty. I asked what the charges had been and they told me it was for willful abuse of government property, his body.

These guys must have really appreciated my keeping them warm on cold nights. They put me under a very hot shower and held me there while the water hit my sunburned skin, feeling like needles. This was intended to open the pores to better receive the salve that they would rub on afterwards. This procedure was followed three times a day for about two weeks. During this time, someone always covered for me to make sure that none of the sergeants or officers would see the way I had abused this government property, that I preferred to think of as my body.

PREPARATIONS FOR THE WAR GAMES THAT WERE to take place in the Yakima Desert seemed to go on forever. I really had not concerned myself with the upcoming four week military exercise, figuring that, as an essential Fireman, I might be exempt from participating. As usual, I guessed wrong. All of the military units in the Main Post of Fort Lewis were going to take part in this mock war. The Yakima Training Range is about 150 miles inland from Ft. Lewis, and we had to travel in a military convoy on the mostly two lane highways.

Lieutenant Lee was directly under Captain Englehart and he was in charge of putting together our Battalion's part of the convoy, which required more truck drivers than we had in our motor pool. I had taken tests, when we first arrived in Fort Lewis, that related to the skills necessary to drive large trucks with trailer hitches that pull artillery guns. After seeing my peripheral vision test, which went beyond the charts on the down side, the instructor excused me from the rest of the tests. I reminded Lieutenant Lee of those test results when he suggested that I drive a deuce-and-a-half pulling a 155 Howitzer for the convoy. He had even offered to give me a 4503 MOS number, which was the truck driver designation, and was apparently desirous to some soldiers, if I would drive for him to Yakima. We went through my files to review the test results, and the scores spoke for themselves. The P.V. test was graded from 1 to 100 with the higher number being totally unacceptable. My test score was in the neighborhood of 530. He reluctantly let me off the hook, but immediately assigned me to ride shotgun for one of the other recruited drivers.

My driver's name was Vance. I knew him from seeing him around the Battery. He was an ammo handler and was delighted with the change in job designation. I knew him as a pretty flighty guy with a weird sense of humor. He was good looking, sort of a Johnny Mathis look-alike with a thinner nose, and he bragged about his conquests of lady friends a lot, but he had a warm and engaging personality. I was enjoying his company as we drove up and down the mountainous roads as part of the convoy. We seemed to have plenty to talk about and he knew most of the pop songs that I knew. Before the trip started, we were instructed that the convoy would be sharing the roads with civilian traffic and that it was our duty, since the size of our vehicles would block the view of most civilian drivers, to keep an eye out for breaks in the oncoming traffic and to wave the cars behind us on when the coast was clear.

After we had gone about eighty miles, Vance asked me if I wanted to take over and give him a rest. I reminded him that I was not qualified to drive a two and one-half ton truck, with or without a Howitzer trailer. He had not forgotten, he said he just thought I might enjoy being behind the wheel. He was getting a kick out of waving the civilian traffic on to pass us. After a while, he would chuckle every time he waved someone on, and then I would hear honking of horns, screeching of tires, and a plethora of four letter words. The convoy was ordered to stop and I saw Lt. Lee stomping toward our truck with murder in his eyes. He proceeded to chew out Cpl. Vance like I had never seen the usually mild-mannered officer do to anyone. He then focussed his attention on me. "Was I not aware of what Vance was doing?" I asked to be told what the Lieutenant was referring to.

Apparently Vance had gotten bored. He had started to wait until there was oncoming traffic before he would wave the cars behind us on, which explained the sounds I was hearing after he waved someone on. Vance was told that he was immediately demoted to PFC, which he opted to accept in lieu of a court-martial, and was not allowed to continue driving in the convoy, even though he promised to behave. I pleaded his case to no avail, fearing that I would have to take over the driving chores on an emergency basis. As the intentions of Lt. Lee became clear, I reminded him that I had never driven with a trailer before, and I brought up the Peripheral Vision test scores, but he was not to be swayed. According to him, this was a combat condition and I had to learn to grow with the challenge. "Good Training," was Lt. Lee's predictable response to put an end to the discussion.

Vance tried to make conversation as the convoy continued on, but I was much too preoccupied with driving that huge vehicle, and worried about the cannon it was pulling. Every bump in the road seemed to have an effect on the stability of the load we were pulling. Each time the cannon started veering from side to side, I had to slow down to a snail's pace until the trailer had gotten back in line with the truck. The convoy drivers behind us were less than patient with my inexperience. By the time we arrived at our destination, I felt like I had been sweating bullets. I got out of the cab and told Vance that he would have to back our vehicle up. I knew the basic principals of backing up a trailer, but didn't have the experience or desire to risk plowing the Howitzer into a vehicle on either side of our parking space.

Lt. Lee thanked me for agreeing to "on the job training" to get him out of a bind, and he looked kindly on my suggestion that someone else be found to drive the vehicle back to Fort Lewis at the end of the war games. There was a shortage of drivers for ammo delivery to the gun positions, so Vance was reinstated as a truck driver with the admonition that if he screwed up one more time, he would be court-martialed. He did not get his corporal's stripe back.

The war games were going to be one long bivouac. We were going to be living out of two man pup-tents and Vance was designated to share a tent with me. I hate to admit that I was actually afraid to sleep in the same tent with Vance at the beginning. I liked him, but he had done some unpredictable things in the convoy that were pretty scary. As it turned out, we got along famously. We spent many of our evenings around a fire with a group of black soldiers, one of whom had a guitar, singing blues and other popular songs. I still consider one of the greatest compliments ever paid me was when Vance told me that I had been accepted in the group, because they felt that I sang with soul, as if I were a black man.

Yakima Training Center is a desert. The days were excruciatingly hot and the nights were relatively cold. Our daily routine was patterned to be as if a war was going on. We followed orders, delivering ammo to the gun positions. What I couldn't figure out was how the game worked. Our guns could not have been shooting at the "enemy" positions, so what were they shooting at, and why the live ammo? I was told that mine is not to reason why, mine is but to do or die. I left the worrying about the "war effort" to the people in charge, and I went about my business of surviving in the heat, and trying to find ways to occupy myself in the evenings, which occasionally were free.

The word was out that there was a big poker game going on nightly in the mess tent. I hurried over there only to find that there was a waiting line for seats in the game. That turned out to be less of a problem than anticipated. The game was no limit, table stakes poker, which can be real cut throat and can dry up a player's money supply quickly. It didn't take long before a seat was available and I sat down with the confidence of a non-swimmer in a deep pool. I had never played table stakes, much less no limit poker before, although I knew the rules. As confident as I was with my poker skills, I found myself playing much more cautiously than I normally would have played in a typical poker game with limits on the bets. I was staying about even when the guy sitting next to me dropped out and our drill sergeant sat down in his place. I had no love for this sergeant. As a matter of fact, I disliked him intensely. He didn't strike me as much of a poker player either, but he was really drawing some good hands and winning in spite of himself.

Almost every dealer chose seven card stud, high-low, because two winner games seem to make for larger pots. I played cautiously, folding if the hand was not showing much promise after the fourth card. The first two cards were face down, so the second bet was after seeing the fourth card. I had just folded an awful four card combination and sat there watching the hand progress from the sidelines. Sarge's hand looked promising from the cards showing. The betting was getting heavy, and Sarge, who had been feeling good about his hand, was beginning to question whether he should call the large raise by a Corporal across the table. All of a sudden he nudged me, showed me his three hole cards, and asked me to advise him on whether to call or go out. This was not a penny ante game, where kibitzing is not frowned upon, yet this was my drill sergeant who could make me regret not advising him correctly or not advising him at all. I reluctantly glanced at his cards, and after he pressed me again for advice, told him that if the hand were mine, I definitely would at least call.

Sarge won the hand, which had the biggest pot of the night, and thanked me for my advice. The corporal, who had made the large raise to scare Sarge out, was not so pleased. He got up from the table, stood at the entrance flap of the tent, and motioned for me to come outside. I asked Sarge to hold my seat for a moment and went out to talk to the Corporal, whom I knew from our singing group. I figured he would be unhappy with me, but I felt that he might understand the predicament I had been in. He stood me up against the tent, looked me straight in the eye, and said in a very stern voice, "Don't you ever pull a stunt like that again if you want to stay alive! Consider yourself lucky that I know you and I like you, otherwise I would kill you right now for advising that jerk to call my bluff. You cost me big." There was nothing I could say. I was convinced that he meant every word. I liked poker, but this game was for blood. I thanked the corporal for his magnanimity and decided I had enough poker for the night. I left the game and did not play poker again for the remainder of my stay in the state of Washington.

I don't even remember if our side won or lost the war games. What I do remember is that several participants lost their lives in various forms of accidents. I heard two soldiers were fatally bitten by rattlesnakes when they crawled into their tents, unwittingly cornering the snakes. I also heard of explosions of heaters used for warming water in garbage cans to wash mess kits. At least one soldier died in this type of explosion, or, rumor had it as high as three. Total fatalities, according to the grapevine, may have been as high as eleven. However, no official information was ever made available to us. For a mock war, the casualties were unusually high.

The return convoy to Fort Lewis was uneventful. Vance drove like a sane person. Our unit was no worse for the wear except for Vance's stripe. Before Yakima, I had been told by the motor pool mechanics that my car would have to have a ring job. The "Ramblin Wreck" had been parked for a month, and lo and behold, it had stopped burning excessive amounts of oil. The mechanic said that the rings must have settled while sitting for a month. To celebrate, he started looking for the short in the car's electrical system and found it in less than thirty minutes. The car was getting shaped up. Now all it needed was a brake job, new shocks, a paint job and seat covers.

WITHIN A WEEK OF OUR RETURN FROM Yakima, the whole Battalion was in a dither over the upcoming I.G. inspection. I had never seen so many officers and non-coms worked up over an inspection before. I had seen all kinds of inspections, but apparently this was going to be the big one. The Battalion was given several weeks lead time to prepare and make sure that everything was in ship-shape order. The I.G. inspection was not limited to outward appearances, it included, among other things, the matching up of job profiles with the qualifications and intelligence quotient of individuals assigned to specific jobs.

I had been going about my business of tending the furnace and painting signs, oblivious to all the excitement involved in preparations for the inspection. A young sergeant working in G-3 at Battalion Headquarters called and asked to see me. He had a certain urgency in his voice. We had met before to compare notes, since both of us had entered the army with two years of college under our belt, and both of us majoring in architecture. In previous conversations, he had led me to believe that the training he had received during his two years at U.C.L.A. was superior to what I had received at Georgia Tech. This was to explain why he had acquired his position at headquarters, supposedly as a draftsman, and the promotions that came with the job, as opposed to me, who had similar schooling yet was initially assigned, after sixteen weeks of basic training for something else, to the position of ammo handler. We both had volunteered for the draft, but apparently he had found the opportunity and had done a good job of selling himself.

The reason he asked me to see him at headquarters was not social. He had been handed an assignment that had to do with the I.G. inspection. An assignment that, his superiors assumed, he was eminently qualified to complete. The Battalion C.O. wanted a brochure on the make-up of the Battalion, complete with drawings, graphs and charts to impress the inspection team. The former U.C.L.A. architectural student had done a better snow job on his superiors than he had done on me. He now confided in me that he could not draw. He had no natural talent, and contrary to his original boasts, the first two years of architectural studies at U.C.L.A. were only academic, without any drawing labs. In other words, there was no way he could produce the brochure and he wanted me to do it for him on the Q.T., without letting anyone know that he had not done it.

He was familiar with my graphics and design work and knew that I had the ability to produce the brochure. He also knew that I had the free time to do it. To get me interested, he offered to pay me two hundred dollars cash to do the job, and as an extra incentive, he offered to get me any information from headquarters, within limits, that I might need, information that would otherwise have been inaccessible to me. While the deal sounded very tempting, I told him that I needed a couple of days to think it over and that I would call him.

I had mixed emotions about the offer. It would be fun to do, but I disliked the idea of not getting credit for my work. The main issue bothering me was that this guy had conned his way into the kind of job that he was not qualified for, and that by doing this work for him, I would be helping him maintain his sham. On the other hand, two hundred bucks was a little more than two months pay for me, and if I really did have a need for any info from headquarters, I probably would not have even hesitated. I decided to sleep on it for a day or two.

Things started happening quickly. The next day, Captain Englehart summoned me to his office. "Great news, Hirsch. I just got word from headquarters that you have the highest Area One score in the whole Battalion." He watched me for a reaction, but I was fairly nonplussed. This information couldn't have been new, there had to be a follow-up to this revelation. Sure enough, there was. "The Battalion Commander can't understand why the soldier with the highest I.Q. in the Battalion has a job profile that could be filled by a chimpanzee, and he doesn't think the I.G. inspectors are going to understand either." I decided against responding until all the cards were on the table.

For the past week, or so, I had been in the midst of painting a large organizational chart on plywood for the Battery during my sign painting time, listing each soldier in the Battery and his M.O.S. (Military Occupational Specialty). There had been discussion about which M.O.S. to put down for me, since there had been no designation for Fireman, or for sign painter, and I was no longer an ammo handler.

"The bottom line is," Captain Englehart continued, "that you can choose virtually any job profile in the Battalion that would be more commensurate with your ability. This comes directly from the Battalion Commander." I wondered how I could respond without being flip.

"Do you and the C.O. really mean it when you say that I can choose any job in the Battalion that falls within my rank?" I was setting him up, but I was sincere about what I had in mind.

"Of course, you can choose. This is your opportunity to make up for the many months that you have been working at a job that is so beneath your qualifications." He tried to sound convincing, but we both knew what a crock this whole issue was. Were it not for the I.G. inspection, both the Captain and the First Sergeant would have been just as happy to see me on garbage details until my discharge.

"In that case," I responded, "I would like to continue what I am currently doing. While it doesn't take much brain power to be a Fireman, I do the job well, and the free time allows me to pursue more intellectual interests."

The Captain was starting to unravel. He knew that I knew what this was all about. Something had to be done so that the Battalion would not look foolish, but he had no answers. "You can't do that!" He tried to keep from loosing his cool. "This entire discussion has to do with changing the status quo, not keeping it!"

I started thinking to see if I could come up with a way to make everybody happy. I sat down at the First Sergeant's desk to help my thinking process along. I closed my eyes, trying to concentrate on the problem. When I opened them, I noticed some paperwork on the desk that appeared to be transfer orders to Germany for a couple of soldiers in Service Battery. I was so surprised that I blurted out, "I don't mean to change the subject, but I didn't know that enlisted men from Fort Lewis were ever sent to Germany. I was under the impression that overseas from here was limited to the Far East."

In response to my comment, the First Sergeant said that assignments to Europe were rare, but that requests occasionally came in based on the need for a specific M.O.S. That little tidbit of information was enough to inspire the thinking and scheming process. I stood at attention as I addressed the Captain, "Sir, I think I have an idea. I feel confident that the C.O. and the I.G. inspectors could understand a Special Duty job profile of Battalion Artist and Graphics Designer even though there is no such M.O.S. designation. Further, I could select an M.O.S. that would fit in the charts even though I was being assigned to special duty. In the meantime, I could continue my Fireman duties, off the record, and perform the special duties on a Battalion level on my weekdays off." I was making an effort to protect my weekends off.

Captain Englehart raised his eyebrows. I could tell he was thinking over my proposal to see if it could work. "And what M.O.S. will you be selecting?" he asked, sounding like he was afraid that I might have something else up my sleeve.

I was prepared for the question. "I haven't made up my mind yet. However, I'll make a request to you, Sir, before the chart I'm working on is finished."

The Captain seemed satisfied, "Looks like you've come up with a solution that everyone can live with, Hirsch. I like that about you." I saluted him, made a snappy about-face, and walked out of the office trying to contain the excitement I felt over what could potentially be a fantastic sting in the making.

I ran over to Headquarters and called on the U.C.L.A. man in G-3, who had been getting pretty nervous waiting for my answer. I asked him if he had a chance to see requests for specific M.O.S.'s from Germany, before they would be sent to Service Battery. After he responded in the affirmative, I told him that I would do the brochure on one condition. He would have to contact me the next time a request for a specific M.O.S. came from Germany, that would need to be filled by Service Battery. He would then have to see to it that delivery of the request to Service Battery would be delayed by at least an hour, after he told me, which M.O.S. was required. The rest was up to me. He agreed, without questioning what I had in mind, and we shook hands on the deal. I went about my business, waiting for a call from G-3.

The call came within a week. There was a request for 4503 M.O.S., which was a truck driver for an ammo handling Artillery Battery, and it was for Germany. The adrenaline had really started to flow. I reminded my source that he should delay the delivery of this request to Service Battery for at least an hour, and preferably more. He promised he would do the best he could, but guaranteed me that the delay would be at least an hour.

I gathered all of my courage, and walked around for a while to contain my nervousness. When I felt I was ready, I walked into the office, ostensibly to continue painting on the organizational chart. I asked the First Sergeant to tell the Captain that I had decided on which M.O.S. I would like to select for myself, per our previous discussion. Captain Englehart overheard and came out of his office. "Well, which M.O.S. has the Prima Donna selected?" His remark was intended to needle me.

"Sir, with your permission, I would like for the M.O.S. on my records to be for a 3/4 ton ammo truck driver, I believe that would be 4503." I looked at the chart I was painting, "Yes, that's right, 4503 is the M.O.S. number."

He was a little surprised at my selection. "I would have expected something less mundane from you, Hirsch, but I have no problem putting you down as a truck driver, as long as you don't drive a truck for me." He nodded at the Sergeant and it was a done deal. Next, I needed to find a way to get the Captain and the First Sergeant to start needling me, as they usually did when I was in the office working on sign painting.

I overheard the First Sergeant remark to the office clerk that he had just learned that Seattle was not the capitol of Washington. This opened the door for a little obnoxiousness on my part. I told him that we had learned states and capitols in the fifth grade and that I still remembered them all to this day. He took the bait and challenged me by insisting that I could not name the forty eight states and capitols in ten minutes, if my life depended on it. I asked him how much he would like to wager on that challenge. He was quick to pull out a ten dollar bill and offer me ten to one odds, his sawbuck to my dollar. I didn't even have to ask if there were any more takers. There were six other people in the office, including the Captain, and they each put up ten bucks. I had done this exercise so many times in the past that I may have been overconfident. Everyone gathered around while Sarge picked up a pencil and pad, along with a stop watch, and motioned for me to start. I shut my eyes and imagined a map of the United States and started in the NE corner with Augusta, Maine. In less than three minutes, I had rattled out forty seven states and capitols, and couldn't, for the life of me, figure out which state I had left out.

Sarge had really been concerned for his bet as I was rattling off the first forty seven. Now he was enjoying the agony of my search for number forty eight. He started calling out the ticks of the clock and jabbing at me with comments like "You know why donkeys are not allowed to go to college?, 'cause nobody likes a smart ass." The onlookers laughed with him, as I kept running the map through my mind. Finally, I asked for a piece of paper and started sketching the map of the U.S. from memory. I had less than two minutes left as I was frantically sketching away. It worked. With less than a minute to go, I realized that I had left out Lincoln, Nebraska.

Sarge tried to hide the fact that he was impressed as he begrudgingly handed me the money. "You know, Hirsch, you really know a lot of stuff. But that doesn't mean you have to be a smart ass about it." I guessed that was his way of paying me a compliment, but compliments were not what I was looking for at that time.

I turned to the Captain. "Cpt. Englehart, Sir, do you think that I'm a smart ass too?" The Captain was not above swapping jabs with me, I just had to be careful to show the proper respect for his rank, not to mention age.

"Hirsch," he responded, playing the role of antagonist, "you not only are a smart ass, you're probably the biggest f--- off I have ever seen!"

"You really would like to get rid of me, Sir." I baited him on, "I must be a real pain in the ass to you." The same group that had gathered around to watch me sweat out the bet on states and capitols, started taking an interest in the verbal combat.

Captain Englehart didn't hesitate to respond, "If I could find someone to take you off my hands, you'd be out of here so fast your head would spin." This was the opening I was looking for.

"Sir, you mean to tell me that if a request came in from another outfit for my M.O.S., that you would ship me out, regardless of how many other men in this outfit have the same M.O.S.?" It was going well, but I was getting a little nervous about the time factor. I was afraid that he would stop to think about his answer, but apparently this was my lucky day.

"I should be so lucky, that a request would come for someone with your M.O.S.," he retorted, then he put in his disclaimer, "However, I would have to find a way to keep you here long enough to have you complete all of the signage and artwork you are doing for the I.G. inspection."

I approached him while everyone was still in the office, and offered my hand as if to make a deal. "Well I'm sure that if such a long shot came in that we could work out the details of getting your artwork done." He looked at me strangely, as if he knew that I might have something up my sleeve, but he took my hand anyway and we shook on it.

Ten to fifteen minutes later, a messenger came in from G-3 with a request for a 4503 M.O.S. to be shipped to Germany. He handed it to the First Sergeant, whose eyes seemed to indicate that he could not believe what he was reading. "Whatcha got there Sarge?" I couldn't resist taunting him.

"Captain, I think you'd better come take a look at this request," he said half in shock.

Captain Englehart came out of his office again and read the request. "You realize that our conversation was all in jest, don't you?" He looked sheepishly at me, waiting to see if I would hold him to his word.

"A deal is a deal, Sir. You want me out of your hair and I really want to go back to Germany." I said in an effort to let him know there was no personal animosity there. "We have at least six witnesses, but you are a man of your word and I'm sure that you meant at least part of what you said about me."

He asked me to come into his office and to close the door so that we could talk privately. "Now, Hirsch, what is this all about? You know I think highly of you in spite of your antics, and that I don't want to lose you. I don't know how you managed to pull this off, but it was masterful. As much as I want to keep you here, I don't want to go against my word, if you don't want to stay. What I can't understand is why you want to go. You have it easier here than anyone else in the Battalion. Why don't you want to stay?"

"Sir, if I may say so, you have been as close to a father figure to me as anyone I can remember in recent times. If I didn't have an agenda in mind, I probably would never want to leave this outfit as long as you were the C.O." I was really being serious, and I felt comfortable in talking to him this way. "I feel that I have to get to Germany to see if I can find my little brother and sister. I realize that I was told that they were killed with my mother in Auschwitz, but I have seen no documentation to substantiate that, and I simply cannot accept the idea that they are dead."

He reached out and clasped my hand with both of his hands and said, "May God be with you, son. I dearly hope that you are successful." He had a tear in his eye and I had to turn around to contain mine. My orders were going to be cut so that I would leave Fort Lewis in two weeks. That would be plenty of time to complete all the work I was doing for the I.G. inspection, which would take place during my last week, including the brochure for G-3, which I had almost completed. I was relieved from my post as Fireman and someone else was sent to train for the job. Actually, there was little, or nothing, for a Fireman to do in the summer anyway.

I spent the next two weeks saying goodbye. I didn't realize how many people I would miss. Steve was the hardest one to say goodbye to. He was happy for me, that I was going to Germany, but he let me know in no uncertain terms that I was abandoning him. He had introduced me to a friend of his from New York, about two months before, who insisted on believing the rumors that I was Kirk Douglas's brother. I was wishing there was a way that I could tell him that it wasn't true, without causing problems. This guy came from a very well to do family, and had a lot of connections. He also had a black book of lady friends in New York that was his pride and joy. When I mentioned to him that I would be in Fort Dix, New Jersey, before boarding the boat for Europe, he actually gave me his black book, complete with notations. I told him that one or two numbers would be more than I could handle, but he insisted on giving me the whole book.

I let the word out that the "Ramblin Wreck" was for sale, and surprisingly had quite a few bites. The soldier who ended up buying it didn't close the deal until my last day at the base. I sold the car for ninety-five dollars and was very happy to get it, since I had already decided to leave it with Steve if I couldn't sell it. My first car had served me well, I was going to miss it.

My orders were to report to Fort Dix in October, which meant that I could go home for a forty day leave before reporting there. The day I was scheduled to leave, I went by to say goodbye to Captain Englehart. The I.G. inspection had gone well. Everyone was happy with the artwork I had done. My pal in G-3 got a commendation for "his" brochure and he probably got another promotion. As excited as I was about getting to go to Germany as a United States soldier, I was feeling pangs of separation. I really liked a lot of things about Fort Lewis. It was clean and scenic, but most of all, I had made a lot of friends, most of whom I probably would never see again. Saying goodbye to Cpt. Englehart and Lieutenant Lee left me choked up. Several people, including Cuddles, said they would write. The guy who bought my car took me to the airport as part of the deal. I waved goodbye to those who came to see me off, got in the car, and decided not to look back.

7

WHAT WILL I FIND AND HOW WILL I FEEL?

I HAD BEEN ACCUMULATING LEAVE TIME WITH the hope of using it in Europe, halfway expecting to get the opportunity to go there. My orders were cut indicating the date I was to leave Fort Lewis, Washington, and the date I was to report to Fort Dix, New Jersey, in preparation for the TransAtlantic voyage to Europe. When I reviewed the orders and noticed a forty-two day span between the two dates, I ran to Captain Englehart to let him know that I had not requested, nor desired, a 42 day leave. I was told that mandatory leaves of three weeks and up were S.O.P. (standard operating procedure), in the case of G.I.s being sent overseas, and that there was nothing he or I could do to change that. I was anxious to get home and see my family and friends. My sweet sister Sarah, in whose house I had been living from my senior year in high school, until entering the army, gave birth to her third child, Eddy, while I was in Fort Lewis. Although I hadn't seen her older children, Thyle and Neal, for almost a year, I felt that a two to three week leave would have been sufficient.

My older Sister, Flo and her husband Herb, had been living in Kodiak, Alaska, and occasionally took trips to Seattle. I had been looking forward to a visit from them on one of those trips, and it finally happened in my last month at Fort Lewis. I mentioned to Flo that I would most likely be serving the remainder of my army term in Germany, and she got real excited. She contacted my two brothers and my sister to discuss how I could help sell our parents' house in Frankfurt. The house, located at 30 Grünestrasse, had been confiscated by the Nazi government and was being used by what was left of the German military. It was the only house left standing of a one block long group of rowhouses on both sides of the street. My brother Asher, while stationed in Germany in 1946, was able to get the house back into our name.

Landowners who resided on another continent did not make much profit, it seemed. A rent ceiling kept the income level down, while the cost of maintenance and taxes kept going up, leaving us with a negative cash flow, and we had no one whom we could trust to look after our interests. My brothers and sisters made a decision to give me Power of Attorney to sell the house. I was instructed to meet with Mr. Klibansky, an attorney in Frankfurt am Main, who had been my father's friend and attorney. I was to sign over the Power of Attorney to him, and ask him to try to sell the house as soon as possible. I couldn't understand how owning our parents' house could lose us money when it was 100% occupied, but my siblings had made a decision, and I, the youngest of the family, usually went along with my elders' decisions. The fact that I was not consulted on this matter never registered with any of them.

My flight to Atlanta was on a commercial air line. I had to change planes in Chicago and almost missed my connecting flight. In a thirty minute span between flights, I had to run from one end of the airport to the other, while carrying my duffel bag. When I finally collapsed in my seat, with a sigh of relief, I realized that all of the army restrictions, and sickening minutia, were suspended for a while. I started looking forward to forty plus days of rest and relaxation.

Leave was just that, spending time with my niece and nephews, trading war stories with my brother-in-law, Harry, who had served in China during WWII, and hanging around with my boyhood friends, ones who were not away at school or in the armed services. The time went quickly and I almost missed the more eventful existence of army life, regimented as it was. By the time the leave came to an end, I was more than ready to report for duty, and anxious with the anticipation of going back to Germany.

I expected that reporting to Fort Dix, New Jersey would entail a simple processing procedure in preparation for the troop ship across the Atlantic. It was definitely a transitional period, but we were assigned beds in barracks and were assigned KP, guard duty, and other details that soldiers could expect to be saddled with in a permanent situation. The interim period before the ocean voyage was a lot longer than I had anticipated, and the NCOs in charge weren't going to let us get fat and lazy. I didn't know a soul on the base, which had its good and bad points. The best part was that I could forget about the Kirk Douglas bit, for the time being.

We were kept in shape with a lot of calisthenics and kept busy with a duty roster of mostly busywork, but we were usually free in the evenings. New York City was very close by. My brother Asher lived in the Bronx, my cousin Helen lived in Washington Heights, and if I got bored, I could always fall back on the black book I had been given in Fort Lewis by my friend from New York.

I was looking forward to getting to know Helen better. I had not known about cousin Helen when Jack and I had gone to New York for our sister Flora's wedding, in 1949. I remember looking around the synagogue minutes before the wedding and seeing a very attractive girl with long blond hair on the other side of the room. I turned to my brother Asher and excitedly asked him who she was. He looked at me and laughed and told me not to get too excited, since she was my first cousin Helen. Here I was, seventeen years old, and ready to fall in love, only to find out that the object of my infatuation was my cousin. Damn!

We were introduced at the reception and I found out that we had many interests in common. She was fifteen at the time. Her father, Philipp Auerbach, was my mother's brother. He owned a chemical import-export company in Belgium until he was arrested by the Gestapo in 1940, and sent to Gürs, a concentration camp in France. Helen and her mother were caught trying to escape and were also sent to Gürs, where they stayed for about a year. Helen's mother was able to obtain release papers for the two of them, but she was unable to secure her husband's release, because he was marked for deportation to Germany. Helen and her mother fled Europe and arrived in Cuba in 1941 and ultimately moved to New York. Uncle Philipp was incarcerated in several camps, including Auschwitz, where he survived by using his knowledge of chemistry to prepare medicaments for his fellow prisoners, as well as soap and chemicals for pest control. It was there, as he had told my brother Asher, that he had seen our mother, brother and sister on their way to the showers (gas chambers), in the Fall of 1943. In April 1945, he was liberated from Buchenwald, and he set out for Dusseldorf to avoid deportation to the Soviet Union as a chemist. After surviving the war, he involved himself in politics, divorced Helen's mother and eventually became the first Jew to be appointed to a prominent government position in post-war Germany. A lot has been written about him, including that he committed suicide in a German prison in 1952, after he had been arrested, tried, convicted and sentenced for embezzling restitution funds. Four years later, in 1956, he was fully exonerated, posthumously, of all charges. As colorful a figure as he was, to Helen he was the father who had abandoned her. To me, he was the uncle that I never knew and would never get to know. That angered me because he had made the choice to not reunite with his family, after the Nazis had killed so many of us, and Helen needed him so much.

Helen and I were able to spend a little time together and get to know each other better. It was amazing how much we thought alike. There were two major differences in our upbringing. She had a caring mother who kept a close watch over her and kept her in line. My discipline, on the other hand, had been loosely administered by an occasional social worker, and three older siblings who had little or no experience at parenting. The other difference was that she had grown up in a community of refugees from Europe, and survivors of the Holocaust, while my European background made me more or less an oddity among the people I was in contact with on a regular basis.

While Helen was growing up in Washington Heights, the war in Europe, the fate of European Jewry, and ultimately the Holocaust, were part of every conversation around her. Most of her friends were either child survivors, or children of European Jews who were lucky enough to get out in time, and they all pursued interests that would take their minds away from what was constantly being discussed by their parents. Helen and I shared many interests in the arts and I even had a mild interest in opera, for which she had a passion. But she could not appreciate, at first, my compulsion to delve into the Holocaust, and wanting to discover more details regarding the fate of my immediate family. She later developed an appreciation for what she called my obsession, but she could never share it.

The nicest part of being stationed in New Jersey was getting to spend time with Helen and becoming kindred spirits. She even tried to set up dates for me with some of her friends. As it was, someone had misappropriated that little black book given to me, and I had only been able to make one date from it. "Easy come, easy go," I thought to myself, as I tried to hide my dissapoint-ment.

JUST WHEN I WAS GETTING USED TO the light schedule and liberal policy on passes to town, we were notified that the troop ship was ready and that embarkation was imminent. Packing was a breeze, because we had been living out of our duffel bags in anticipation of being shipped out.

The ship was not as bare as I had anticipated. There were even entertainment lounges on board, with pianos and other accoutrements. The mess hall seemed like it was transplanted from an army base, but compared to the sleeping quarters, it was the Ritz Plaza.

It appeared as if we would have smooth sailing. The weather was mild as we entered the Atlantic Ocean and the waters were calm. I couldn't help but reflect back on my voyage across the Atlantic in 1941, sailing in the other direction. It was in August, and the sea had also been calm when we left the port of Lisbon, Portugal. I remember that it was still calm as we passed the Azores, then gale-like winds started to blow. Our ship, the S.S. Mouzinho, was a large, sturdy steamship, but it started to feel like it was a tin can, in those choppy waters. We had been told not to walk around the decks alone, when the sea was choppy, whether it was day or night. I was a frisky, almost nine year old who had a propensity for questioning orders. To make matters worse, I was a very skinny little boy, weighing about 42 pounds. Also, I hated being cooped up in the cramped compartment that housed what seemed like at least a hundred children.

Many nights, to keep from feeling claustrophobic, I would sneak up to the deck at the bow and sleep on a lounge chair with a blanket wrapped around me. The air was so stale in our crowded compartment that I had a difficult time trying to fall asleep down there. One memorable night, as I was walking along a promenade, I had a horrifying experience. The wind was exceptionally fierce. I had to bend my body forward as I walked to keep from moving backwards. All of a sudden, the strip of carpeting on the narrow promenade deck, broke loose and started moving up and down with the wind, like a sine curve. The force of the wind and movement of the carpet picked up all 42 pounds of me, and I was hurled into the air and over the rail. Had I not been able to grab on to a post and hold on for dear life, I would have been blown overboard. One of the stewards heard me screaming and ran to my rescue. After he helped me down, he scolded me for being up on the promenade at night, and for being out of my quarters in such dangerously windy weather. I pleaded with him not to report me to the Captain, or to my sisters, who were somewhat responsible for me on the journey. We made a deal that I would stay in the compartment below every night until we reached calmer seas, and that he would not report the incident to anyone, including my sisters. He also suggested that I take up eating as a hobby, in order to gain some weight. I think about that experience every time I walk near the railing of a ship, and I find myself holding on to the rail for dear life. I also think about the steward who rescued me, and wonder whatever became of him.

THIS TRIP WAS DEFINITELY GOING TO BE different. It was November, not August. We were sailing to Europe, not away from it, and most importantly, I weighed about 155 pounds.

Things went relatively smooth for the first couple of days. I felt fortunate that I was not assigned to KP like some of the other lower ranking GIs. My assignment was guard duty in front of the NCO lounge. I was to make sure that no lowly privates entered the hallowed premises.

Nobody was overly fond of the sleeping quarters, so most of us spent our free time on the deck getting to know each other. I met all kinds of interesting people. One was a career soldier who had gone back and forth overseas more times than he could count. Another, one of the most fascinating guys I met, was a fellow named Hertz. He was a cartoonist for the *Saturday Evening Post*, among other publications, and they were still accepting the cartoons he submitted while he was in the service. I was particularly interested in him, since I had been staff cartoonist for the newspaper and yearbooks at my junior high school and high school, and I often thought about pursuing a career as a cartoonist. I had even sent some of my cartoons to the *Saturday Evening Post* several years before, without any success, and had made it a point to study the cartoons in that magazine, and others, such as the *New Yorker*. So, I was quite familiar with his work, which made meeting him kind of special.

We had been told that November was not the optimum time to be crossing the Atlantic Ocean and that we might run into some choppy seas, but I had figured that nothing could compare to my voyage of thirteen years before. Once again, I was wrong. The stormy weather came gradually. One good indicator of the severity of the storm was the stability of the food trays in the dining area. If one's tray stayed in front of him long enough to eat the food on it, there was a lull in the storm. For most of the voyage, meal time was like playing musical trays. One never knew whose tray he was sticking his fork into, as the trays slid from side to side. The secret was to sit between two people whose trays had similar contents. That way, I could ensure that what I ate was at least the type food I had intended to eat. Ultimately, all of this didn't matter much because most of the soldiers on board were, at one time or another, too sick to eat.

One by one, people started heaving all over the place. The Day Room for privates and the Lounge for NCO's were made off limits except for rare times when the weather calmed down. I still had to stand guard outside the NCO Lounge, but now it was to keep NCO's out when the place was off limits. The piano had to be tied down with ropes. This was after it had almost been destroyed, crashing into walls while sliding from one side of the room to the other. Twice the ropes broke from the force of the piano's weight. Someone finally procured a steel chain to keep it tied in place. By that time, all recreation areas were off limits for the remainder of the trip.

The GIs who weren't seasick were becoming a rarity. Many of those who had boasted of having strong constitutions, succumbed when they were treated to a vomit shower from a person standing next to them. I was an unusual case. For whatever reason, I rarely threw up, and actually couldn't if I wanted to.

By the fourth day of the voyage, there were only eight non-officers that had not succumbed to sea sickness. We were the chosen few that were assigned for special clean up duties, in other words, the "up chuck patrol." I initially begged off because of my essential duties guarding the NCO Lounge. Eventually, the patrol was reduced to three or four guys and I was forced to pitch in and do my share of clean up. My specialty was keeping the stairs clean. We were all convinced that this was the worst duty imaginable, yet for some reason I felt a little sense of pride at being one of the few that had the ability to keep people from severely injuring themselves. How I survived the "up-chuck patrol," even while wearing a surgeon's mask, is still a mystery to me.

While standing guard at the NCO Lounge, I met all sorts of characters. The most colorful was a master sergeant that had been in the service since the early days of WWII. He had been all over the globe and had traveled on every imaginable conveyance. He opined that modern day soldiers just didn't have what it took to survive, giving the rash of sea sickness on our ship, as the perfect example. He was a battle hardened soldier and nothing like a little nausea could keep him off his feet. To illustrate his point, he pulled a brown paper bag out of his back pocket and explained that if the urge came, he would use the bag, dispose of it, and go about his business. This man was very talkative, and I, unfortunately, was the only one around to talk to. I just nodded agreement to every thing he said. He was in the middle of telling me about one of his military campaigns when he nonchalantly pulled out his brown paper bag, up chucked into it, calmly twisted the top of the bag shut, threw it in the garbage, and then continued his story as if nothing had happened. If I had not been so blown away by his blase approach, I probably would have joined the crowd and lost my lunch.

Hertz came up to my guard post to chat with me the next day. He had really been sea-sick, but he was feeling much better although he had not been able to eat anything for quite a while. As we were chatting, the boat started swaying from side to side and his face turned to a shade of green, somewhere between pale aqua and chartreuse. He leaned over the railing to throw up, but there was nothing in his stomach. As he was dry heaving, the boat suddenly tilted toward his side and he started to slide over the rail. I almost soiled my pants. Fortunately, he was very small and frail. I grabbed hold of his belt and pulled him back aboard. It all happened so fast, no one realized that we almost had a man overboard. Hertz's eyes seemed to be thanking me, but the rest of his body was still quivering from the sea sickness. It took very little prodding to get him to go down to his bunk and lie down.

I was all alone on the deck after Hertz had gone down to his bunk, and I had plenty of time to reflect on what had just happened. My mind kept popping back to the moments when Hertz was leaning over the rail and dry heaving. It reminded me of an incident, from my days in the children's homes network in France that had often crept back to my mind, because of its bizarreness. I cannot, for the life of me, place this incident in an exact time frame, but my guess is that it was in 1939 or 1940. I only remember that it was somewhere in between the beginning of my stay at Villa Helvetia in Montmorency, and the end of my stay at Chateau de Magillier in Creuse. Whoever sent me to this place, which was in a camp setting somewhere in the French countryside, apparently did so to fatten up the skinny little boy that I was. Good intentions aside, the episode was a nightmare from the very beginning.

Arriving at the camp-like facility is the first thing that I remember. I remember it because of the manner in which the people in charge of this camp welcomed me to their facility. They took away my tzitzis, the four cornered garment with fringes that I had been brought up to wear under my shirt, and tore it to shreds in front of my eyes. I was too intimidated to ask why they would do such a thing. I was also very confused because I had been under the impression that these people were Jewish, just like me. It just seemed like such a mean spirited thing to do that it made me more apprehensive about how I would survive this new experience.

Lunch-time had just passed, so they sat me down at a small table in the dining hall, all by myself. I was served a plate that held a large slice of ham, with nothing else, and was exhorted to eat it. I tried to explain that, as a Jew, I was not allowed to eat ham, but my words fell on deaf ears. After it became apparent that I would not eat the ham, someone took the plate away and told me to go to my bunk and unpack.

At supper time, the dining room was full of people, but I was made to sit by myself, at the same small table, with the same plate with the same piece of ham. By this time, we had reached a stand still. They knew that I wasn't going to eat the ham and I knew that there was no point in trying to explain why. The irony of the situation was that they were supposed to be fattening me up, and instead they were starving me. When the evening meal was concluded for everyone, someone took my untouched plate away, without offering any alternative food, and I was told to go to bed. It wasn't easy sleeping with the hunger pains that were gnawing at me, but before I knew it, it was morning. The dining room was full again for breakfast, and again they sat me at the same small table, by myself, and served me the same plate with the same piece of ham, which was starting to show its age. When I continued in my refusal to eat the ham, one of the counselors lost his cool, grabbed my arm and dragged me outside toward a large animal pen, enclosed by a wire fence. Inside of the pen was a huge sow. One of the adults went into the pen with a butcher knife in his hand. The sow was being held down by one person on each end, while the man with the knife knelt down and thrust the blade upward into the belly of the pig. Someone then placed a metal bucket under the bleeding pig to catch the blood. All this time, I was being held and forced to watch the proceedings at the side of the pen. When the bucket was filled with blood, one of the people picked up the bucket and heaved the contents in my direction. The blood barely missed me as I was allowed to jump out of the way. As my feet landed on the ground, I was so nauseated that I grabbed on to the fence and leaned over to throw up, but nothing was in me to regurgitate. It seemed like the dry heaving went on forever. I have no memory of what happened after that, how long I stayed at this "fat farm" or if I finally ate the ham. Maybe I don't want to remember.

Land had been spotted as we neared the European continent and the sea started to calm down as we approached the English Channel. To everyone's relief, the sailing remained smooth through the North Sea, but excitement ran high when the port of Bremerhaven was first sighted. Just a day or so before, we had a boat full of dishrags in army uniform. Now these soldiers were beginning to recuperate and were actually beginning to look like an army unit capable of performing whatever duty they were assigned to, well almost.

We docked at Bremerhaven and no tears of sadness were shed as we lined up in formation to get off the boat. I actually saw several soldiers kiss the ground as they got off the ramp. That thought never occurred to me. I was glad to be in Germany for my own reasons, but I don't think that I could ever kiss the soil of any country in Europe, much less that of Germany.

Most of us were sent to Ausbrucken for processing, and since we were in a foreign country, for indoctrination into what we could expect in the new environment, as well as what was expected of us. We were welcomed to the 7th Army, which was the overall command of the U.S. troops in Europe. Then came the welcome to the 1st Division, the "Bloody Red One." The Division Historian was a master sergeant who probably had been in the army since WWI. He extolled the valorous achievements of the 1st Division in WWII, such as being the first to land at Normandy, the first to suffer casualties, the first to win a battle against the German Army, the first to take German prisoners, the first to have soldiers captured by the Germans, and the list went on. The Division had not left Europe since the invasion of Normandy. It kind of made us proud to be a part of such a macho history. Deep down inside I had a great respect for the American soldier of World War II, most of whom were not Jewish, for their part in defeating Hitler and liberating the camps. I always kept that to myself.

The rest of the lectures were on subjects having to do with how we should act, and take care of ourselves on our own time. We were shown some fairly gross movies on gonorrhea and other venereal diseases, and then treated to a lecture on the legalized prostitution system of Germany and other European countries. We were first exhorted to stay away from prostitutes. Realizing, however, that celibacy was not the order of the day, the lecturer went on to warn us that if any of us could not control our urges and felt compelled to consort with prostitutes, that such contact should be limited to Mondays and, in no event, no later than Tuesdays. His rationale was that since the "Ladies of the Street" were required to have a physical examination each Monday to get a current health card, that Mondays and Tuesdays would be the safest times to have contact with them. In any event, we were told that no soldier should cavort with a lady who could not produce a current health card. I had always wondered what sex education was all about and I wasn't convinced this was it. Then again, maybe this was the army's version.

The next lecture was to prepare us for the difference between German beer and American beer. The beer we had been served on American army bases was 3.2 beer, which related to the percentage of alcohol content and was probably half the strength of beer sold anywhere other than army bases. We were cautioned that the German beer was a lot stronger and the alcohol content was a lot higher. The lecturer cautioned us not to be fooled by the taste because German beer was much smoother and tasted better than its weaker American counterpart.

I listened carefully, although I felt that this valuable advice was meant for the younger recruits who started drinking beer after they joined the army. I, on the other hand, had prided myself on being able to drink everyone under the table when the students and instructors of my architecture lab at Georgia Tech used to go out for an afternoon of "sipping the suds." Needless to say, I had never been affected, beyond feeling bloated, by the pitchers of 3.2 we quaffed on the army bases. I felt justified in feeling smug, even after he cautioned those of us who considered themselves major league beer drinkers not to be lulled into thinking that this advice did not apply to them.

He went on to remind us that the American Army was in Germany as an occupying force and that the attitude of the German population toward our presence varied greatly. Many Germans were glad to have the American armed forces there, both because the army brought a stabilizing force to an otherwise unstable area, and because American servicemen, with their buying power, boosted the economy. But there were just as many Germans that would prefer that we were not there and some that had no compunction about showing their dislike for the occupying forces. This dislike varied from vulgar hand gestures to physical attacks, and on rare occasions, even kidnapping or murder. Our instructions were to be aware that we were guests in this country and to act accordingly toward its citizens, but on the other hand, never to let our guard down in the event a citizen decided to turn hostile. If he had been trying to convince us that we were not in Germany for a vacation, he succeeded.

WE WERE PLACED IN TEMPORARY BILLETS DURING the processing and indoctrination period. When we weren't being lectured to or seeing films, we were given clean up details and other forms of busy work while we waited for our permanent assignments. I had expected to be placed in an Artillery Service Battery as an ammo truck driver, since that was my MOS and ostensibly was the MOS that was in demand in the American occupying forces of Germany. For whatever reason, there were no openings for a 4503 MOS, so, they had to figure out what to do with me.

Our first night in town was sort of weird. We were fresh from the lectures and warnings regarding our behavior on foreign soil, and as a result, were apprehensive about fraternizing with

German civilians. We stuck together in groups of four or five for comradeship, as well as security. The lesser of the evils we were warned about was beer, so the natural place to go was a local Gasthaus, German for pub or beer hall. Sitting there, drinking beer and hearing German spoken all around me was a weird sensation. None of the soldiers with me knew of my background and I had no desire to tell them about myself. I just sat there with the air, filled with rapidly spoken German, hovering over me like heavy steam. I was intent on not letting it get to me. What surprised me was that I found myself being able to understand bits and pieces of what I was hearing, once I got over the harsh guttural sound of the language and started listening to the words.

The more beer I drank, the less harsh the German sounded and the less oppressed I felt. The beer was smooth and better than any I had tasted at home. The GIs with me had been better listeners than I. They all stopped at two or three bottles, but I had no qualms about continuing on, particularly since I was beginning to feel relaxed. When it was time to go back to the base, I was incapable of standing by myself. I was fortunate to have guys with me who were willing to carry me back instead of leaving me for the MPs. I learned two important lessons that night. Everything the man said about German beer was right, and being back in Germany was going to take some getting used to.

I decided to stay off beer for the remainder of my short stay in Ausbrucken. However, I was able to find a poker game to fill up my free evenings. The players were good enough to make the game a challenge, but not so good that I had to be overly concerned about losing money. We found ourselves playing whenever there was free time, and there was a good bit of that since we were all basically were waiting around for our assignments. I found out that Kirk Douglas's new movie, *Act of Love,* was playing at the theater on base, and that it was playing for only one more night. As much as I loved playing poker, I wanted to see that film more, so I excused myself and went to the film with one of the guys in the barracks who didn't play poker.

I was glad that I finally had a chance to see the film and that none of the soldiers from Basic Training had been there to make me uncomfortable. I had hoped that the game would still be going on when I got back, but it finished abruptly about thirty minutes before I got there, and the regular players were waiting to tell me all about what had happened. It seems that a soldier from another part of the base came in and asked if there was an open seat. He was told that I would be gone for at least two hours and that he could play in my place until I got back.

Everyone wanted to talk at the same time. They all agreed that the new player appeared to be just a decent poker player and that he basically held his own for the first two hours. Then he dealt what turned out to be the last hand. He dealt everyone but himself a full house, and he had drawn four cards to the six pat hands. When they told me that the full houses ranged from aces over eights to nines over treys, I remembered a book on card tricks I had read years before and surmised what had happened. When I asked if he had drawn a straight flush, they looked at me with astonishment. To further determine what happened, I asked if he had started the deal with a brand new deck. By this time, one of the guys half- jokingly suggested that I might have been in on the scam. They confirmed that he did have a straight flush, even though the deck was one of ours, and that they had watched him shuffle it. Therefore, they felt, there was no way that he could have rigged the deck. Most of the players were convinced that he cheated but they just could not figure out how. I decided that telling them would only make them feel worse, so I commiserated with them and agreed that we should never again let strangers into the game.

The trick I had read about was an old one, but the dealer had to be a pro to pull it off. I had tried it several times as a card trick, but could never think of doing it in a real card game. The dealer had to be able to shuffle a new deck so that it would end up in the order it was before shuffling. There had to be seven players and he had to deal himself the first and third cards from the bottom of the deck in order to deal a full house to the six other players. Then all he had to do was keep his last card, discarding three deuces and a trey, and draw four cards to the straight flush, from the top of the deck, with everyone watching intently. I wasn't sorry that I had not been there. I later learned that transient bases, such as Ausbrucken, were known to have roving card sharks, and that some of them were dangerous. Had I caught him in the act, the guys might have killed him, or he might have killed them. As it was, they had learned an expensive lesson, but it had only cost them money. For once, I thought, Kirk had gotten me out of a jam, and it was about time.

The next day my orders came through. I was assigned to be a draftsman in an Engineering Battalion in Fürth. The wait seemed to be worth it. I couldn't believe that the army had actually assigned me to a position for which my records indicated I had an aptitude, and for which I had been trained in civilian life.

8

PALACE OF JUSTICE

THE ENGINEERING BATTALION WAS PART OF THE 7th Army, but was not a part of the infamous 1st Division. I really had no idea what that meant and couldn't have cared less. I was just excited at the prospect of finally getting an assignment where I would be expected to utilize my drawing ability, and maybe even my brain. I was hoping that this new assignment might exempt me from such mundane chores as guard duty and KP, and maybe even forced marches, drills, alerts, and all those army maneuvers. Even though I was assigned to be a draftsman for the G-2, a captain whose work was supposed to be Top Secret, my dreams of exemption from unpleasant duties were just that, dreams.

FÜRTH IS A TWIN CITY TO NUREMBERG, in fact I couldn't tell where one began and the other ended. The whole city reeked of history, and the building in which our engineering battalion was housed was no exception. The building had been billets for the German army, and the word was that it had been condemned before it was ever turned over to the American army. If the Corps of Engineers had done any rehabilitation or renovation to the building, it was not noticeable. The facilities may have been acceptable as billets by World War I standards, but it was out of date for that purpose before World War II, and certainly was in gross violation of current building codes.

The most blatant violations were the inadequate hall and stair widths as exit ways. It was bad enough when daily calls to formation would result in bodies frantically squeezing through jammed doorways, but Alerts were another matter. My first experience with a call for an all out Alert, in this milieu, gave me a lasting respect for strict adherence to exit code regulations. This Alert was a call for total mobilization of the battalion, not just our bodies with our personal weapons, but all of the tools and equipment unique to an engineering battalion. The tools and equipment were kept in long wooden casket-like containers, with four rope handle stations on each side. It took eight men to carry each container.

The containers were stored in rooms one floor below street level. The stairs up to street level, which were narrow for normal pedestrian traffic, were virtually impassable for crews of eight soldiers carrying heavy crates, plus their individual weapons. Other soldiers were also rushing in the opposite direction to get more crates. The crates were so heavy that if one soldier let go of his load, the remaining seven would be hard pressed to keep from dropping the container. Given these physical conditions, and adding the component of the frantic pace that is required in evacuating the premises during an Alert, the chaos that ensued should have been predictable.

What was difficult for me to fathom, was how the powers in charge persisted in calling Alerts, on a periodic basis, without investigating ways to improve this impossible condition. It would have been an interesting statistic to have kept records on the number of broken bones that resulted from the mobilization of tools and equipment at each Alert.

I STILL HAD A PICTURE IN MY mind of the Sergeant I had met in pre-basic, who had been a draftsman for Lt. Zimmerman, and all the fantastic drafting equipment that he had at his disposal. I told myself not to anticipate that type of a set-up in Fürth, and to walk into the drafting room full of enthusiasm and appreciation for the chance at the type of work that had not been available to me for over a year. The set-up was not bad. I was taken into the room and introduced to a Corporal Marioneli, who was the chief draftsman. He in turn introduced me to the other two draftsmen, who were also Italians from New York City. The three of them were really tight, and were either related to each other or grew up in the same neighborhood or both. They joked around a lot, called each other "Wops," and they called me a "Kike," which didn't bother me in the context of their joking around.

The room was a large open space with about six drafting tables. It was very spacious, compared to any drafting room I had ever seen, and it had an unusual amount of daylight. After Marioneli introduced me around, he wanted to test my drawing ability. He sat me down at a drafting table and gave me a drawing to copy. It had been a long time since I had used drafting equipment, and I was so used to drawing free hand, that I didn't even think of using triangles and a T-square for this drawing. He looked over my shoulder and told me that free hand drawing wasn't going to cut it in his department. He told me to step aside so that he could show me how it was done, which he did with flair. He was a professional draftsman in civilian life, he was good, and he knew it. I had known that I was not yet a proficient draftsman, so I started over, clumsily using drafting instruments. I had my doubts about the end product, but was relieved that he felt I was good enough to do the job. He said that it made him feel good, since he had no college education, to be training an architectural student, ready to start his junior year. On the other hand, I wasn't too proud to relish the opportunity of learning under such a proficient draftsman.

My primary job was to draw up the designs of the G-2, a Captain whose office, I was told, was in a safe. I thought they were pulling my leg, until Marioneli took me to the Captains office to introduce me to him. "You might wonder why my office is in a safe," he said, looking at me as if he was reading my mind. My eyes told him he was right, and he proceeded to tell me that his work was so top secret that it required this degree of security. I was curious enough to want to know what could possibly be so top secret, but I figured he would tell me in time.

He was an engineer and a demolition expert, and his job was to design the demolition of every bridge between the forces of Eastern and Western Europe, in the event that war broke out. He impressed upon me the necessity of accurate delineation of the design intent. I was relieved to hear that he would double-check all of my drawings of his designs for accuracy.

I went back to the drafting room with a folder full of roughly drawn designs, kind of taken aback by the apparent importance of the work I would be drawing up. I laughed to myself at the irony of the situation. I had been going to school to learn how to design buildings for construction, yet I was going to spend the following months drawings up designs for demolition of existing construction.

WHEN I FIRST ARRIVED AT THE BILLETS, I was assigned to a squad of demolition engineers who, as it turned out, were being trained to do the type of demolition work that the G-2 was designing and for which I would be drawing up plans. I quickly learned that this type of work was hazardous, even when there was no war going on. I had been looking forward to my first Sunday morning in Fürth, so I could explore the facilities of the base, and get to know the soldiers in my squad and company. I was just getting back from breakfast at the Mess Hall when the First Sergeant blew his whistle and yelled out for all of us to fall into formation. I dutifully fell in and asked the guy next to me if this was done every Sunday morning. He shook his head "no," looking just as surprised as I was.

Apparently, I wasn't the only one caught by surprise. Soldiers came straggling into formation in various modes of dress. Some guys were in Class A's, others in civvies, while most of us were in wrinkled olive drab work clothes, ODs. Finally, after everyone was standing at attention, the sergeant started to speak. "Most of you know that we lost two good men last week in an accidental explosion. Although they died during training exercises, the army considers that they died in the line of duty." This was a big shock to me. I had not heard of any accident, much less that two soldiers from my Company had been killed, nor did I have any idea that demolition training was being done with live explosives.

He waited a few seconds to let his words sink in. Then he continued, "I know that not all of you go to chapel on Sunday mornings, and the army don't make anyone go, if he don't want to, but today is different—I don't care what your religion is, and it ain't important what religion those two boys were." He paused for a few moments, then started pacing, from side to side in front of the formation, with his hands clasped behind his back. He returned to his original position, faced the formation of soldiers, and continued his message: "I don't care what army regulations say," he bellowed with a stern look on his face. "I wants to see every swinging dick in Chapel this morning! Now fall out, and go put on your class A's and go to the chapel of your choice. Pray for the souls of your fallen comrades." He started to walk away, stopped in his tracks, and turned back to us before we could break formation. "In case any of you decide not to go to Chapel services, I'm looking for replacements for the men on KP who feel the need to go." As he turned around to walk away, I thought to myself that that was the best argument against atheism I had ever heard.

I thought it was ironic that I would be cajoled into going to Chapel on Sunday morning, especially since I had made no attempt at going to either Friday night or Shabbat morning services on my first Sabbath in Fürth. Since I had not been told of any special memorial services, at the Protestant or Catholic Chapels, for these poor boys, I decided to seek out the Jewish Chapel. I put on my class A's and made some inquiries only to find out that there was no Jewish Chapel on base. There was a Jewish Chaplain, however, and Sabbath services were held in town in some historic building. I contacted Chaplain Pincus Goodblat, introduced myself, and asked if he was leading a service in memory of the boys who were killed. He invited me to his residence where several other Jewish soldiers from the Company were gathering a minyan, the ten men required for a Jewish prayer service, to respond to the First Sergeant's eloquent plea in behalf of the unfortunate young victims of tragedy.

I found it difficult to get into a proper frame of mind to say prayers on memory of youngsters that I had never met nor even knew of their demise until that morning, but I tried nonetheless. The service did get me in touch with Chaplain Goodblatt and his family, an association for which I was the richer. Plus, these were American soldiers.

THE NEXT WEEKEND I APPLIED FOR A pass to go to Frankfurt, and since I had no chance to screw up yet, I was not turned down. The anticipation was great. I had called Dr. Klibansky when I first arrived in Germany, and told him that I would make an appointment with him as soon as I was settled and able to get a weekend pass. I made the appointment and informed him that there would be matters I wished to discuss with him, other than the power of attorney for the house. I was anxious to meet this man who had known my father intimately, as his attorney and close friend.

Arriving at the Banhoff, train station, in Frankfurt was a strange experience. I expected to have explicit memories of the place where I had last seen my mother, a little over sixteen years before, but I didn't. I did feel a chill and I had this feeling of having been there before, but even though I had vivid memories of that day on December 5, 1938, I could not superimpose those memories onto that bustling train station in 1954.

I was told that it wasn't particularly safe for an American G.I. to stay in a German hotel, and that there was a serviceman's hotel in Frankfurt that was run by the army. This hotel became my base of operation for all the trips I later took to Frankfurt.

My appointment with Herr Klibansky was at 10 in the morning. I left the hotel at 9:00 A.M. just to make sure that I wouldn't be late, in case I got lost. I arrived so early that I walked around the block a couple of times, before going in. I was still about twenty minutes early and was told that Herr Mueller, Klibansky's partner, who was to be at the meeting, had not arrived yet. After a few minutes, Herr Klibansky ushered me into his office and proceeded telling me of his close relationship with my father. He was a very large man, corpulent would describe him better, with a mustache and a pair of red suspenders that held his pants up, just below his protruding belly. It was special hearing him speak of my father, although he didn't hold back on his criticism of my father for failing to heed the warnings, and not taking advantage of opportunities to escape Germany. When I asked him why he stayed, he said that his was a totally different situation. I wanted to like him, but I suddenly became very suspicious of him, and nervous to the point that I wished I had the choice of not giving power of attorney to sell our house to this self-righteous son of a bitch. I particularly did not enjoy seeing him lean his rotund body back in his chair while passing judgment on my father for not leaving, when he supposedly, had a chance. I wondered about how genuine his friendship with my dad was, and I couldn't help but wonder how he had stayed alive and was able to maintain his corpulent body, although almost ten years had passed since the end of the war.

He asked me how I managed to get sent to Germany for duty, while the United States armed forces were involved militarily in Korea. I sketchily told him of the circumstances that brought me to Germany, and of my efforts toward that end, and then I told him why it had been so important for me to come at this time.

Herr Klibansky was a very blunt man, and just as he wasn't shy about criticizing my dead father to my face, he had no compunction about telling me that I was on a wild goose chase. He added that if I had contacted him from the States, with regard to Werner and Roselene, he could have saved me a lot of time and anxiety. He had known my uncle Philipp well, and could verify that Philipp had watched from afar, behind several rows of electrified barbed wire fences, as his sister, my mother, with her two youngest children walked naked into "the showers" for delousing. Uncle Philip, in his position as chief chemist while interred in Auschwitz, came upon a list that included a Mathilde Hirsch ne Auerbach, and two children, Werner Hirsch and Roselene Hirsch. Recognizing their names, he ran out, to be as close as possible, to verify that this was in fact his sister, niece and nephew.

I stared at him in disbelief. I was beginning to understand why ancient Greeks used to kill the messenger of bad tidings. I had asked him to give me leads to help me find Werner and Roselene, instead he confirmed, with an air of certainty, that the reports of their death, that I had refused to believe, were true beyond a shadow of a doubt, as far as he was concerned. I was too numb to let my bad feelings for him surface.

As he spoke, Herr Klibansky began to realize that what he was telling me so matter-of-factly was having a traumatic effect on me.

He assured me that, according to my uncle, Philipp Auerbach, my mother, sister, and brother had no inkling of their pending fate, that he had seen them from afar as they were waiting in line to enter and he felt sure that they thought they were to be deloused in the showers, not gassed. It was small comfort, but it was at least something to grab on to, at a time when I needed to hear anything positive to keep me from total despair.

Herr Meuller's entrance was almost a welcome intrusion, but I wasn't quite ready to get down to business. They proceeded to prepare the required paperwork for me to sign over the Power of Attorney while I was slowly returning back to earth. By the time they finished the paperwork, I was better able to focus on the business I was there for, but I was a bit reluctant when they gave me the papers to sign, because I had only been instructed to give the Power of Attorney to Klibansky. I was being asked to give it to Klibansky and/or Mueller. Herr Klibansky explained that he planned to go in for surgery in the very near future, and that Mueller should be able to take action in his absence, in case a buyer showed up while he was incapacitated.

Mueller spoke excellent English and was amiable enough. I just had a queasy feeling about turning over the Power of Attorney of what once was our family home, to a German national who was not Jewish. By this time, I didn't fully trust Klibansky, and I was totally uncomfortable with Mueller. Klibansky, sensing my inner turmoil, assured me that he was the one who would be in charge and that adding Mueller to the document was only to facilitate matters. I reluctantly signed the papers, and then wrote to my siblings to keep them abreast of what I had done in their behalf, then I went back to the base feeling that I had accomplished step one of what they had asked me to do, even though I was not particularly in favor of selling the house. I sat on the train back to Fürth limp as a dishrag. My expectations of finding Werner and Roselene alive had been dashed so abruptly that I had been unable to prepare myself for the letdown. In retrospect, I can't imagine any scenario that would have prepared me for such a devastating letdown. I actually was glad to be going back to the mundane army existence. Regimentation and mindless busywork was just what the doctor ordered to keep my mind off of the confirmation that my younger siblings were indeed dead.

I RETURNED TO THE BASE VERY DEPRESSED. I, for the first time, realized that finding Werner and Roselene was a pipe dream at best. I just didn't expect the search to end so quickly. I resolved to refocus my energies and make the best of my stay in Germany by pursuing other goals and activities with my spare time. I enrolled in an advanced calculus correspondence course under the auspices of the army, even though I had all the calculus credits required by Georgia Tech for an architectural degree. Some of the material was review of what I had taken at Tech, but there was plenty more to sink my teeth into. I actually found myself waiting with anticipation for each lesson to arrive.

The U.S.O. in Fürth gave all sorts of classes. I availed myself of the art class, which turned out to be an opportunity to draw or paint in virtually any medium, with very little, if any, instruction. This was good for me because all I really wanted to do was try my hand at oil painting again and I had in mind certain portraits I wanted to do from photographs. The first painting was from a photograph of my parents' engagement. Since the photograph was in sepia tones, I had to fly by the seat of my pants to guess what colors to use. The portrait took less time than either I or the instructor had anticipated. The colors were dark and somber which made the whites of their eyes stand out on the canvas. It was far from a masterpiece and barely respectable for a first try at portrait painting, but as soon as it dried, I wrapped and sent it to my sister Sarah in Atlanta.

My second effort at portrait painting was more ambitious than I had imagined. Sarah had sent me a picture of her two oldest children, Thyle and Neal. It had been done by a professional photographer, in color, and seemed easy enough to paint from. The problem for me was that they both were smiling with their mouths open, and try as I may, I could not get the hang of painting open mouthed smiles. They were probably 3 1/2 and 1 1/2 years old in the picture, and as I got more frustrated at failed attempts of getting the mouths acceptable, I surmised that they would be teenagers by the time the portrait was finished. As it was, I never finished it. By the time I received orders to report to Schweinfurt, I decided to wrap up the unfinished portrait, which only lacked finished mouths, and sent it to my sister.

My tour in Germany was going to last less than a year which was plenty of time, so I thought, for me to find and visit the O.S.E. children's homes in France, in which I had stayed while hiding from the Nazis. That became my next quest. Unfortunately, it would also end up leaving me totally frustrated. This time, my frustration was with the absence of resources available to me, as one who didn't speak the language, while I was making efforts to revisit places of my youth. On my next trip to Frankfurt, I visited several travel agents, and though my German was sufficient to get by in most situations, I might as well have been speaking Chinese for all those folks cared. Throughout my stay in Germany, I also visited travel agents in Nuremburg, Fürth, Würzburg and Munich. They all said the same thing, "There are no such places as Montmorency, Chateaux de Margelies, or Chateaux de Morrell in France." As far as they were concerned, my past was a figment of my imagination. I was positive they were wrong, but I could not find a source of better information in the limited time available on my occasional passes from the military base. To the army's credit, all of the mindless crap they threw at us, when we were recruits in basic training, trained this soldier to cope with being stonewalled and with the general frustration of dealing with the bureaucratic nature of Germans, whether at civilian or governmental levels.

THE FIRST FRIDAY EVENING THAT I WASN'T on some kind of duty, I went with Chaplain Goodblatt to services, which I had been told

were being held at a municipal building in Nuremberg. When I
got there, I remember being impressed with the aura of history in
this apparent courthouse building. I was surprised to see that
there were over thirty worshipers in the room that was being
used for the Jewish Chapel, one of the largest congregations I
had seen at a regular Friday night service related to an army
base. Some of the congregants were American civilians and there
were even one or two German civilians. The Chaplain handed me
a tallis (prayer shawl), and a sidur (prayer book), and instructed
me to lead the services.

Reluctant as I was to question the direct order of an officer, I
looked at Lieutenant Goodblatt with chagrin, and explained that
I had not led a service in many months, and that I was just not
prepared to lead this august body of worshipers, which included
the captain of my engineering company, my commanding officer,
who I had not realized was Jewish, in prayer. The Chaplain put
his arm around my shoulder and gave me a fatherly look, and
said that I should not be nervous, that he had all the confidence
in the world that I was up to the task. He later confided to me
that there had been no one else to lead the service besides
himself, and that he felt that he had to train me so that he could
concentrate more on his sermon.

Had this not been the army, I never would have accepted such
a dubious "honor," without prior notice. I followed orders and
led the service, though I was unsure of which melodies to use and
was quite rusty on the Hebrew recitations. I hesitated several
times during the service, looking toward the Chaplain for
guidance on which parts to repeat out loud and which tune to
use. Each time he just waved his hand for me to go on and decide
for myself. I began to realize that I was on my own, and just
continued on as best I knew how. When the service was over, I
was embarrassed. I felt that I had botched up the service by
being ill prepared, but the congregants were very kind, and told
me that I had done a wonderful job. I knew better, but it was nice
to hear a good word even thought I felt I had screwed up. I made
a promise to myself to practice before the next Friday night, to let
the congregants know that their confidence in me was not
misplaced.

On our way back to the base, the Chaplain asked me if I had been aware of the significance of the building in which our services were held that evening. I remarked that I had admired the classical architecture of the structure, and commented that it appeared to be an important civic building, but other than that, I had no idea of what he was getting at. He knew that I was a survivor of the Holocaust, and of my recent disappointing meeting in Frankfurt with Herr Klibansky. "There was a reason that I pushed you to *daven* from the *omed* (lead the services) tonight," he said with a look on his face that indicated that he knew something that I didn't know. "Tonight, you just led *Kabolos Shabbos* (ushering in of the Sabbath) services at the Palace of Justice, where the Nuremberg Trials were held six years ago. He looked at me to see my reaction. I was speechless. Not another word was spoken until we arrived at the base. We exchanged greetings of "Good Shabbos" as he went his way and I went mine. I didn't sleep much that night, reflecting on the irony of the situation. I couldn't help but wonder, if my mother could see what I was doing, how she would react to the situation.

9

GERMAN DOCTOR

I BECAME A REGULAR AT LEADING THE Friday night services at the Palace of Justice and each time I recited *Shema Yisroel* (Hear O Israel), the affirmation of the oneness of the God of Israel, my voice rang out several octaves louder than I had thought I was capable of. I was hoping that Hitler, and his henchmen who were tried in that very building, could hear me in the depths of Hell.

Weeks later, when I was advised of a pending transfer to the artillery in Schweinfurt, I realized that, of all the things, I might miss in leaving Fürth, the main thing I would miss was the satisfying feeling of standing at the Bema and leading Sabbath services in the very building in which major Nazi war criminals were tried and sentenced.

THE THOUGHT HAD CROSSED MY MIND, ON many occasions, to buy a pair of boots in my size at the PX. I had actually tried to do that in Ft. Lewis on more than one occasion, only to find out that they did not have my size in stock. Boots were not cheap, and I had worn out my army issues, so now they were reasonably comfortable, as long as I didn't have to wear them for long marches. I had been assured that my assignment as the draftsman for the Captain was of a crucial nature, and would exempt me from most of the routine marches that were periodically scheduled.

The Saturday morning that we were called to formation and told to quickly fall out, gather our gear in our backpack, and fall back in formation for a forced march should not have come as a surprise to me, but it did. I tried to explain to the Field Sergeant that I was on a crucial, top secret assignment, and that I should be exempt from this march. He took great pleasure in telling me that no one was exempt from this march, which had been called by the Company Commander himself, to see if his men were ready to mobilize at a moment's notice. I looked around for the Captain, who had just complimented me on leading the Service the night before, but he was nowhere in sight. Pleading my case to him, apparently was out of the question.

The march was for ten miles, five there and five back, and to my surprise, my boots fared pretty well. My calf muscles didn't cramp and my feet were only a little sore. I was more than anxious, however, for the opportunity to take off those boots and soak my feet in hot water. When the sergeant blew his whistle and screamed at us to fall out, I made a bee-line to my bunk and broke all records in taking off my boots, expecting to have the rest of the day off. With a sigh of relief, I sat there rubbing my aching feet when all of a sudden there was another whistle and a call to fall in for inspection, by the Company Commander.

Everyone made a mad scramble to put their boots back on and get back into formation. My feet had swollen to the point that it was physically impossible to put my boots back on, without surgery. I frantically tried to put on my low cut dress shoes, to no avail. Finally, in desperation, realizing that missing a formation was tantamount to being AWOL, I put on my shower clods and ran down the steps as fast as my floppily clad feet could carry me.

I was the last man to fall in, and as I passed the Captain and Field Sergeant, I tried to make eye contact with them in the hopes that they would not look down at my feet. It didn't work. The Captain took one look at me, shook his head in disbelief, turned to the Sergeant and told him to tear up the paperwork for my promotion to PFC.

I had no idea that I was up for promotion. In fact, I had about given up hope of ever making PFC. However, hearing the Captains remark really got to me. The formation had just been called so that the Captain could see that everyone made it through the hike unscathed, and after everyone had a few laughs at my expense, we were dismissed for the rest of the day. That is, except for me. I was told to put on some shoes and report to KP. I asked the Captain for permission to explain. He looked at me and shook his head, and told me that he had wondered why a soldier with my ability and so much time in service had not made PFC. I tried to explain my predicament with ill fitted army issue boots and my flat feet, but I could see that it was of no use. He turned to walk away and as a parting shot said, "Hirsch, you have made screwing up an art form. You'll be reviewed again for promotion in two months, but don't hold your breath."

THE ENGINEERING BATTALION IN FÜRTH WAS THE first outfit I had served in that was located in the midst of a city that was substantially urban. There were many advantages to being situated in a non-rural area, not the least of which was the proximity of a number of Gasthauses (local pubs) that were frequented by local females looking for companionship. No matter which direction any of us went, upon leaving the base, a Gasthaus was only minutes away.

After my initiation into drinking German beer in Ausbrucken, it didn't take long to get adjusted to German beer, which in addition to being stronger than American beer, also tasted better. The important thing was knowing when to quit. We had been warned of the dangers of getting soused in a foreign country, especially when we were considered an occupying force. Even though it was obvious that the ladies in Gasthauses were looking to meet American GIs, the local men did not always take kindly to this scene. Heeding the warnings, we made it a practice to always go in groups of no less than three or four GIs.

I was not much of a Hell-raiser, but I enjoyed getting off the base, on occasion, and going with a group to local Gasthauses. However, it wasn't the same as going to the bars in the States, where I felt free to open up and party. Even though the beer was much better, I never felt much like drinking more than one or two beers in the Gasthaus environment. I found myself taking in the atmosphere and watching the local people who frequented these drinking establishments. I studied their faces and their mannerisms, but most of all, I wondered what they did during the war, and how they had treated their Jewish neighbors. My visual probing didn't go unnoticed. It wasn't rare for a man to get up and leave when he became aware that I was watching him. Somehow, that didn't make me feel guilty.

At some point in the evening, almost every time we went Gasthaus hopping, we inevitably ended up in the company of a group of local girls. The guys called them *shatzes* which, though it may not have been the most respectful German term, they responded to. I had little or no interest in flirting with these girls, but I got a kick out of watching my fellow GIs operate. The *shatzes* all spoke fluent English, but when they spoke to each other, they spoke in German. To my surprise, I found that I could understand enough of what they were saying to get the gist of their conversations.

I became the guy to go with, once the word got out that I could tell my compatriots what the girls were saying about them behind their back. The girls never suspected a thing, and the guys had the advantage of knowing when they were being misled, which was the case more often than not. Occasionally my undercover work helped match up a GI with a *shatze* that had confided to her friends in German that she liked him.

ONE OF THE STRANGEST PHENOMENA OF MY tour in Germany was the periodic reaction of German civilians, often ordinary pedestrians, to my history as it relates to the Holocaust. To this day, I cannot fathom how anyone knew that I was a survivor who had lost immediate family members to Hitler's war against the Jews. It was not that they knew details of my experiences, which they did not, but somehow they seemed to know that I had been very adversely affected by the actions of the German people, and their allies, during that period of madness between 1933 and 1945.

It was not an uncommon scene for me to be walking the streets of Fürth or Nuremberg and to have a stranger approach me, put their arm around me, and start crying and bemoaning the "fact" that they had been helpless to act in the face of Hitler's reign of terror.

Whether I was in uniform or walking around in civilian clothes made no difference. I was constantly picked out in a crowd by individual Germans seeking absolution. But how did they know? For the most part, they all said that they had no idea what was happening to the Jewish people, that it was all the act of one madman who had cast a spell on his followers and that they, the unsuspecting German citizenry, were shocked when the truth of the concentration camps and killing centers "was discovered" by the allied troops and made public.

The first time this happened, I actually felt bad for the woman crying on my shoulder, and had I not been so dumbfounded by the fact that she approached me in the first place, I probably would have instinctively tried to comfort her. Although this was not an every day occurrence, it happened often enough that I found myself repulsed at being a designated crying post for absolution that was not within my power to grant.

I was beginning to feel pretty comfortable in the 15th Engineering Battalion. I felt good about the work I was doing and I had a lot to keep me busy in the evenings and on weekends. There were only a handful of Jewish soldiers in the Battalion, at least ones who identified to the point of going to services on an occasional Friday night. I met a corporal at services one Friday night, who had been a pharmacist in civilian life, and was in charge of sick bay for the Battalion. We started hanging around together and had fun sharing "war stories."

I developed my own afflictions in the army. Almost all the soldiers in my outfit had developed hemorrhoid problems to one degree or another. Mine were beginning to bother me to the point that I went to see my buddy in sick bay, unofficially, one evening.

He chose not to check me out, since, as he put it, they didn't teach him how to check people for hemorrhoid problems at pharmacy school. They did, however, teach him how to treat painful hemorrhoids with medicine, which he said he could not dispense to me unless I went on sick call and let the doctor examine me.

I went on sick call the next morning, and while I was waiting to see the doctor, my friend came to chat with me for a brief moment. It seemed he had neglected to tell me that the doctor in the infirmary was not an army officer, but a German civilian. At first, I didn't know what to make of this tidbit of news. I sat patiently awaiting my turn, expecting the doctor to examine my posterior and prescribe some medicine to shrink the hemorrhoids and ease the pain. That was before the doctor became a person.

I was called into the examining room and came face to face with a man in his mid-forties with a short graying crew cut. He spoke perfect English, but with a distinct German accent. My friend had told him that I was born in Germany, without going into much detail about the fate of my family. He also told the doctor that I had a relatively mild case of swollen hemorrhoids that could easily be treated with medication. No longer face to face, the doctor examined my area of discomfort and proceeded to disagree with his medical assistant. He told me that I needed an operation and wanted to schedule it as soon as possible. Trying to get over my shock, I asked who would be performing this operation, and Herr Doktor said that, of course, he would.

The doctor left the room while I was supposed to be thinking about when to schedule this "simple operation." My friend looked at me sheepishly and shrugged his shoulders. "What the hell is going on here?" I shouted, as he motioned that I keep my voice down. "I thought you said that going on sick call was just a formality so that I could get the medicine I needed!"

"Between you and me," he said in a hushed voice. "This guy must have his own agenda for prescribing surgery in this case. He is not a surgeon, in fact, he is a certified dermatologist. He is, however, the doctor in charge of the infirmary and he can order you to have the surgery, according to army regulations."

The doctor re-entered the examination room with his appointment calendar and wanted to know if I had selected a date yet. I told him that my pain had gone away and that I no longer needed any treatment, therefore, there would be no need to schedule surgery. He looked at me sternly and said that in order for me to function as a soldier, without constantly going on sick call, that the surgery was mandatory. I promised him that I would not ever go on sick call again for anything relating to hemorrhoidal problems, if he would just dismiss me and allow me to get back to work.

By this time, the doctor sensed that I might be questioning his authority and possibly his ability to perform this operation. There was no way to avoid a direct confrontation. I told him that it was my body and that I simply did not want to be operated on. He responded by ordering me to have the operation and threatening to have me court-martialed if I did not comply.

That threat was all I needed to set me off. I looked him straight in the eyes and said, "I don't know what you did during the war, but this is one Jewish body you are not taking a knife to! The Nazis killed my mother, father, brother and sister—and there is no way that a German doctor is going to put a knife to me. If you want to have me court-martialed, go for it. I'm leaving."

I stormed out of the infirmary and went to my room to cool off, waiting for the s--- to hit the fan. Nothing happened. About twenty minutes later, my friend from the infirmary came in and told me that I had more guts than the law allowed, but that the doctor did not have the stomach for court martial proceedings in such an emotionally charged controversy. He said he would drop his demand for surgery and that he did not want to see me again. I had no problem with that request.

10

NAZI BABY KILLER

I NEEDED LITTLE TIME TO DEVELOP A drafting technique for the demolition plans I was working on. There was no design involved. That was taken care of by the G-2. The more I worked on delineating these plans, the more I realized the top-secret nature of the work I was doing. Corporal Marioneli made a point of impressing on me the importance of accuracy in preparing these drawings, which were first checked by him, then by the Captain, after I had finished with them.

Everyone seemed happy with the work I was doing, and even I was getting a feeling of accomplishment from this work, which was a far cry from what I had been trained for in architectural school. I was plugging away one day when I overheard the other draftsmen comparing their security clearances. I wondered when they had obtained these clearances, and whether it was for the work they were doing in this office. I asked and was told that they were thoroughly checked out for security before they could report for duty as draftsmen in Headquarters & Service Company, of the 15th Engineering Battalion. That made a lot of sense to me, but then why, I thought, was I not given a security check, and why was I not required to have security clearance. After all, the man generating the top-secret data that I was drafting up, had his office in a safe.

Marioneli could only shrug his shoulders when I posed the question to him. The other draftsmen were actually peeved that I had this top-secret assignment and was not required to have security clearance. I decided not to let them in on the other absurdity of the situation. Aside from the fact that my drafting board was in a large room with ordinary door locks, and large accessible windows, I was not a citizen of the United States yet. In fact, having been born in Germany, I was legally an alien.

I became very self-conscious about my status, in light of the work I was doing. At the end of the workday, I walked over to the captain's top secret safe and broached my dilemma with him. He was totally flabbergasted. He could not believe that such a lapse in security had taken place. He was quick to let me know that he was more than pleased with my work and that losing me would be a real hardship on him, but he felt that I needed to report the situation to the G-3, his immediate superior, a major who was in charge of security.

I had been introduced to the major when I was first assigned to H&S Co. and had run into him on several other occasions. I particularly remember the night the entire battalion was on a map reading field exercise. The exercise was for everyone regardless of rank. We were divided into teams of two, given a map and compass, dropped off at various points in the countryside, and we had to find our way to a given destination. We had to assume that we were in enemy territory, therefore any source of light other than the moon was not permissible. Map reading and mathematical or geometric calculations were strong points of mine, and the moon was relatively bright. It took a little while to figure out the azimuths, but once I got the hang of it, we were breezing right along.

We were just beginning the home stretch when I noticed what appeared like two lost souls in a clearing. We cautiously approached them, to make sure they were on our side, and saluted as we recognized the major with our company commander. They were not too ashamed to admit they were lost and were eager to receive any help that would direct them back to their course. As I was explaining the azimuth system and the directions to the major, I noticed my captain looking at me, the soldier he would not even promote to PFC, instruct the Battalion G-3 on map reading. I had to keep my feeling of satisfaction to myself, as they went on their way in accordance with my directions. The major thanked me the next day, but the captain never once mentioned the incident.

When I went to see the major, he was happy to see me, as he always was when I wasn't being called on the carpet for one screw-up or another. The Major was a very distinguished looking black man with a full mustache. "Always good to see you, Hirsch," he greeted me as I saluted him, and asked for permission to speak with him. "What's on your mind?"

I tried to explain the concerns of the G-2. I asked the Major if he was aware that I had absolutely no security clearance, that I was not a citizen of the United States, though my application was in, and that my drafting of the Captains Top Secret designs were being done in a wide open room, with ordinary locks and large accessible windows.

His eyes opened wide as if he had seen a ghost. Virtually every soldier in Headquarters had some clearance, and all of the other draftsmen had high-level security clearance. There was a long silence as he was thinking of what to say or do. He must have been wondering how I could have slipped through the cracks, without even being asked about my background. After a long pause, he looked at me and smiled. "That's alright, Hirsch, we trust you." I was totally flabbergasted. It was nice to be trusted, but this was ridiculous. In retrospect, the major must have had advance knowledge of the fact that I would be transferred to the Big Red One within a few weeks, and calculated that by the time security clearance procedures were completed, I would be out of there.

AMONG THE SOLDIERS IN OUR OUTFIT, TRADING stories of our various sorties into the local cityscape, mostly Gasthauses, was a favorite pastime. One night, one of my buddies came back with a very disturbing story. He had been at a large Gasthaus in the heart of Nuremberg, which he had frequented with his girlfriend before. Most of the beer drinkers were regulars, German civilians who often shared experiences of the war. Very few GIs ever went there, especially not in uniform.

That night, one of the regulars, who according to my friend, had quite a bit to drink and decided to share some of his more memorable experiences as a member of the S.S. Among the things he bragged about was taking Jewish babies, holding them by their feet, and smashing their heads against a wall until their brains spewed out.

My fellow soldier had not realized, as he was recounting this story, that I was among those listening. When he saw the look on my face he quickly clammed up. I was so filled with rage that the tears that were welling up inside me could not come out. I insisted on being led to this Gasthaus. My demands were refused. I pleaded that he should at least show me where this place was located on the street. Again he refused.

By this time, I was crying and begging him to give me a chance to avenge my family. "That's why I can't," he finally said to me. "If you go there and confront this animal, you'll either kill him or he'll kill you. Either way your life is over, and I can't allow myself to be a party to your ending your life." I felt like I had just been given a whiff of ammonia. He was right. He was so much smarter than I. How could I even think of wasting my life to get revenge on someone whose only legacy is his memory of murdering babies. I thanked my friend for knocking some sense into me and went straight to bed, totally drained.

11

LAST NIGHT IN FÜRTH

ONE OF THE PERKS FOR ENLISTED MEN serving in the army overseas, was the E.M. clubs. In the States, every army base had an officers' club. There may have even been N.C.O. clubs, but I never heard of an enlisted men's (E.M.) club, until we arrived in Germany. These were great places to hang out with other enlisted men, drink American beer, and partake in American style fast food. Even though the prices were relatively cheap, the E.M. club near our base made a substantial profit every month.

Although the club was not on the army base, it was officially attached to it, and therefore, not allowed to make a profit. Prices were sufficiently marked up to avoid losing money. Once a month, the managers of the club had a "Free Beer Night," at which they either served free pizza or some other food from the menu. The amount of beer and food dispensed was directly related to the amount of profit the club garnered the previous month.

During my first couple of months in Fürth, I avoided the E.M. club. I preferred German beer, and the guys I drank beer with frequented the Gasthauses in the hopes of meeting local females. Strangely enough, I had never tasted pizza before, and it didn't sound particularly appetizing to me. At the first "Free Beer Night," the party ended in a riot which had to be quelled by the M.P.'s. I was told that the fight was between black soldiers and white soldiers, what some people called a "Race Riot," and that such things happened quite often on "Free Beer Night."

That was enough to keep my interest in partaking in this monthly ritual at a low ebb. My best friend was Corporal Featherstone, who incidentally was black. We had about the same level of education and shared interest in the arts, music and sports.

Among the many places we had gone together, the E.M. club was never even discussed. After word came that I would be transferring out of the 15th Engineering Battalion, Featherstone suggested that we partake in at least one "Free Beer Night," before I left for my new assignment. There had been no riot since that one during my first week in Fürth, and it appeared that the frequency of these disturbances had been greatly exaggerated. We both were low on cash, so it seemed like a good idea.

The E.M. club was understandably crowded. We were able to find a small table in a corner, big enough for only two chairs, which was just fine with us. For the first two hours everyone seemed to be having a good time. Beer was plentiful. Featherstone was enjoying the free pizza, which didn't appeal to me, especially after watching the grease dripping from every slice. I had no choice but to make up for it with beer consumption.

We were having a nice conversation, talking about our respective plans after our tour of duty in the army. I told him that although I had reservations about my future, I finally had come to the decision that I should continue studying architecture at Georgia Tech. Featherstone was telling me about his plans to go into pre-med, then the shouting started. Some white guys were yelling "M----- F---ing N----r" at blacks, who were in turn yelling the same expletives preceding "Honky" and added an occasional "white bastard" for good measure.

At first it was amusing to watch these grown men, who normally work and fight side by side, berating each others race, while in a very drunken state. They could barely stand, but they were ready to fight for any reason they could conjure up. The amusement was short lived. Before long, chairs and beer bottles were flying across the room, and people who had not been involved in the fracas up to then, began taking sides based on their race.

Featherstone looked at me and I looked at him. We both agreed that this was not our fight and that neither one of us was interested in hitting the other, or in joining the fray on either side. We shook hands and took the only prudent course of action, since we were too far from the exit. We both ducked under the table and stayed there until the M.P.s arrived and calmed the situation down. That was the last evening Featherstone and I spent together. I was leaving for Schweinfurt in less than a week and I had to see a lot of people before leaving. We walked back to the base together, convinced that we were the most sensible people in the E.M. club that night. I often wondered what ever happened to Featherstone. My bet would be that he became a good doctor.

I HAD FINALLY LEARNED TO ADAPT TO my place in the 15th Engineering Battalion and to the environs on the base, as well as the city of Fürth. I got along with the personnel in the drafting department, as long as I remembered to keep my place. The Captain and I seemed to get along, as long as I didn't expect to ever make PFC. I had even been feeling comfortable with the G-3, who for some reason, thought everything I said was meant to be funny. I was even able to avoid the German civilian doctor, whenever I needed to go on sick call. Between the service club, the art studio, the PX, the gymnasium and volunteering at the Chaplain's office, there were plenty of on base facilities to occupy leisure time without leaving the compound.

The occasional passes to town were taken up with visits to the many Gasthauses, or an occasional movie or even a concert, depending on who accompanied me. Friday nights at the chapel gave me that spiritual shot in the arm that was needed to keep me in line. I was getting much too comfortable in my surroundings for things to stay at status quo, so I should not have been surprised when the Major called me in to explain "Operation Gyroscope."

"The Big Red One," the 1st Division of the 7th Army, had been in Europe since the invasion of Normandy on D-Day, and now, the Major explained, after eleven years, the entire division was going to be transferred stateside. To fill the void, the 10th Division, then at Fort Riley, Kansas, was going to be transferred to Germany while the 1st Division would replace it at Fort Riley.

This massive troop movement was being called "Operation Gyroscope," and every outfit in Germany had been ordered to purge their personnel files for "short timers," who were due to be discharged on or shortly after August of 1955, and were not essential to the operation of the unit they were in, to fill openings in the "Big Red One."

Up until that conversation, I actually believed what I had been told time and again. That I was doing an essential job and that I was considered indispensable by my superiors, even though I had no security clearance. The major, trying to soften the blow to my ego, assured me that I was doing a bang up drafting job and that the G-2 would be hard pressed to find someone with my abilities to replace me. He finally admitted that it was somewhat awkward, however, having to explain having a non-citizen, without security clearance, and whose current citizenship was from a country that had recently been at war with the U.S., drawing the top secret demolition plans for the bridges connecting Allied occupied Europe with Soviet occupied Europe. I had to chuckle at the "new found" reasoning that all of a sudden made my job non-essential. At the same time, I hoped there would be a good side to this news.

My two year term in the army would not have been over until October 21, 1955, Yet I was being told that by becoming part of "Operation Gyroscope," assuming that I would be able to resist the inevitable pressure to re-up for another year in Fort Riley, the chances of my getting discharged in August were virtually assured. It wasn't as if I had a choice about the transfer, but the thought of an early discharge was music to my ears. To my dismay, the M.O.S. in my records had not been changed to that of a draftsman for the Corps of Engineers.

The service battery of the 7th Field Artillery Battalion, a part of the 1st Division, had need for an ammo handler to replace one that had been recently discharged, and because of "Operation Gyroscope," was limited in finding a replacement. They had to locate a soldier, already stationed in Europe, with the required M.O.S., that was scheduled to go back to the States within a few months after August, 1955.

THE DIE WAS CAST, I WAS GOING to be transferred to Service Battery of the 7th Field Artillery Battalion, that was housed in what used to be a Luftwaffe base in Schweinfurt, Germany, a town about forty kilometers south of Würzburg. Schweinfurt was the city with the ball bearing factories that the Allied air forces continually bombed, in the later years of World War II. In spite of the bombing raids, they sprang back into operation within hours of the bomb blasts. Those were the same bombers that made bombing raids on the I.G. Farben synthetic rubber plant in the town of Auschwitz, less than ten kilometers from the Auschwitz/Birkenau death camps. Aerial photos taken by U.S. Air Force photographers clearly showed the railroad transports entering the Auschwitz/ Birkenau compound. Pleas from Jewish and other humanitarian organizations to bomb the rail lines to the death camp, in order to thwart the Nazi's push to murder the one million Jews of Hungary before the wars end, were denied. The ostensible reason given for this denial was that the rail lines to Auschwitz/Birkenau were "not military targets." While the bombing raids on the I.G. Farben plant and the ball bearing plants in Schwienfurt were going on, the killing of Jews in the gas chambers of Auschwitz/Birkenau was being carried out at such a pace that the crematoria could not burn the bodies fast enough and piles of bodies were burned to keep up the pace of destroying the evidence.

The day after my conversation with the good Major, I received my official orders to report to Service Battery, 7th Field Artillery Battalion, 1st Division, 7th Army in Schweinfurt, Germany, within one week of the date on the Order. This barely gave me enough time to get all of my things in order. I had some drafting assignments that needed to be completed, as well as a couple of personal projects in the arts and crafts area. I also had to say goodbye to my lady friends at the U.S.O., the Chaplain, my military buddies, and my favorite gasthause waitresses.

After a week of running around and seeing everyone I could, I decided to spend my last night in Fürth relaxing at the Service Club and maybe drink a few beers in town after it closed. Chaplain Goodblatt had made me promise, however, to come spend some time that evening with him and his family. Strangely enough, the ladies at the Service Club and Chaplain Goodblatt were the people I was most comfortable with, although they represented very different influences on my leisure time. The Service Club had provided the GIs of our base many opportunities for relaxation and diversion. They provided all sorts of games, some requiring more skill than others and some more competitive than others. They had a piano and sheet music of every popular song of the last decade. The U.S.O. ladies worked hard at designing programs that would be available and enjoyable to the soldiers that frequented the club.

My favorite pastimes at the club were singing popular tunes at the piano and playing Scrabble. My combination of luck and skill at the game made me the guy to beat, and in very short time few people were willing to play Scrabble with me, except for the U.S.O. ladies and one other soldier I'll call Frank. Frank, two of the ladies and I, played at least once a week during my stay in Fürth, and we thought that including this activity, along with a little bit of warbling at the piano, on my last night would be fitting.

The two U.S.O. ladies were reasonably attractive, but mostly they were just fun to be with. There was never any romantic interest between the tall blonde and me. She was taller than I, for starters, and she was going steady with a special duties basketball player. The shorter brunette and I used to tease each other, but I had felt that was all in fun. The day that Frank left, she showed me the diamond ring that he had given her to seal their engagement. I was very happy for her, although I had never been aware of any romantic interest between the two of them. I knew that Frank was not very demonstrative, in fact he was genuinely timid, but he really faked me out on that one. The biggest surprise to me was that he, who professed to hating army life, was going to re-up (meaning to re-enlist), with the stipulation that he would be sent back to Germany so that he and his fiancée could be together.

It was a fun night and I realized that I was going to miss my friends in Fürth more than I had imagined. We sang a few of our favorite songs, drank coffee, ate donuts and played Scrabble. A combo got together and started to play some dance music and I took turns dancing with my U.S.O. lady friends. It was getting close to 9:00 P.M. and I reminded the girls that I was supposed to be at the Goodblatts' apartment before the kids went to sleep. We agreed on one last dance before I said goodbye. On the last dance, the brunette held me closer than usual, kissed me on the cheek, and asked me to come back before closing time, so that we could go out for a drink.

Ordinarily, I would have jumped at the suggestion. Knowing that she was supposed to be engaged to Frank made me hesitant, and I told her so. She assured me that she and Frank had agreed that they each would not stop seeing other people until they had a chance to get together again and finalize their commitment to each other. I believed her and told her that I would be back by the time the club closed at 11:00 P.M.

I told everyone else goodbye as I rushed off to the Goodblatts. The Chaplain's wife had been concerned that I would not get there in time to see the kids, who were in their pajamas when I arrived. I took the kids to bed, read them each a story, and gave each a big hug. I snuck out of the bedroom and found that the Goodblatts had waited to eat dinner, until I had arrived. I really wished I hadn't eaten donuts and coffee at the club, but I didn't let on that I wasn't particularly hungry. The food was so good that I soon forgot that I had not been hungry.

After a delicious meal, we sat on the sofa and started schmoozing. I mentioned to Chaplain Goodblatt that I was going to meet one of the U.S.O. ladies for a drink after the club closes, so that he would realize that I was on a fairly tight schedule. He acknowledged my comment and suggested that I would be much better off spending the evening with him, learning about the Torah portion of the week. He brought out two Chumashim, books containing all the Torah portions, with English translation, and we proceeded to read the text and commentary, and to discuss our understanding of what we read. At about 10:30 P.M., he looked at his watch and said that we had better stop, because he wanted me to draw several illustrations for his Chanukah bulletin.

I had been doing all the artwork for his bulletins since we met, and he knew that I would not disappoint him on this last bulletin. The paper, pen, and pencils were already on the dining table and he had already made notes regarding the illustrations he needed. I quickly sketched out everything in pencil for his approval and proceeded to do the ink drawing over the pencil sketches. I finished the drawings in less than 40 minutes. As I reached for my jacket, he asked if I had time for one more illustration. If I had any doubt of his motives, they quickly disappeared with this latest ploy. I felt the need to confront him.

"You're really trying to keep me from going back to the club, aren't you?" I looked at him, without anger, but a little peeved at being manipulated.

He had a sheepish grin on his face as he responded unsheepishly, "I'm just trying to keep you from doing something you might regret for the rest of your life."

I was mad at myself for confiding in him about my mixed feelings of anticipation and guilt in regard to the date, for which I was already late. Even though I had trepidation about this date, I cared enough about her to not stand her up. I desperately tried to call the club but there was no answer. I said goodbye to the Chaplain and his wife, thanked them for the wonderful meal, and told him that while I should have appreciated his looking out for my welfare, I felt that I was capable of deciding for myself on how to deal with this sticky situation. Had I not felt that way, I would have asked for his intervention.

I shook his hand and ran to the Service Club. It was a little past 11:30 P.M. when I arrived, all out of breath, and no one was there. I found a telephone and called her at home, trying my best to apologize in such a way that would make her believe that I really had wanted to come back and have a last drink with her. To my surprise, she sounded very understanding but somewhat miffed at the influence that she felt Chaplain Goodblatt had on me. She said that when I was not there at 10:45, she knew that I was being pulled by whatever forces brought me to be friends with a Chaplain in the first place. She continued that while she was really looking forward to spending time alone together, that she realized that this was just not meant to be, and therefore was not inviting me over. We wished each other well, and I started back to my quarters.

As I was walking to the billets, I began to realize that Chaplain Goodblatt could never have manipulated my evening, if I had not gone along with it.

12

HERO BY DEFAULT

I ARRIVED AT SERVICE BATTERY HEADQUARTERS AROUND noon. It was a beautifully sunny day and I couldn't get over the difference in the setting of this army base compared to the urban squalor of the one in Fürth. This base was actually prettier than any army base I had ever seen. The buildings were masonry and stucco and were arranged in a layout that provided ample distance between buildings and plenty of open spaces for outdoor activities. The thing that caught my eye as we drove in was the line of high caliber bullet holes in one of the stucco walls of the dining hall, which actually looked like the results of a strafing by a fighter plane.

I was introduced to Master Sergeant Rambo, the first sergeant of Service Battery, who apologized for not having time to show me around the base because of a mad scramble to get ready for the division wide alert. This was scheduled to start at 17:00 hours and go on through the night. I asked him about the bullet holes and he explained that the base had been a Luftwaffe base during World War II, and the strafing dated back to that time. Orders were never given to repair the bullet damage and it had sort of become a historical symbol.

In spite of the frantic rush that seemed to involve every officer and enlisted man in the battalion, Sgt. Rambo found a little time to chat with me, regarding possible assignments. My records indicated that my MOS was that of a 3/4 ton ammo truck driver, but that I had little or no experience at this specialty. They had no use for a draftsman in the artillery, or for that matter, a sign painter. Even though my training records as a gunner for a 105 mm Howitzer indicated that I was top man in my class, Service

Batteries don't use gunners, there were no openings for a gunner in Abel, Baker or Charlie batteries, and they were 155 mm Howitzer batteries anyway.

He offered that since my Area One scores were so high that he would try to find an opening in the office or the supply room. In the meantime, he said that the timing of my arrival, being just before the big alert, was indeed fortunate. Since I had not yet met anyone in the battalion, I would be perfect as an "aggressor" for this evenings official war games. He told me where to report to get instructions on what to do that night, and cautioned me not to introduce myself to anyone and not report to my squad leader, or even put away my duffel bag, until after the alert. After I had completed my job of posing as the enemy, and been repatriated, as it was a foregone conclusion that I would be captured almost immediately, I was to report back to him and he would make the necessary introductions and assignments.

I REPORTED TO AN OFFICER WHO WAS from another base and temporarily assigned to the battalion, just to command the aggressors for these war games. The two other new men that arrived with me earlier were the only other aggressors who were not imported from bases outside of Schweinfurt.

We were each given a weird looking helmet that appeared to be a dime store version of those worn by the army of Alexander the Great. It had a raised portion down the center of it, starting high at the front of the helmet and tapering off down the rear. The rest of the uniform came from our own army issue wardrobe and equipment. The idea was that our uniforms were to be so different from the official uniform to make it obvious to anyone that wasn't asleep, that we were the dreaded enemy, the "aggressors." We had to wear our Olive Green shirts, normally used as undergarments in cold weather, instead of field jackets, and our ammunition belts were to be worn outside of the O.G. shirt. In case our uniforms were not obvious enough, every soldier, noncom and officer, had been given a complete description of us, which included poster sized pictures, of what the aggressors would be wearing.

The officer in charge explained to us that we were there to test the alertness and efficiency of the 7th Field Artillery Battalion, while other aggressor units were similarly testing the various components of the 1st Division. Our job was to act as enemy forces, infiltrating the battalion's positions, and whenever possible, putting them out of commission. He explained to us that Schweinfurt was a mere twenty kilometers from the Russian troops in East Germany, and that if the battalion's regular troops were not proficient enough to capture the make-shift aggressor, then the lives of these American soldiers would be in danger in the event of a Russian attack.

He emphasized that we had a job to do and that we had to take it seriously. If we were doing our job to the best of our ability and got caught, it would bode well for the battalion troops, and we would have nothing to be ashamed of. But if we were captured because we had not been a formidable enemy, then there would be Hell to pay. To this end, we were issued our weapons. A handful of tags, about a dozen, and some M-80s.

The paper tags were supposed to be our primary "weapon." Whatever or whomever we encountered as we infiltrated the battalion's positions, could be rendered dead, destroyed or captured, by tying one of our volatile tags on it. In the event that one of us should run out of tags, he should resort to lighting the M-80 fire crackers, which looked like cherry bombs, and toss them at targets as if he was tossing hand grenades. The officer then instructed us where to meet, in case we were not captured by the end of the exercise.

My mind had started to wander before the last part of our instructions. It appeared to me that, with the absolutely ridiculous looking uniforms we were wearing, being the only soldiers not carrying a real weapon, and knowing that our adversaries had been trained to identify aggressors by our uniforms, early capture was inevitable, and I would get some long awaited rest while the war games were being concluded.

After dark, we were each dropped off at different points along the perimeter of the position that the 7th Artillery Battalion had taken up in the woods. I was left off at the outskirts of Baker Battery's position. Not knowing exactly what to do, I scanned the area, under cover of trees, to get an idea of the activities that I could consider disrupting. I noticed that a Lieutenant was laying out the battery, that is, he was using a transit, similar to the kind used by surveyors, to position the six Howitzers under his command. This mandatory procedure would make it possible for the gunners to respond to firing orders from the FDC, fire direction center, to lob artillery shells at the given coordinates, in support of infantry troops. I watched for a few minutes, marveling at how engrossed the officer was at his task, while other members of the battery were just hanging around, waiting for him to finish.

Chancy as it seemed, I couldn't resist the temptation of going for the transit. I started walking through the open field towards the Lieutenant, waving at the other soldiers who were too preoccupied, with whatever they were doing, to notice my uniform in the moonlight. I approached the officer and tapped him on the shoulder. He swung his arm around as if he were shooing away a dog, "Can't you see I'm laying the battery, don't bother me!"

I ignored his protest and tied a tag to the epaulet strap on his shoulder. He took his eye off the instrument and glared at me. He was able to blurt out, "What the Hell do you think you're do----" before I put my left hand on his mouth and the index finger of my other hand to mine as I responded, "Sir, your dead. Please don't try to alert the soldiers around you, because that would break the rules of the game. This tag is official, Sir. You are dead and this battery of Howitzers is out of commission."

The officer was fuming. "Who are you?" he whispered, as he came to the realization that he was supposed to be dead. "I'm just your friendly aggressor, Sir. It was a pleasure making your acquaintance. Not another word, please, while I make my get-away." By this time he was shaking his head not knowing whether to laugh or cry. I walked away waving at twenty or so artillery men staring at me with eyes wide open. They appeared astonished as they watched me tag each Howitzer, and they waved back, somewhat dazed, as I waved at them.

I was more surprised than the Lieutenant that no one took the initiative to take me into custody. That incident was like a shot of adrenaline for me, it made me feel indestructible. I started walking through the woods, without bothering to take cover, and tagging every truck that was parked along the way, while advising the driver that he had been blown up, with his truck, and was dead. Many of them had been asleep and just groggily nodded their assent.

Finally, I ran out of tags. I reached for my M-80s as I approached the headquarters tent for Able Battery, and realized that I had a problem. Not being a smoker, I had no matches, and never expecting to get to the point of using the M-80s, I didn't think ahead to get any. It was like having a gun without bullets. I figured that I was due to get captured anyway, so why not try something bizarre.

I entered the Able battery HQ tent, in my aggressor sartorial splendor, and asked if anyone had a match. There were about four people in the tent, including the first sergeant. They looked at each other and each shook his head. The sergeant spoke up, "No matches here, soldier. Check with one of the truck drivers. If you gotta smoke, be sure to stay away from an ammo truck, and be sure to cover up the lit cigarette. Not only is smoking during this exercise against regulations, but an aggressor may spot you and render you dead."

I thanked him for the advice and told him that I would have my eyes open for aggressors, as I backed out of the tent. Heeding the sergeants advice, I approached the first truck I saw and banged on the cab to wake him up. As he was shaking out the cobwebs, I asked him if he had a match. He checked all of his pockets, reached into one and handed me a cigarette lighter. What the Hell, I thought to myself, this can't last forever, just go with the flow and see what happens. I took the lighter, thanked the driver, told him I'd give it right back, stepped down to the ground, took out an M-80, lit it with the lighter, and threw it at the hood of the truck. The explosion probably could be heard over a half mile away. I handed the lighter back to the driver whose eyes were popping out of his head, and told him that his truck was blown up and he was dead. The astonished look on his palid face almost made me think he was.

I started walking toward Charlie battery to see what could be blown up there, with the assistance of the victim. A squad of men came running in my direction and I figured that the jig was finally up. The squad leader stopped while the rest of them kept running, with their rifles in hand. "There's an aggressor in the area," he blurted out, almost out of breath, "have you seen him?"

"Is that what that noise was?" I responded, scratching my head. "I know what they look like, so I'll keep my eyes open. If I see him I'll yell for you, cause I doubt if I could capture him by myself."

"Thanks!" he shouted, as he ran off to catch up with his squad. He ran about ten feet and stopped, as if he had been hit by a bolt of lightning. "Hey, wait a minute, you're the aggressor, you S.O.B.!" I had taken off running as soon as he had turned his back. He yelled for his squad members to turn around, and they took off after me, in hot pursuit. Speed was never one of my attributes and I was soon overcome by the squad leader.

I was taken to the prisoners' compound and met up with my fellow aggressors, who had already been captured. We shared escapades and it became apparent that my ease of infiltration was not unique. One aggressor had even taken out the battalion headquarters, leaving the commanding officer screaming obscenities and vowing that heads would roll. The total breakdown in the battalions ability to deal with a foreign infiltrating force was going to have to be dealt with, and I only hoped that my superiors for the next eight months would not take it out on me.

13

RESTRAINT WENT OUT THE WINDOW

I OFFICIALLY REPORTED FOR DUTY THE NEXT day and was introduced to various people in the battery. Sergeant Rambo thanked me for filling in as an aggressor and patted me on the back for a job well done. It turned out that Service Battery was the only outfit in the battalion that didn't suffer "casualties." I confided that I would hate to depend on the soldiers of this battalion in a war effort. He wasn't all that shook up by the disastrous showing, except for the fact that Division Brass was raising Hell. It was his opinion that these same men would be up to the task in the event of actual combat. I told him I admired his faith but couldn't bring myself to share it.

I was shown my sleeping quarters and was only allowed to park my duffel bag, without time to unpack. There was much to do and I could unpack after hours. I was introduced to my squad leader, a Filipino sergeant who seemed nice enough. Then I was taken to the supply room and introduced to the supply sergeant and his assistant. It appeared that I would be getting another chance to work in a supply room, and I made a promise to myself that I would not blow it this time. The supply sergeant and his sidekick were pretty shifty guys. I could feel from the beginning that they were casing me out, but I was intent on not making waves. However they wanted to run the supply room was not mine, a mere private, to question.

That night, I had a chance to meet the guys with whom I was sharing a room. They were all ammo handlers who would happily trade jobs with me. While unpacking, I told them what I had done with my supply room assignment in Ft. Lewis, Washington, and I assured them that I would not make the same mistake again. Everyone in our room seemed relatively happy at this base. The town of Schweinfurt, they said, left a lot to be desired. Most guys went either to Würzburg or to Frankfurt on overnight passes. In the evenings, however, they felt that there was more activity available on the base than in the town of Schweinfurt.

I was a short-timer and this seemed to be as good a place as any to wait out my last eight or nine months in the army. I was intent on not making waves and going with the flow, particularly as far as my assignment to the supply room was concerned, and that was no easy task.

The supply sergeant and his assistant seemed to enjoy making busy work for me and challenging my every decision. They made little effort to hide their sexual preference, and continually tried to feel me out, to see if I was inclined in their direction. I wasted no time in making it obvious that I was not interested in sharing their private lives. They, in turn, began to lose patience with me and found fault in almost everything I did. Nevertheless, I was intent on making this assignment work.

No matter what the task, I did it to the best of my ability, and redid it to their liking, whether I agreed with them or not. After a relatively short while, my diligence paid off. For over a week I had not been able to please the supply sergeant, then all of a sudden he began to express appreciation for my work. As a result, his assistant began to look at me as a threat, although I bent over backwards to assure him that I was not after his job. Within one more week things started to run smoothly. The supply sergeant had already decided that I was an asset to the supply room, and the assistant had finally become convinced that all I wanted to do was stay out of trouble. Things were looking good and I promised myself that this time I would not screw up.

Whoever said, "we are the masters of our own destiny," undoubtedly had never served in the U.S. army. After less than three weeks as a supply clerk, I was notified that a corporal in my squad, who had less time to serve than I did, told Sergeant Rambo that he would re-enlist for three years, with the stipulation that he would be assigned to my position as supply clerk. He then would be in line to take the supply sergeant's place, after he was discharged.

I couldn't believe what I was hearing. I knew this corporal. He was a very quiet, short, skinny, and somewhat nerdy guy, but he wasn't dumb. In fact, his "area one score," which is supposed to be the equivalent of an I.Q., was 155, and he was a college graduate. I later asked him why he didn't do this before I came on the scene. He admitted that he had no idea he wanted this position until I had it, and I appeared to be having it better than the ammo handlers, and the truck drivers.

The supply sergeant expressed regret. Actually, I felt that he had mixed emotions. I finally had been trained to do things his way, yet he could sense that I was humoring him, and that deep down I had little or no respect for him. Actually, I felt sorry for him. If he had been concerned that I would laud education or I.Q. over him, he would have his hands full with his new supply clerk. For better or for worse, this was no longer my problem.

IT WAS FRIDAY AFTERNOON WHEN THE NEWS came of my change of assignment to ammo handler. I tried to tell myself that there was no point in dwelling on this unfortunate turn of events, but I couldn't get over the feeling of helplessness, as if some outside force was controlling my life. I decided not to dwell on feeling sorry for myself, and to just bide my time until August.

There had to be a bright side to this new turn of events. Most of the ammo handlers in our outfit had developed muscular upper bodies, and I saw no reason why I could not benefit in the same manner, if I worked at it. This was only one of the inane thoughts that raced through my mind that night, as I was on my hands and knees, scrubbing the wood floor of our room. Friday night was G.I. night, and it was my turn to scrub the floor. I was scrubbing away, deep in thought, when I noticed a pair of shiny boots in front of me that belonged to a pair of legs spread about two feet apart. I looked up and saw that the legs belonged to my Filipino squad leader, who was standing over me with his legs spread and his hands on his hips.

While I was the supply clerk, my squad leader had very little to say to me. As short as he was, from the perspective of my hands and knees, he looked like Colossus of Rhodes. Our eyes met, but he just stood there staring at me with an angry look, the basis for which I had absolutely no clue. I was sure, however, that I didn't like the looks of this. I had been told that I would be serving as an ammo handler under him, but I couldn't figure out what I had done to make him angry. I broke the ice by asking him if I had done anything wrong. He stared at me in silence, for a few more seconds, then let it out.

"You think you're smarter than me because you have two years of college!" he paused to catch his breath, "I'll have you know that these stripes did not come easy. If you get one inch out of line, I'll show you what these stripes mean, and what these boots can do."

My mind started reeling. Was this *deja vu* or was I dreaming? I prayed that I would wake up and that this wasn't really happening. Didn't I go through this once before in Camp Chaffee? He stood there waiting for a response, but I felt that anything I would say would get me into more trouble than I seemed to be in.

One of us had to break the silence, and he was only too glad to be the one. "I'm gonna watch you like a hawk, Hirsch. I know your kind. You think you're too smart to do a days work. You're in my squad now, and I don't give a s--- how smart you think you are. You goof up and your ass is mine! You got that, Private?"

"I've got the picture, Sergeant." I responded, in a voice that was mixed with defeat and disgust. "I'll try to give you nothing to complain about."

He gave me one last parting shot, as he turned around to walk out of the room, "I doubt that, you poor excuse for a soldier. You'll never make PFC in this squad, if I have any say about it." Frankly, that thought had never entered my mind. I had given up on a promotion long ago and could care less if one never came. As he left the room, my fellow soldiers gathered around me to lend whatever support they could. They had never seen the squad leader come down on someone this hard before. He was no Mr. Congeniality, but for the most part, he got along fairly well with his squad. A couple of guys offered to take me under their wing after I told them that I had no experience as an ammo handler, and was afraid of the sergeant's attitude toward my learning on the job.

The first free moment I had the next day, I asked Sgt. Rambo for a few minutes of his time to alert him to the friction between my squad leader and myself, and to look into the possibility of a transfer to another squad. He responded that learning to cope with adverse situations was what the army was all about. "You mean this comes under the category of 'good training'?" I asked him. "You got it, Hirsch," was his response.

The next few days were my own private hell. Everywhere I turned, my squad leader was there to badger me. He made it a point not to touch me, but he was usually within a fraction of an inch, his chest to my stomach, with his breath, reeking of his last meal, shooting up into my face as he proceeded to chew me out for my every move. Every disgusting detail was assigned to me, but he limited the assignments to ones that he had complete control over, leaving guard duty and K.P. for the days he had off.

It was obvious to everyone in the squad, that for whatever reason, I had been singled out for special treatment, to be an example of what can happen to a soldier when he crossed a superior. The fact that I had resisted punching him out made me a candidate for sainthood among my peers in Service Battery. I wasn't the only one, however, that had suspected that the squad leader's agenda was to goad me into hitting him, in order to have me court-martialed. It was that suspicion and the fear of its consequences that kept me from going over the deep end.

THE MORE I STOICALLY TOOK EVERYTHING HE threw at me, the angrier he seemed to get. I was hoping that Sgt. Rambo or one of the officers would see what was going on and intercede. I was looking at the bulletin board outside of the office one morning, when my squad leader came storming at me, accusing me of telling lies about him to the Captain. He refused to believe that I had never even talked to the Company Commander since being introduced to him on the day after the Alert, and looking around to see that no one was there, he proceeded to pick a fight with me. I refused to hit him back, without witnesses that he had hit me first. He continued with his verbal abuse, and finally crossed the line when he called my mother a Jew-bitch whore. All restraint went out the window. I could not contain the rage that had been building up in me since he started harassing me on G.I. night.

If he thought he was going to run away and report me after one punch was thrown, he was sadly mistaken. I had been holding a lot of anger in for much too long. He finally had pushed the right button to unleash my fury and I wasn't about to let him off easy. There were still no witnesses when I jumped him, threw him to the floor, and started pounding his face with my fists. Sgt. Rambo came running out of the office and put a stop to the fight. He held us apart, then he motioned for the sergeant to step in the captain's office, and then gave me a look that seemed to say "Now you've really done it."

I was told to sit in a chair by Sgt. Rambo's desk, while he was in the captain's office getting my squad leaders side of the story. About forty-five minutes later, my squad leader was ushered out and I was asked to come in and explain myself. The captain started off by asking me if I was not aware that hitting a non-commissioned officer was a court-martial offense. I told him that I was, and that for that reason I had restrained myself from responding to his torture as long as I had. I reluctantly told him what finally provoked me to violence along with chapter and verse of all the harassment that had preceded my indiscretion. I told him that I realized that there were no witnesses to the fight, but that he could talk to other members of the squad to confirm the special treatment I had been getting.

Sgt. Rambo and the Captain looked at me sternly for several minutes. "What you did was inexcusable and a very serious offense," the captain said, with Rambo nodding his head. "If it were not for the fact that we had heard several complaints about what your squad leader has been doing to you, and for the fact that the company clerk had overheard the verbal battle that preceded the fisticuffs, you would be court-martialed, and you would spend a year in the stockade. A year, that incidentally, would not have counted toward your discharge. Justified or not, you did hit a non-commissioned officer and that type of action cannot go unpunished. You are hereby put on fourteen days restriction, during which you will not be eligible for any passes, and this incident is going on your record, in the event that you ever commit another court-martial offense."

I tried to hide my emotions, but I was almost ready to cry from relief, and my renewed faith in justice. Sgt. Rambo started walking out of the captain's office toward his desk. He stopped, turned around and looked at me. "Oh, by the way, your request for assignment to another squad has been granted, but I'm going to be watching you. You have no idea how lucky you are this time. Don't push your luck." I had hoped that Sgt. Rambo would be sort of a mentor. He made it clear that he would be my warden instead.

14

"THE MAN"

MY NEW SQUAD WAS A WELCOME CHANGE. The personnel were different, but we were still ammo handlers. My new squad leader looked like a slightly thinner version of Fats Domino. He was fairly easy going for a squad leader, but he made no bones about letting everyone know who was in charge. He had heard that my previous squad leader had felt threatened by my "area one" score, and was quick to let me know that he was cool about that and that he would be using me as an encyclopedia. He would let me know when my input was desired, and that I should not offer suggestions, unless asked. With these ground rules we were sure to get along famously.

Two weeks confined to the base was not so bad. I had been to the service club and it was every bit as nice as the one in Fürth, including the personnel. The U.S.O. ladies were avid Scrabble players, and they worked hard on programming to give the soldiers a variety of activities. I had asked them if an art studio was available, so that I could continue working on some of the oil paintings I had started in Fürth. They told me that an art instructor was scheduled to come two to three days a week, but if I could develop a relationship with him, he might let me have a key to the studio, so I could work whenever I had the time.

The art instructor was a German, from Würzburg, in his early 30's. By the time I had a chance to meet him, he had already found out a lot about me. It was the first weekend of my 14 day restriction and he had been advised by the U.S.O. ladies that I would be coming to chat with him about signing up for his painting studio. He was wearing a white smock when I was introduced to him, and his black hair was combed straight back.

Trying to make idle conversation, I looked at his spotless smock and commented on the German penchant for uniforms. This allowed him to get what he wanted to say off his chest.

"I know you were born in Frankfurt am Main and that many of your family members were killed by the Nazis. That was a terrible time in Germany, but I will not apologize for it, because I was not a Nazi." There was no apology in his voice. He was direct, as if he were making a statement of position. "Jews," he continued, "ought to get on with their lives and quit fixating on the guilt of the German people."

We argued for a while and I could see that this man had a mind like a steel trap, except someone had locked it and thrown away the key. Realizing that we could never reach a level of understanding, he concluded that "I am not a Nazi and I was never a Nazi, however, I strongly dislike Jews and I find myself very uncomfortable around them." Having said that, he told me that I was welcome to join his art studio. He would have been relieved if I declined, therefore, I told him that I would think about it and let him know. I didn't want him to be as comfortable as I was in knowing that I would never participate in his studio, even if he were Da Vinci.

A SPECIAL DIRECTIVE ON HYGIENE CAME DOWN from 7th Army Headquarters that caused quite a stir. Apparently, there had been a rash of penile infections, as well as venereal diseases, among American soldiers serving in Europe. Studies had shown that an overwhelming majority of soldiers that had contracted these infections and diseases were not circumcised. Therefore, the directive was sent to promote voluntary circumcision among the uncircumcised masses of soldiers. Any soldier submitting to voluntary surgery would be granted a fourteen day leave, immediately after the circumcision. The first day that the directive was posted in the 7th Field Artillery Battalion, pandemonium broke loose. The line of volunteers queuing up for sick call was so long that soldiers who were really sick could not get medical attention. To alleviate the problem, volunteers were instructed to schedule their medical procedure through the office of each battery. That took the scheduling pressure off of the daily infirmary personnel.

Whoever dreamed up the fourteen day leave carrot to encourage this voluntary procedure was a genius. As it turned out, the normal recuperation time for an adult after being circumcised happened to be fourteen days. The large number of volunteers who actually went through with this hygienic procedure spent their leave recuperating. As a result, many of those on the tail end of the schedule decided not to go through with it. All in all, the program was a success. The men that were circumcised complained of the pain, and of not being able to take advantage of the bonus leave time, but when the pain was gone, they were glad they had it done.

The V.D. rate of our battalion was abnormally high, and although it was hygienically advantageous, circumcision alone was not going to be the answer for that. There were mandatory lectures with graphic movies, to no avail. The frustrating part of the problem for the medics was seeing the same soldiers coming in for treatment, time and time again.

I watched these activities with great interest and marveled at the irony of the situation, from my perspective. When I was a young boy in Germany, during the Nazi era, being circumcised branded any male as a Jew, which ultimately was tantamount to a death sentence. Less than ten years after the defeat of Nazi Germany, non-Jews in the American armed forces occupying Germany were being encouraged to get circumcised for hygienic reasons. Does God have a sense of humor, or what?

Charlie, a former squad leader in Baker Battery, who had planned to be a career soldier, was one of the most jovial guys you could ever meet. When I met him he was a PFC. He had actually been a sergeant several months before. When I became aware of his obsession with a German girl, he was a Pvt. E-2, the lowest rank a soldier can have after basic training, the same rank I had.

Charlie had a little blonde companion in Schwienfurt and she had the clap, known in medical circles as gonorrhea. She refused to get treatment and he just couldn't stay away from her. Every time Charlie got an overnight pass, he would come back with the clap, go on sick call, get treated with penicillin and then be put on 14 days restriction, which was the punishment for contracting a venereal disease. Aside from this indiscretion, he had been a good soldier. At the end of his restriction, he would apply for an overnight pass, which was almost always granted with the provision that he would be careful and at least use a condom. While it was a mystery to Charlie's friends why his little Fraulein would not seek treatment, it cost Charlie his career. He was not allowed to re-enlist. And though he didn't recognize it as a blessing, she would not come back to Alabama with him.

MY FOURTEEN-DAY RESTRICTION WAS OVER, BUT I continued to frequent the Service Club. There were quite a few regulars who enjoyed chess, bridge and Scrabble, and there was a good piano player from New Jersey. In civilian life, he was a professional accompanist and he could play almost every popular song without sheet music. With all this, who needed to chance the disease of the week in Schwienfurt? Life in Service Battery was tense, the politics and back-biting was too much for me, so I made the service club my retreat.

The talk of the Battalion was the upcoming Winter Indoctrination in Grafenwöhr, a God forsaken place that reportedly boasted 30 below zero(F) temperatures. The word was out that no amount of gold-bricking could get anyone out of participating in this exercise. Every one made jokes about ridiculous scenarios that would allow someone to bug out of this dreaded two week winter training, but no one, including myself, had any serious thoughts of avoiding the big chill. This was the main topic of discussion during a hot Scrabble game one weekend, when one of the U.S.O. ladies suggested that I enter the talent contest the following night.

I had no desire to get up in front of my fellow soldiers and make a fool of myself, and I told her so. She was persistent and insisted that it wasn't that they needed more participants to make the contest interesting, she wanted to have someone represent popular music lovers. Virtually all of the talent that had signed up for the contest had been country music, bebop, or rock and roll oriented. She let on that she had listened in on several of my singing sessions accompanied by the piano player from Jersey. She felt that we would make good contestants.

I kept refusing. I had no qualms about singing in front of a group, as long as I had a good accompanist and a good microphone. Maybe I was playing hard to get. I facetiously asked what the prizes would be for the winners. She brought me a flyer that spelled out all of the details of the contest, which was titled "The 1955 All Army Talent Contest." The third prize was money, about $25. Second prize was an overnight pass with all expenses paid in a Schweinfurt hotel. The first place winner got a $75 cash prize, and a three day pass to attend and represent the 7th FAB at the All Army Semi-final Talent Contest, in Würzburg, all expenses paid.

I burst out laughing when I noticed the date of the Semi-finals in Würzburg, then I protested that this first prize was a farce. I explained that the winner could never attend the Semi-finals, since they were scheduled to be on the same date as the beginning of Winter Indoctrination in Grafenwöhr. She admitted to not having thought of that, but she could not imagine any scheduled army activity being so sacrosanct. How could they disqualify a winning contestant in one of the annual All Army Contests from participating in the semi-finals. We continued our game without her while she made a few telephone calls to clarify the matter.

She came back a few minutes later with a smile from ear to ear. She had called all the way to 7th Army Headquarters to get the official answer. Each winner of an All Army Base Contest would receive official orders from the Commanding General of the 7th Army, and that took precedence over anything else.

The stakes were beginning to sound interesting. Less than an hour before, we could only joke about the possibility of getting out of Winter Indoctrination. All of a sudden the impossible became, at least, a long shot. I agreed to enter the contest to the cheers of encouragement from my fellow Scrabble players. Luckily the man from Jersey was playing away at the piano, and from the smile on his face, as he looked in our direction, I realized that he was instrumental in this push to get us in as contestants.

We finished the game and I went to converse with my accompanist. We needed two songs and I felt they should not be the same tempo. He had a great ear, so I asked him for suggestions from the songs we had been singing and playing recently. Of all the songs we had done together, his favorite was "Lost in Loveliness," and he was insistent on using it. Having selected our slow, Dick Haymes type love song, we had to select a faster number out of the music sheets that were available. After flipping through pages of sheet music of songs, we finally ran across the music for "Rags To Riches," which neither one of us was crazy about, but which, we both agreed, had popular appeal.

There was virtually no time to rehearse, so it was good that we had selected two songs we both knew and felt comfortable with. I was excited about trying for the brass ring, but after hearing that other contestants had been rehearsing for a couple of weeks, I had no expectation of winning. Supposedly, the other contestants were serious about developing their talents. For me, just the chance, remote as it was, of getting out of Winter Indoctrination was enough of a challenge to get my adrenaline flowing.

At first, I thought about asking all of the guys in my billets, or at least in my squad, to come and cheer me on. I changed my mind when I thought of the ribbing I would get if I came in last place. If anybody from my outfit would hear about the contest, it wouldn't be from me.

The next day was just like any other, tedious details interrupted by predictable meals. That evening, I went to the Service Club, sang a few warm-up numbers with my accompanist, and started a game of Scrabble with the U.S.O. ladies. There had been no time to build up anxiety over participating in the talent contest. The relaxed state I was in could have been misinterpreted as over confidence. The opposite was, in fact, closer to reality. Just being able to talk about taking a shot at penetrating the impenetrable wall around the winter exercises was enough to satisfy me, and I felt good enough about our act, particularly with such a fine accompanist, that I had no fears of making a fool of myself.

The first contestant was a Hank Snow impersonator, although he wasn't billed as such. The crowd, which was somewhat larger than the usual for a Monday night, was not particularly partial to Country music. His reception was in no way comparable to what it might have been at Camp Chaffee. Next came a trio that must have been influence by the Ink Spots. I thought the imitation was good, but not very original. The crowd seemed to share my feelings and gave them polite applause.

We were on next. I finally began to feel a little nervous as I grabbed the mike, but as soon as my accompanist started playing, I felt good about being there. We finished "Lost in Loveliness" to a surprising round of applause, although I did notice some of our friends encouraging the crowd reaction. The applause was almost as loud after our second number, then it was over. We had given it our best and were well received. What else could I ask for.

As I was walking away from the stage area, shaking hands with well-wishers, one of the next contestants came rushing over to me and he seemed distressed. He was really decked out for his performance, a handsome black man in an outfit that would never be allowed during duty hours. "Hey man," he said in a raised voice, pointing his finger at me. "You stole my number, now what am I gonna do?" I had no idea that he, or any one else, had planned to sing "Rags to Riches." I really felt bad, even though I had no way of knowing what his repertoire was going to be.

I took him over to the U.S.O. lady in charge and suggested that he be put on last, so people could forget that we sang the same song. He offered that his rendition was going to be drastically different anyway, and exuding confidence, added, "with a lot more class."

As it turned out, had I been judging, he would have taken first prize. He had a great stage presence, apparently was a seasoned performer, and was well received by the audience. He was as disappointed as I was shocked when it was announced that he came in second, a formidable prize for someone less sure of themselves. The Ink Spot imitating trio had won third prize, and I tried to figure out who the judges could have thought was better than the second prize winner.

The lady in charge asked for a drum roll to lead in to the announcement of the first prize winner. I really didn't have a clue, since I was so sure that the second prize winner had it in the bag. She announced my name and I was dumbfounded. People started rushing up to me, shaking my hand, patting my back or giving me a hug. I snapped out of my daze, and started thinking that maybe I deserved it, after seeing the approval of the crowd.

Then the reality hit. My God, I thought, I've done it, if I don't blow it somehow, I will be in Würzburg while everyone else is in Grafenwöhr. After the euphoria settled, I decided that I would not say a word, until, and if, orders from 7th Army Hqs came.

After celebrating our success with a few beers, my accompanist, our friends from the Service Club and I all went our separate ways to our respective quarters. A handful of guys from my outfit had been there and they were kind in their appraisal of the contest outcome. None of them had any idea of the possible implication of winning first prize, in relation to the upcoming winter exercises in Grafenwöhr. In fact, my squad leader was ecstatic when he heard that a soldier in his squad had taken first prize in the talent contest for the whole base. He expressed a new found admiration for me and wasted no time in relaying the news to Sergeant Rambo, who in turn, took pride in passing on the news to the captain.

My fifteen seconds of fame lasted a couple of days. I was glad that my immediate superiors felt good that I would be representing the entire base at the All Army semi-finals, but I did not dare let on that I was aware of the pre-scheduled date of the semi-finals, and that it was in conflict with Winter Indoctrination. I calmly waited, at least outwardly, for orders to arrive from 7th Army Headquarters, and I fully expected total cooperation and support for my trip to Würzburg, when the orders arrived, from those same superiors who had been so proud of me.

I WAS BEGINNING TO GIVE UP ON receiving orders. Almost two weeks had past since the local contest. Our squad had been pulling a detail in the motor pool, when my squad leader hand delivered a piece of mail to me, because of its apparent importance. The return address on the envelope was that of the Commanding General of the 7th Army, and a large note stamped on the envelope read "Direct Orders inside, deliver immediately."

The squad leader stood over me as I opened the envelope and read its contents. I was just as anxious for him to see the orders, as he was curious about the contents of the envelope. I took my time reading the orders, however, to make sure I had the details straight in my mind and to verify that I had not been told wrong about the dates of the semi-finals. The orders were exactly as I had anticipated. I felt like I was holding a piece of gold, and with some reluctance, handed it over to my squad leader to digest. He seemed quite impressed as he was reading the orders, but his smile abruptly disappeared when he saw the dates for the All Army semi-final talent contest. He handed the piece of paper back to me and offered that it was a shame that I would not be able to attend.

I was shocked at the matter-of-fact dismissal of direct orders from the Commanding General of the armed forces in Europe. I followed him as he turned to leave. "Corporal, these orders are from the Commanding General himself, I can't believe you plan to ignore them."

He stopped and looked me straight in the eye, "Nobody gets out of Winter Indoctrination. I'm sure that if the general was made aware of the conflict in dates, he would rescind the orders."

My disbelief at what I was hearing was turning to anger. "So that's it?" I yelled, "Case closed!"

He gave me an impatient look that was bordering on anger and said, "As far as I'm concerned, Hirsch, it's a closed issue. If you have a problem, feel free to discuss it with Sergeant Rambo." I turned around and started to head toward Rambo's office. He grabbed my shoulder and spun me around until we were face to face. "I'm in charge here, and you go when I say go. The first sergeant isn't going anywhere. If you want to talk to him, you do it on your time or when I give you permission to go."

I got the distinct impression that my squad leader was not too enamored with me for questioning his decision, but his decision needed to be challenged, and it was having much more of an effect on me, than anyone else. I realized that finding Sgt. Rambo in, after hours, would not be easy, and I figured that the corporal couldn't get any angrier with me for asking, so I walked over to him and asked, "With your permission, Corporal, may I go see the first sergeant now, and get this issue behind us?"

He was exasperated. The anger had gone from his eyes, but he was still annoyed. He began to wonder, though, if he had not over-stepped his bounds by over-riding the orders of a four star general. Whatever the reason, he let me go. I was being a smart ass and I knew it, but I couldn't let go of this reward I had so looked forward to. For some reason, fighting this battle became a raison d'etre. I felt I was right, but I was beginning to wonder if being right is what it took to win a point in this army.

I took off before he could change his mind, clutching my orders from 7th Army. I was very confident of the outcome of Sergeant Rambo's review of the situation. It seemed so cut and dry. An order from a four star general takes precedence over anything else, short of war.

I approached the first sergeant's desk and told him I had permission from my squad leader to show him the orders I had received from above. He glanced at them and raised his eyebrows when he noticed who signed the orders. "Looks good to me, Hirsch, what's the problem?" he asked, sensing that there was a reason that I was bringing this to his attention in the middle of a work day.

"My squad leader says I can't go, no matter who signed the orders," I blurted out in a somewhat indignant tone, that probably was not too wise.

"What have you done wrong this time, are you on restriction again?" He looked me in the eye like he was the head counselor of a school for wayward boys.

"Sarge," I responded, "I've worked hard at keeping my nose clean, I think even my squad leader will vouch for that. His concern is that the date of these orders conflict with Winter Indoctrination, and he would rather ignore orders from the Commanding General of the 7th Army than allow me to miss any days from those exercises."

I got the feeling, that if my squad leader had not objected, Rambo would not have had a problem with my going to Würzburg. However, he was not one to over-ride the decision of a squad leader for fear of having the squad leader's authority constantly under question. He handed me back my orders and said, "If your squad leader says you can't go, you can't go." He turned his attention to some paper work and motioned for me to leave.

I held my breath and counted to ten, to keep from saying something that I would live to regret. I was really angry at being jerked around so cavalierly. "Is that your final decision, Sergeant?" I asked him while standing at attention. He responded in the affirmative.

Still standing at attention, and remembering my rights on addressing grievances, I requested permission to see the captain. Sergeant Rambo was visibly shocked that I would even think of going over his head. He had that "so that's the way you want to play the game" look on his face, got up from his chair, pointed at me and said, "you stand right there at attention." He then walked into the captain's office and closed the door behind him.

I was probably only standing there for about ten minutes, but it seemed like an hour. Finally, he came out and said "the captain will see you now," while he nonchalantly went back to his desk. I fully expected that they had been discussing my situation, and made a decision before I ever stepped into the captain's office. I positioned myself in front of the captain's desk, stood at attention, saluted, and held the salute until he casually saluted me back.

While I was waiting outside, I realized that as the first sergeant backed his squad leader, so would the battery commander back his first sergeant. I also remembered what the optometrist in Fort Lewis had taught me.

The captain was predictable. He listened to my story as if he knew nothing about it in advance, and weighing all considerations, sided with the first sergeant and the squad leader.

I was prepared for this outcome. I continued to stand at attention and spoke, "Request permission to see the I.G., Sir."

By the stunned look on the captain's face, I could tell that he was not expecting this. "What did you say?," he almost growled looking me straight in the eye.

I repeated, "Request permission to see the I.G., Sir!," still standing at attention and knowing full well that my request could not legally be denied.

I had mixed emotions seeing my commanding officer squirm like that. It felt good standing up for my rights, yet I was afraid that I might live to regret questioning his right to be wrong, at my expense. He composed himself, made it a point not to appear intimidating, and said he would have Sergeant Rambo make the appointment and travel arrangements for me.

Sgt. Rambo either overheard, or the captain notified him by intercom. The look on his face as I left the captain's office did not speak well for me. "You're sure you want to go through with this?," he queried, looking like Clint Eastwood saying "make my day." I nodded in the affirmative and went back to my squad.

I didn't know what to expect. My squad leader had already gotten the word that I was "fighting the system." He shook his head at me and said, "Boy, you must really want to do this talent thing real bad." I felt relieved that he didn't start harassing me. For the next few days, every non-com from squad leader up, and every officer in the outfit gave me sneering looks. I started getting a lot of moral support from the regular troops, however, for taking a stand. I felt good knowing that it wasn't going to be me against the world, at least not totally.

Three days later I was on my way to Würzburg, wearing my class A's, to see the I.G., inspector general, who was the last word on the rights of any member of the military, regardless of rank. Up to this point, I had been positive that I was right in my stand. As I lingered in the I.G.'s waiting room, I began to get nervous and have some doubts. Not on the merits of their arguments, but on the fact that no one had agreed with me, from squad leader up to battery commander.

The I.G. had no pompous airs about him, he seemed more like a chaplain. You could tell he was "The Man." He asked me what my complaint was. I took out the orders from the Commanding General of the 7th Army and handed them to him, then told him about the squad leader who insisted that winter maneuvers superseded these orders, and the chain of command that were insistent on backing him up. Our meeting lasted less than ten minutes. He ruled that the issue was cut and dry. The orders from headquarters had to be followed. He wished me luck in the talent contest and told me not to worry about repercussions from having asked to see him. He added that asking to see the I.G. was any soldier's right, even if he turned out to be wrong.

The captain's jeep driver had not asked why I went to the I.G. and I chose not to offer any information on my reason for going, or on the outcome of the meeting. We had a friendly chat on the way back, without delving into any substantive issues. He did express surprise, however, at how short the meeting had been. At first glance, everything seemed normal when I returned to the base. I reported to Sgt. Rambo and he did not seem fazed at the I.G.'s ruling. I assumed that he had either gotten word beforehand or he knew all along that the General's orders were going to hold up. The interesting thing was that neither he, the captain, or my squad leader showed any emotion in regard to this issue. It was as if there had been an honest difference of opinion that had been resolved to everyone's satisfaction. I didn't believe it for a minute, although that would have been the best scenario, so I decided to play along and just wait around for the first shoe to drop.

I WAS SCHEDULED TO LEAVE FOR WÜRTZBURG on Friday. The entire battalion was busy packing up to leave for winter indoctrination on Saturday, and I was told to pack my equipment too, since I would have to report directly to Grafenwöhr, after competing in the semi-finals of the All Army Talent Contest, and join in the winter training. No one expected me to compete beyond the semi-finals. That didn't hurt my feelings, since I had never expected to even make it that far. With the exception of a few smirks from my squad leader and Sgt. Rambo, my immediate superiors behaved exceptionally well toward me. If they were trying to make me wonder what they had up their sleeve, they were succeeding. Most of my peers were happy for me, and some were even excited at the prospect of my winning and going on to the finals. For the most part, the privates and PFCs were just glad that one of theirs didn't allow the non-coms, backed up by the officers, to push him around, and take away something that he had rightfully earned. I had anticipated some sour grapes over my opportunity to miss some of the winter exercises, but what I encountered instead was admiration for pulling this thing off.

With my duffel packed for Würtzburg, as well as for Grafenwöhr, and with more good wishes than I could have hoped to expect from my fellow soldiers, I boarded the truck for Würzburg. I was housed in guest billets of Headquarters Company, and then was allowed to do some sightseeing before having to report to the theater at which the competition would take place. Würzburg was a beautiful city that had not been a major target of the allied bombers during the war. The extraordinary Rococo style churches were breath-taking even though I was not able to see the magnificent interiors I had studied in architectural history classes. As an architectural student, I was delighted that these monuments to the overly ornate successor of the Baroque style had been spared the devastation of American and British bombers. But as a German Jew who had watched his magnificent synagogue being destroyed on Kristallnacht, by Germans, I couldn't help but feel a twinge of mixed emotions over the fact that these impressive examples of Rococo architecture had been spared.

That evening I had the opportunity to meet the other contestants and listen to some of them practice their repertoire. I was disappointed that my accompanist from New Jersey had not received orders to attend the Semi-finals with me. I had hoped to meet the accompanist assigned to me and give him the sheet music for my number, so that we might have a chance to rehearse. I was told that he had been delayed, so I decided to relax and enjoy the entertainment provided by the other contestants. With very few exceptions, they were extremely talented entertainers. I was almost glad that my accompanist was running late. I felt like a sandlot baseball player hobnobbing around with major leaguers. Not having grand illusions about my singing ability, allowed me to put things in perspective, relax, and enjoy the experience.

Fifteen minutes before the theater was to be closed down, my accompanist arrived and was introduced to me. I handed him the sheet music and asked him when he felt we would be able to rehearse. The contest was scheduled for Saturday afternoon. He suggested that we come about forty-five minutes early, but he assured me that even if we didn't get a chance to rehearse, that we would do fine. He had enough confidence for both of us. I was convinced that he was sincere about his ability, but I was sufficiently unsure of myself to feel the need for at least one rehearsal.

Saturday morning I sought out a Jewish chapel for Shabbat services. I felt a little guilty for missing Friday night services, but it would have been ill advised to miss the rehearsal session, even if, as it turned out, I did not get a chance to rehearse. I had not been to a Sabbath service since I had left Fürth, and I really missed the spiritual connection. I was given the honor of being one of the seven people who get called up to say the blessing over the Torah before each portion of the weekly Torah reading is recited. After I recited the blessing, the Chaplain whispered that he wanted to talk to me after services.

The Chaplain was an orthodox rabbi, one of the few I had met in the army. He pulled me aside and told me how excited he was to finally run into a soldier who appeared to read Hebrew fluently. Predictably, he wanted to know how much time I had left to serve before being discharged. I suspected that he was looking for a Chaplain's assistant, and I hated to tell him that I was a short timer with less than six months to serve. I don't know who was sadder, he or I. He was desperately looking for an assistant who could meet the minimal qualifications he required, and I had been wanting this type of position from the day I had entered the army.

Finally, the opportunity was there and I had too little time left to serve to qualify, unless I wanted to re-up. That suggestion was so absurd that it had to have been made in jest. We schmoozed for a while and he introduced me around to the regular attendees as "the one who got away." I couldn't even accept his invitation for a Shabbat meal, for fear of being late to the theater. I wished him Shabbat Shalom and expressed regret that we had not met earlier. He said he shared my sentiments and wished me luck in the contest.

I got to the theater almost an hour early and waited for my accompanist to show. He finally came about twenty minutes later, and sensing my anxiety, put his arm around my shoulder and told me not to worry about a thing. One of the contestants, a very talented black quartet, was on stage rehearsing. He went up to the senior member of the quartet, a tall lanky man with a very deep, rich voice, and asked him if we might rehearse our number since we had not had the opportunity to do so before. He and his group graciously obliged and I got my opportunity to familiarize myself with the microphone and with the stage-fright that had to come with seeing the number of seats in the theater.

I was so nervous I could hear my knees knocking and my voice quivering. The accompanist was very good and his calm demeanor helped me cope with my stage-fright. The quivering in my voice started to diminish as the number went on, but I was still a little embarrassed at being such an amateur in the midst of the other contestants, who, at least in my eyes, could pass for professionals. The accompanist patted me on the shoulder and told me he thought I would do fine, now that I had a chance to get the rust out of my vocal chords and got a feel for the stage. If that was supposed to make me feel like a winner, it didn't come close. But then, I never really expected to be a winner, I just wanted to do the best I was capable of doing.

As I walked to the rear of the stage to take my place with the rest of the contestants, the tall lanky bass singer came over and shook my hand. He must have sensed my nervousness and was kind enough to want to give reassurance. He asked me for the name of the number I had sung and I told him it was entitled "Lost In Loveliness."

He put his hand on my shoulder and said, "Man, I really like that song, and I like the way you sing it." It didn't matter to me whether he was just trying to make me feel good or not. The fact was he succeeded in making me feel almost comfortable in taking part in this competition. I thought to myself that when someone as accomplished as this gentleman would go out of his way to say a kind word to a nervous, aspiring and competing performer, this was not only the mark of a professional, but that of a real mensch as well.

The theater filled up and the show got underway. We were given a program to make sure each of us knew when his number was up. It was a long program broken up into four categories. First came instrumental solos with ten contestants, then specialty acts with eight contestants followed by a five minute break. Next was vocal solos with ten contestants of which I was third. Last was Group acts with eight contestants. I thought all of the acts were good, some better than others, but only two stood out as exceptional. The black quartet—I think they were called the Diamonds—sang rhythm and blues type songs and they performed them in a style that was distinctly their own. The lead singer was a young tenor, who could have passed for a fourteen-year-old, with the voice of an angel. With the standing ovation that they received, I felt they were a shoo-in for first place.

The other outstanding performer was a deep rich baritone, whom I had heard was a divinity student when he was drafted. He sang a spiritual called "Shadrach, Meshach, Abednego," and got a standing ovation for it. Then, to show his versatility, he sang "September Song," which he did very well, but not with the level of performance of the spiritual. As good as he was, I was shocked when his name was announced as the first place winner. From the reaction of the audience, I could only assume that they shared my preference for the rhythm and blues quartet, who took second place.

I joined the throng of well-wishers to congratulate the winner, then made a bee-line for my new friends to let them know that I felt they were robbed. Although they were in agreement, they were good sports about the system of judging. These guys had talent and they were going places. A little setback like this was not going to deter them, they were too good for that. The bass singer told me that if he had been judging, I would have come in third. I told him that meeting him was a real boost to my moral, and even though I didn't believe a word he was saying, it was nice to hear. As we were saying our good-byes, he tried to elicit a promise out of me to pursue a singing career. I gave him a big hug and promised that I would think about it. To my chagrin, I never kept up with his group.

I left the theater to repack my duffel bag in time to catch the transportation that would be waiting to take me to Grafenwöhr. It was a real change of pace from being part of a theater group, to going back to the field for winter training. It had been an exhilarating experience for me, and I remained on a high from it until I rejoined my Battery.

15

KING OF THE GUARD MOUNT

GRAFENWÖHR WAS COLD, BUT THE SKY WAS clear and the sun was out. I reported to Sgt. Rambo, who was very matter-of-fact about my arrival. After all, the winter exercises were for two weeks and I had only missed three days of the festivities. I actually had expected a lot of ribbing, especially from Sgt. Rambo and all the other non-coms, and I was pleased that no one even asked me how I had fared at the semi-finals. Rambo pointed out my squad's barracks and I hot footed it over there to change into my fatigues before the rest of the squad returned from whatever duty they were on. My hopes were to try to fit into the outfit, as if I had not been absent for the last three days.

Entering my barracks, I quickly realized what Sgt. Rambo meant when he said that I would be able to figure out which bunk was mine. My bed was full of movie magazines, the walls were plastered with photos of singers from entertainment magazines, and there were home-made posters and strip slogans welcoming back their hero, the crooner. The gaudy display was a lot of fun at my expense, but I thought it was actually funny, though embarrassing. I expected to see people jumping out from under the beds yelling "surprise!," but mercifully, that did not happen. I did however hear some giggling going on outside. Looking out of the barracks window, I saw the captain, Sgt. Rambo, and several other officers and non-coms cracking up with laughter. They seemed real pleased with themselves.

Rambo came into my barracks, still giggling a bit, and put his arm around my shoulder and told me that the officers wanted me to know how proud they were of me, and the way I represented the Battalion in the talent contest. He continued that, as a final gesture, he had something to show me in his office. He asked me to follow him, as if I had a choice in the matter. He sat down at his desk, opened the top drawer, reached in and pulled out what appeared to be an official document, which he handed to me. I was startled to see that it was the paper-work for a court-martial, with my name on it. Rambo studied the quizzical look on my face, took back the forms and proceeded to explain, with a threatening smile on his face. "I hope you noticed that the forms are all filled out except for the cause. I'll be watching you like a hawk, Hirsch. The first time you screw up and give me a cause, the paper-work goes through channels and your ass is grass."

He stared at me, waiting for a reaction. I was too stunned to respond, other than to snap to attention, salute, and tell him that I would make him proud of me as a soldier. "You'll have plenty of opportunities to show me what a good soldier you are" he responded. "From here on out, you will be on guard duty and K.P., once a week each, and one weekend every month. I've checked it out and that is the maximum that these duties can be assigned to a soldier, before he can complain to the I.G. about being singled out for special treatment."

I got the message. I had been expecting repercussions from my visit to the I.G., and this was it. I thought to myself that as a short timer I could take as much crap as they were going to throw at me, and survive, knowing that in a little over six months, I would be a civilian again. I stood at attention, saluted again, and held the salute until Sgt. Rambo returned it. "Will there be anything else, sergeant, I need to get back and clean off my bunk, so that I can unpack?"

He returned the salute and looked down at some paper-work on his desk. "That will be all soldier, you are dismissed. Oh, by the way, I've made a notation on the pass list. You will not be eligible for a pass until you have proven to me that you are worthy of having one."

I rushed back to the barracks and started dismantling the display around my bunk before everyone returned from duty to clean up for chow. I didn't bother to ask if anyone wanted to save any of the magazines or posters, and proceeded to trash everything from my home-coming display. By the time the rest of my barracks mates returned, I had unpacked and changed into the uniform of the day, fatigues over O.G.s over long johns, to combat the forecasted 30° below zero temperature. The guys had seen the display that Rambo and his cohorts had put up for my homecoming, and wondered what my reaction had been.

After the reception I had received from the officers and non-coms, it was heart warming to see that none of my fellow soldiers had resented my attending the talent contest. In fact, they were supportive and wanted to hear about Würzburg and the contest. They were more disappointed than I that I didn't fare well enough to continue on to the finals. It was difficult for me to make them understand the level of talent I had been competing against, but they were drinking in my words as if I had just returned from a dangerous combat mission.

I began to realize that these guys were looking at me as some sort of hero. Not because I had won a local talent contest, but because I had stood up to "the powers that be" and lived to tell about it. To put things in perspective, I told them that I was off the pass list for the unforeseeable future, and that I would be pulling guard duty and K.P. once a week, and one weekend each per month. No one had any idea that this fell within the limits of what was allowable in army regulation, but I assured them that Rambo had checked it out before informing me of my fate.

The reaction of my fellow soldiers was nothing short of amazing. They were even angrier than I. It was as if Sgt. Rambo had slapped them in the face and they rallied around to find ways of giving me support in my battle to survive the next few months, without getting court-martialed. One guy had a great idea. We all had heard of Corporal Strand of Baker Battery, who was a legend in the battalion. He had made Colonel's Orderly twelve times straight, which was a record that was almost as impressive as Babe Ruth's sixty home runs in one season.

Everyone pulling guard duty was required to report for guard mount, a formation/inspection conducted by the officer of the guard for that day, along with the sergeant of the guard. Approximately thirty soldiers would report for every guard mount with shined boots, pressed uniforms, clean weapon and shined brass. The inspecting officer would select the six or so soldiers whose appearance was the sharpest, pull them out of formation and let the sergeant of the guard drill them. The officer would then pose questions to the leading candidates, after which he would select the top soldier of the guard mount and make him "Colonel's Orderly." The two runners up would be the "Supernumeraries."

The Supernumeraries were allowed to stay in the guardhouse and be in charge of waking the guards up for their shifts at walking guard. They did not have to walk the four-hour guard shifts. The Colonel's Orderly was allowed to sleep through the night and report to the base commander the following morning, and be his driver for the day. At the end of this duty, the Colonel's Orderly was granted an automatic forty-eight hour pass.

Corporal Strand must have been somewhat of a rebel to have had to stand guard duty at least twelve times. The word was that he had made Corporal only because of his impressive guard mount performances. The important thing was that Strand was going to be discharged soon, and that he would be leaving for the States in less than three weeks. The plan was to convince Strand to take me under his wing and teach me, along with a couple of guys who would be willing to be my helpers, the tricks of the trade, the ins and outs of how to make Colonel's Orderly. Strand didn't know me from Adam's house cat, but the theory was that once he was told that I had stood up to Sgt. Rambo, and that, as a result, I was off the pass list and would be on guard duty at least once a week, he would agree to help.

Rambo wasted no time. My first guard duty assignment came while we were still in Grafenwöhr, followed by K.P., as soon as the guard duty was over. Cpl. Strand and I had not had a chance to get together before my first guard mount, but I did get a chance to see the master in action. As luck would have it, his last guard mount was my first one, and it turned out to be an educational experience. The formation of prospective guards was almost ready for inspection when Strand came walking toward the formation as if he were floating on air. I had never seen a G.I. look so sharp. He could have passed for a guard at the tomb of the unknown soldier at Arlington Cemetery. His uniform was immaculately pressed, his brass was shiny, you could use his boots as a mirror for shaving, his red kerchief had been pressed and was puffed up perfectly under his chin, and his pants were bloused over his boots with machine-like precision. There were others who tried to compete with him. It wasn't much of a contest for Colonel's Orderly, but they had their chance at being Supernumeraries.

I paid attention throughout the guard mount, figuring that if this was going to be a weekly activity for me, that I might as well learn the ropes and do the best I can for myself. The drill was not different from our daily routine. The questioning of the select few "sharper soldiers" was interesting. The questions were basically about army regulations and procedures. What seemed to interest the Officer of the Day was the sharpness of the response to the questions. Strand easily made Colonel's Orderly for his 13th consecutive time while the competition for Supers was stiffer. Needless to say, I was not in the running. After I started my second shift of walking guard, I promised myself that I would make every effort to learn and perfect the secrets of preparing for guard mount, in spite of my reputation of being a soldier who had trouble taking orders.

There wasn't going to be much time to schedule a meeting with Strand. I had K.P. the next day, and he was leaving about ten days after we were to return to Schweinfurt. Kitchen duty had never been fun, but coming directly off of guard duty, without rest, made it particularly grueling. My concerns about finding time to talk with Cpl. Strand, and to have him commit enough time to train me in the art of guard mount preparation, weighed on me as I plodded through my duties on K.P. I left the kitchen that evening and I plopped into bed, totally exhausted. Two guys from my squad who, up until then, had very little use for me, sat down at the foot of my bunk. They had been patiently waiting for me and asked if I needed to catch a couple of winks before listening to their report about my scheduled meetings with the "King of the Guard," Corporal Strand, himself.

I couldn't believe what was going on. There I was, exhausted and filthy from cleaning greasy pans and floors, yet blown away at the idea that Crenshaw and Flanders would go out of their way to help me in my battle to survive against Rambo and the system. Not only did they set up instructional sessions for me with Strand, they planned to attend themselves, so they could help me make a good thing out of being on guard duty once a week. Both of these guys were intelligent, Crenshaw was a college graduate, and Flanders was a Junior in college when he was drafted. They kept their noses clean, but they despised the way officers and their non-com support staff used their knowledge of army regulations to harass the rank and file soldiers. Crenshaw told me that he admired how I had stood up to Sgt. Rambo's heavy handed tactics, and was appalled at his reaction of maximum punishment within regulations, to the legal exercise of my rights as a member of the U.S. armed forces.

It was really kind of strange. Cpl. Crenshaw, PFC Flanders, Cpl. Brumbelow and a handful of others had a sub rosa clique operating in our billets, with the goal of finding legal ways to get back at those in leadership that were abusing their power. They had been keeping an eye on me since the fracas with my Filipino squad leader, and decided that I would be their cause celebre when they heard that I would be assigned to guard duty and K.P. once a week. My head was reeling as I took a hot shower. "Wow, I'm not going to have to fight this battle by myself, on the other hand, I can't depend on anyone else to stand up for me, then again, they did set up those sessions with the illusive Cpl. Strand." I decided that I would not look a gift horse in the mouth. Whatever help these guys offer I'll be glad to accept, however, I will not rely on help from anyone. I thanked Crenshaw for setting up things for me with Strand and expressed appreciation for the moral support and any other kind of help I may be getting, then excused myself as I laid down and fell into a deep sleep.

MY FIRST GUARD DUTY IN SCHWIENFURT WAS the day after we returned from Grafenwöhr. More importantly, it was before I had a chance to meet with Strand. I felt I had learned enough on my last guard mount to make an effort at competing, such as devoting special effort polishing my boots and brass, and making sure that my Class A's were pressed. I even borrowed a set of chains to weigh down the blouse of my trousers over the boots, and had someone help me tie my red kerchief. Looking in the mirror, I was pretty proud of myself. For a guy who often scoffed at soldiers who spent inordinate amounts of time polishing boots, and working hard at looking sharp, I was surprised at how accomplished I felt, looking like a gung-ho soldier. Crenshaw and Flanders quizzed me a little to prepare for rapid fire questioning, saying they were convinced I would reach that level, and wished me much needed luck.

I felt very much out of character, strutting from the billets to guard mount, dressed to the nines, with my spotless Carbine M-1 rifle strapped over my shoulder. Anticipation of the upcoming test was beginning to make my adrenaline flow. Looking around guard mount formation, I could spot six to ten guys who appeared to be serious about competing for colonel's orderly. The juices really started to flow when I was one of the six selected for further consideration.

The sergeant of the guard started drilling us with rapid fire orders. "Left face!, right face!, about face!, present arms!," etc. Unbeknown to him or anyone else, I was carrying a small rock in my left hand to help me respond to the sergeant's orders, without having to think. I had learned to do that in basic training to compensate for my inability to tell right from left, without having to pause to think. In less than ten minutes, the drill was over and I was one of the four left to be inspected and to respond to rapid fire questions from the Officer of the Day.

It was not often that spectators would show up for a guard mount, but as I glanced through the corner of my eyes, I spotted Crenshaw and Flanders checking out their new protege. The earlier practice drill of questions prepared me for the O.D.'s questions and kept me from being intimidated by his rapid fire technique.

The Officer of the Day gave the sergeant his decisions and walked away. I had made first supernumerary, which was only slightly disappointing. Crenshaw ran up and congratulated me, pointing out how proud I should be, considering that I had not yet met with Strand to get the finer points.

He was right. It had been a good effort. I wasn't going to have to stand guard, although I was responsible for seeing that all guards were up and ready for their shifts every four hours. In between, I could read, sleep, or play cards with the other super. A far cry from walking a guard route every second four hours, during twenty-four hours of guard duty.

I finally met with Cpl. Strand, and of course, Crenshaw and Flanders had to come along to make sure that I wouldn't miss or forget any fine points. Strand had heard about my last guard mount and opined that, with his coaching, I could conceivably break his record of making colonel's orderly thirteen times straight.

We left the session with Strand, having a game plan in hand. I would have a special Class A uniform that would be used only for guard mount. The brass would be kept shined and would only need to be rubbed with a cloth before the mount, a separate pair of spit-shined boots would be set aside, and not used for any other occasion. Throw away the chains and get two #10 cans from the Kitchen, with tops and bottoms cut out, to blouse the pant legs over the boots. Strand showed me how to tie the kerchief so that it would puff up just the right amount under my chin. My weapon would have to be kept ready for inspection at all times, to avoid a lengthy cleaning session before each guard mount. We were ready.

My next guard duty was preceded by K.P., to spice things up a bit. I was allowed to leave the kitchen early enough to give me thirty minutes to prepare for guard mount. To Rambo's chagrin, I was not only ready on time, but I made Colonel's Orderly. Having enjoyed a full night's sleep in the guard house, I reported to the battalion commanding officer, and served as his driver until about 5:00 P.M. As soon as the C.O. dismissed me, even before I went to the mess hall, I ran in to see Sgt. Rambo to get my forty-eight hour pass, which was automatically for the next two days. He was expecting me and did not give me a hard time, but as I was leaving, he couldn't resist reminding me that my court martial papers were already drawn up, just waiting for the cause and date.

16

Russian Peasant

I TOOK OFF TO FRANKFURT ON MY first forty-eight hour pass. This would be the first time I visited Frankfurt since I had been moved to Schweinfurt, and I was looking forward to checking with our attorneys regarding the efforts to sell our house on Grünestrasse. I checked into the special hotel for servicemen and immediately called Herr Klibansky's office. Klibansky, I was told, was in the hospital and Herr Mueller was handling the efforts to sell our house. He was able to meet with me within the hour, at which time he told me that Herr Klibansky was very ill, and that he has been unable to find a suitable buyer for the house. I asked him to explain why there had been no offers in the months that he had the power of attorney. He cited a slow real estate market and repeated his earlier statement, emphasizing the term "suitable buyer."

I left his office dissatisfied and dejected and walked back to the hotel to take a nap. On earlier trips, I had become friendly with the elevator operator in the hotel who was a Russian emigrant. I was very impressed with his drive to make something of himself. He held down three jobs and lived on a little farm that was run mostly by his wife and children under his supervision. He noticed that I didn't seem too happy as I entered the elevator and asked me why I appeared dejected, when I should be enjoying my time off. He was easy to talk to, so I shared my frustrations with our German attorney and his apparent lack of effort to sell our house.

To my surprise, the elevator operator sounded genuinely interested in the house, and asked me for the address and any other information I could give him. He proceeded to tell me that he had escaped from Russia through East Germany with his wife and two children, with just the shirts on their back, about four years before. Since then, they all worked at any jobs they could find until they had saved enough to buy the small farm. By working several jobs and long hours, he had been able to put aside money for investment purposes, and our house sounded like the perfect investment to him.

This was exciting, a prospective buyer without having to go through a real estate agent. I wanted to stay in Frankfurt and try to wrap the sale up, but since I had to get back to Schwienfurt, I gave the prospective buyer the address of the house as well as Herr Mueller's address and phone number. I told him to contact Mueller if he wanted to get inside the house. I also told him that I would call Herr Mueller to have him draw up the necessary sales papers, and that I anticipated to be coming to Frankfurt at least once every two to three weeks, on the assumption that I could make colonel's orderly at least once out of every two to three times I was assigned to guard duty. We shook hands and I went to take a nap so I could have a big night on the town before going back to the base early in the morning.

Luckily, I caught Herr Mueller before he left for the day. I told him that I had found a buyer, and he initially was skeptical. After hearing the price and that the potential buyer was able to pay cash, he agreed to meet with the buyer and draw up the papers. He expressed surprise that the buyer agreed to the market value at a time when the real estate market was supposed to be soft. Since no loan would be involved, Mueller suggested that we should be able to close the transaction on my next trip to Frankfurt.

I MADE IT TO THE BANHOFF IN PLENTY of time to make the 2:00 A.M. train to Schwienfurt. The train system in Germany had a reputation for efficiency and it was well deserved. I was able to plan my passes around the clockwork precision of the train schedule, but once on the train back to the base, my mind would wander as I listened to the clickety-clack of the trains' wheels.

Were these the sounds that deported Jews heard on their way to whatever concentration camp or death camp they were sent to? Were these the same tracks my family traveled over? Eventually, I dozed off, waking up just in time to get off at Schwienfurt. It ended up being a good trip after all. I couldn't wait to check the guard duty roster and speculate on my next opportunity to earn a forty-eight hour pass.

Rambo greeted me as I made my way past his office, "I see you made it back in time, but I have confidence in you, Hirsch. Sooner or later you'll screw up." I told him that it was comforting to know that he was paying so much attention to my every move. I suppose I should have felt intimidated by Rambo's obsession to have me court-martialed, but I was beginning to enjoy the role of underdog against the system.

As expected, I was scheduled for guard duty in one week. Crenshaw and Brumbelow looked on as I prepared for guard mount, to make sure that I didn't miss any of the sartorial nuances, and grilled me on the AR's and SR's once again, for good measure. We had decided to treat each guard mount as a separate challenge, so as not to get complacent. They figured that each time I would make colonel's orderly, it would be a thorn in Rambo's side.

The guard mount went smoothly. There was less competition than usual, and by the time that the Officer of the Day turned to leave, after he told the Sergeant of the Guard who had won, there was no doubt in my mind, nor in the minds of my friends watching, that I had made colonel's orderly again. Before dismissing the guard mount, the sergeant announced that I had made first supernumerary, and that one of the least impressive finalists had made colonel's orderly. My friends and I were flabbergasted. At Crenshaw's insistence, I asked the Sergeant if there had not been a mistake, and he assured me that he only announced what the O.D. told him. If I had any questions, I should address them to the O.D. We knew he was bluffing, figuring that no private would risk going over the Sergeant of the Guard's head.

I waited for the Officer of the Day to return, saluted him, and asked for permission to speak. He remembered me, and he had a quizzical look on his face when I asked what I could have done better in order to increase my chances in the future to make colonel's orderly. He suggested that there must have been a mistake, because he had instructed the sergeant that I had made colonel's orderly. He assured me the error would be straightened out, and he went directly to the Sergeant of the Guard to have him rectify the situation.

The recipient of the sergeant's blunder was less than happy with me at the reversal of his first colonel's orderly selection. He called me greedy for not being able to give up the top position once in a while. At the O.D.'s insistence, the sergeant apologized for the misunderstanding. By the look on his face, I was sure that this was not inadvertent, but I wasn't sure if his reason was to help the other guy or to stiff me as a favor to Rambo. I did not loose any sleep over that issue and the next morning I reported to the colonel, with whom I was becoming a regular.

My PASS WAS WAITING FOR ME THE following morning. I decided not to mention the guard mount incident to Rambo, being fairly sure that he was a party to the shenanigans. Over a week had passed since my last trip to Frankfurt, and I was looking forward to closing the sale of the house and celebrating. I checked into the hotel and took the elevator to my room. My Russian friend was at his post and was surprised that I was not aware that my attorney refused to complete the necessary documents to close the sale of the house. I assured him that I didn't know what he was talking about, and asked him to start from the beginning.

He had gone to see Herr Mueller, as I had suggested, and gave him all the background information necessary for the closing documents. Since he was going to pay cash, everything should have been very simple. After interviewing the prospective buyer, however, Herr Mueller informed him that he would not be able to buy the house. When my Russian friend asked why, Herr Mueller only responded that it just was not possible. My friend was disappointed, but assumed that I had changed my mind and that was the end of the matter.

I was confused and angry. I would have at least expected to be notified by my attorney if there was a problem with the sale. I called Herr Mueller and asked to see him right away. He could not understand my agitated state, and proceeded to explain what seemed perfectly obvious to him, or anyone who was concerned with upholding the integrity of class distinction in the Reich. It was very simple, the would be buyer was a peasant, not even German, and he should not be allowed to become a landowner.

By this time my blood was beginning to boil. How in the hell did Klibansky hook up with this bigot, and how could he entrust the power of attorney for my parents' house to this German, whose bigotry could qualify him for the Nazi party? I asked to speak to Klibansky and was told that he was very ill and may not survive his illness. I tried to control myself. I told Herr Mueller that while I may understand his strong respect for class distinction, that I was the client, and that only I could make the decision of whether or not to sell the house to a given buyer. "You cannot sell a German house to a Russian peasant," he protested. It was his only response.

I slammed my fist on his desk and put my face within an inch of his. "Yes I can, and I will," I screamed back at him. "And you will prepare the necessary papers, or I will find another attorney!"

He defiantly looked me in the eye and said "Ich farshtei nicht." Literally translated, the phrase he spoke means "I understand nothing," meaning "I don't understand." That was the first time he had said anything to me in German, and his previous statement turned out to be the last time he said anything to me in English. This pitiful excuse for a human being, who was fluent in English, insisted now that he could only deal with me in German. I turned and left in frustration, not knowing what to do.

I took a long walk to cool off and headed back to the hotel. My Russian friend seemed to be more inured to the German class system that somehow survived the war. I refused to accept the situation and promised that I would seek legal assistance through the U.S. Army. He appreciated my outrage at this discrimination against him and said that he would welcome any intercession, but it was apparent that he was resigned to the fact that he would not be allowed to purchase my family's house.

As soon as I returned to the base, I started looking into the legal status of Herr Mueller's refusal to sell our house to my buyer. I met with attorneys in the 7th Army HQ, only to find out that the situation was hopeless. Even though we were the owners of the house, we could not, as absentee owners, force our German attorney to sell the house to someone he did not feel was fit to buy it. Incredulous as it was, he told me that my hands were tied as long as Mueller would not willingly return the power of attorney to me.

I got up to leave and turned back for a parting shot. "Didn't we fight this war to put an end to the German bigotry and hate that almost destroyed Europe? Didn't we win this war? Don't we have any way of protecting American citizens' rights to deal with their property, particularly if that property is all that is left of the possessions of their parents who were murdered by Germans?"

It probably wasn't fair to put this guilt trip on him. He shrugged his shoulders and made a gesture of helplessness. "I wish there was something I could do to help you, soldier. I know it's not right, but it's the policy of the United States Army, we are not allowed to interfere in local legal matters."

If I wasn't so angry, I probably would have cried. I saluted the Lieutenant, made an about-face, and left with whatever dignity I had left.

17

BRUMBELOW'S MISTAKE

I SHARED MY DILEMMA WITH ANYONE WHO would listen. Even Sgt. Rambo commiserated with me, using a few choice words for "Nazi aristocrats" like Herr Mueller. He then informed me, that as a soldier of the Jewish faith, I was entitled to a special leave for Passover. He was quick to add that this even applied to an eight-ball like me. My brother Asher had told me that I should try to spend a Jewish holiday with our cousins in Basel, Switzerland, and until this news came, I did not think I would be able to do so.

Max Meyer was my father's first cousin, and he was the one who had ransomed my father out of Buchenwald some time after his arrest and incarceration on Kristallnacht. Asher had visited the Meyer family in 1948, when he was serving in the American army in Europe. He fell in love with Max and Meta's oldest daughter, Henrietta. They were married in 1949.

Meta Meyer was excited to hear from me and that I would be able to stay in Basel for the first days of Passover. Arrangements were made without difficulty, and this was going to be a treat. I had not been to Switzerland since I was sent there by my parents one summer, when I was either three or four years old. I vaguely remember that summer in Basel, and for some reason I only remember the girls. This was probably because they were the oldest, and most of their five brothers were either babies, or not yet born.

I was made to feel very much at home. Justin was the oldest son and ran the family furniture manufacturing business. Max had, by this time, passed away. Justin was the steady, level headed member of the family, who tried to keep a semblance of order among a family of divergent personalities. Jack, the next in line, liked to give a happy go lucky appearance and made an effort to entertain me at every available moment. He had a joke for every occasion and professed ambitions to become a professional entertainer, as a standup comic.

Next was David, who was serving in the Swiss militia and was home for the Passover holidays. He told me that there was no professional army in Switzerland, but that every able male, within the ages proscribed for military service, had to serve in the militia a certain number of weeks of active duty every year. The militia reservists kept their weapons at home and were responsible for keeping them in operating order, while they were not on active duty. I thought this system was unusual. Fortunately for them, it had never been put to the test.

The youngest were Beno and Manny, who were unable to compete for attention. If ever there was such a thing as getting too much attention, this was it. The Seders were very nice. Justin tried to keep everyone on a religious plane in spite of Jack's puns injected at almost every sentence of the Haggadah.

For the morning services, we went to the first synagogue I had seen in Europe that had not been damaged by the War. I had brought my civilian suit, and since I was not accustomed to wearing a hat when not in army uniform, I had just brought a kippa along. Justin suggested that I wear his father's Homburg, an honor which I tried to graciously decline. The whole family insisted that I should wear the hat in honor of my dad's cousin. It turned out to fit perfectly, so I couldn't refuse. I do believe that was the first time I wore a Homburg—a black felt hat with stiff curled brim and high creased crown—or for that matter, any civilian hat except for a Basque beret or a rain hat. They were all very proud of the way I looked in Max's Homburg, as we walked to the synagogue. I was feeling very self-conscious. I couldn't help but wonder if my father would approve.

I RETURNED TO THE BASE FEELING GOOD about having been with family. I had only been away a few days but I felt like I was walking into a changed milieu. I soon found out that my absence was not without incident. Apparently, Corporal Brumbelow had been flaunting his knowledge of ARs and SRs once too often. He had a complaint about one of the drill sergeant's directives, feeling that he had been singled out for a larger share of strenuous duty. This particular sergeant was more laid back than most. He was a master sergeant with almost twenty years in the service. He was black and very personable, intelligent and liked by almost everyone. Why Brumbelow chose to give him a hard time was beyond me. There were so many other sergeants deserving to be baited, why did he pick on the one man everyone liked?

Be that as it may, I was told that Brumbelow had followed the drill sergeant to the office, quoting him army rules and regulations to justify his point. Whether he intended to goad the sergeant into hitting him or not, Brumbelow riled him to the point that he turned around and pushed Brumbelow away, just as he was about to enter the battery office. That may not have been so problematic if Brumbelow hadn't been standing at the top of a short run of steps. The witnesses said that although Brumbelow was a little banged up from the fall, his pride was more bruised than his body. The sergeant realizing what he had done, tried to help him to his feet, but Brumbelow would not accept his help. Instead, he threatened to file a complaint and have the sergeant court-martialed for hitting a soldier under his command.

Corporal Brumbelow got up, brushed off his uniform and stormed into the first sergeant's office to file a complaint. Sgt. Rambo, who apparently was aware of what had transpired, handed Brumbelow an order to deliver ammo to Baker battery, before he could get a word in edgewise. Brumbelow requested permission to file a complaint before leaving for the ammo run, but Rambo told him to save it for when he came back. Baker battery was on field exercises, along with Able and Charley batteries, about four to five hours away by ammo truck. Not wanting to disobey a direct order, Brumbelow saluted, did an about face, and proceeded to drive his ammo run with his crew of ammo handlers. That was the day before I came back.

Corporal Brumbelow and his crew returned from the mission about two hours after I arrived back in camp. He filled me in on the story not realizing I had already heard it from more than one source. He cleaned himself up and determinedly marched to the office to file his complaint. As he walked through the door to Sgt. Rambo's desk, the first sergeant handed him orders to deliver ammo to Able battery, telling him that whatever problem he had would have to wait until he finished the assignment at hand.

Undaunted, he returned to the barracks to prepare his crew to leave for their assignment. In the midst of preparations, he told me that Rambo's tactics to keep him too busy to file a complaint would not work. He was determined to go through with it, as soon as an opportunity presented itself. Trying not to show his annoyance, he gathered his crew, had them load the truck with ammo, and took off for Able battery. The scuttlebutt around the barracks was that Rambo figured Brumbelow would cool off after a few days, and lose his enthusiasm for having the drill sergeant court-martialed.

The next day, a tired, yet more determined Brumbelow returned with his ammo handlers. Again he dismissed his crew, cleaned himself up and made his way to the office. The path was lined with spectators waiting to see the fireworks. He walked into the office and stood erect as Sgt. Rambo handed him orders to deliver ammo to Charlie battery. He must have been anticipating Rambo's move, because he didn't blink an eye or try to say anything. He just saluted, did his about face and walked out of the office. If there was any resignation in his resolve, he didn't show it.

His crew of ammo handlers was beginning to suspect that something was going on. Three ammo runs back to back was not normal, even during field exercises. He told them that their efficiency was being tested and that so far they were getting high marks. Whether they bought it or not, they prepared for the run one more time, as if we were in an actual war situation. As they drove off, Brumbelow made a point of not showing any emotion, although he and his crew were exhausted and he was annoyed. He knew he was being manipulated, but he felt he could last until Rambo ran out of delay tactics. If he ever had any thoughts of easing up on his charge against the drill sergeant, they were gone. These tactics of the first sergeant, which obviously had approval of the captain, angered him and hardened his resolve to stand up for his rights.

They came back the next day totally worn out. The crew went straight to their bunks and collapsed. Brumbelow, on the other hand, washed up, changed his uniform and marched straight into Sergeant Rambo's office to formally issue the complaint against the drill sergeant. He had taken the time to type the complaint so that there could not be any miscommunication. Rambo read the complaint carefully, as if he had no inkling of what it was about. After reading it, he looked up at Corporal Brumbelow and told him that the matter had already been taken care of.

Brumbelow was thrown for a loop. "You mean the drill sergeant has already been court-martialed, without me there to testify?" He was yelling so loud that the crowd gathered outside of the office could hear every word.

Rambo explained that was not quite the case. The drill sergeant had reported the incident himself, and threw himself at the mercy of the commanding officer. The Captain and Sgt. Rambo, after hearing testimony from witnesses, decided to put the drill sergeant on three days of house arrest, where he would be relieved of all his duties and privileges for that period of time. The three days, which ran concurrent with Brumbelow's three ammo runs, were just over and the case was closed.

Brumbelow tried to protest. He was told that the sergeant was tried and sentenced and that the sentence was served. Seeing that he was getting nowhere, he asked for permission to file his complaint with the Inspector General, a request that could not be denied. Rambo had done his homework. He knew that once the sergeant was brought up on charges, tried and sentenced, and the sentence was carried out without any complaint from aggrieved parties, that there was no way to have him retried on the same charges.

Brumbelow had picked the wrong battle to fight. He put on his class A's and was allowed to borrow Rambo's Jeep to drive to the I.G. He came back several hours later, a dejected man. He had been beaten at his own game. He had thought that he was the master of army regulations in this outfit, but Rambo showed him that when it comes to non-coms sticking together, they too can figure out how to work the rules in their favor.

18

COLONEL'S ORDERLY, A NEW KING IS CROWNED

TIME WAS MOVING ON AND WE WERE getting closer to Operation Gyroscope, which for Crenshaw, Flanders, Brumbelow and me meant an early discharge from the army. As Rambo had threatened, I had been assigned the maximum in K.P. and guard duty, within regulations. On the brighter side, every time I made Colonel's Orderly, I was awarded a forty-eight hour pass and that turned out to be almost every week. I had actually tied Corporal Strand's record of thirteen straight, and we still had a few weeks to go. Rambo was taking it all in stride. He was very complimentary regarding my guard mount performances, but he jokingly would remind me that my uncompleted court martial papers, lacking only the cause, were still in his desk.

The thirteenth time I made Colonel's Orderly was on a Wednesday. Therefore, I drove the Colonel around on Thursday and took my forty-eight hour pass on Friday and Saturday. Of course, I was scheduled for weekend guard duty on Sunday, which meant that I would have to be back on the base and at guard mount by 6:00 AM, Sunday morning. Rambo must have stayed up all night planning the assignment schedules to make sure that I would be maximally inconvenienced. One solution would have been to forfeit my pass, or to take it in beautiful downtown Schwienfurt, to avoid the risk of being late for guard mount. I had worked with tough schedules before and knew the train schedules by heart. I was confident that I could rely on the 2:00 A.M. train from Frankfurt to get me to Schwienfurt early enough to make it back to the base, change clothes, prepare for guard mount and have time to spare before reporting for guard duty.

Like almost every other forty-eight hour pass, as Rambo anticipated, I went to Frankfurt. I had a wonderful time and planned my trip judiciously to make sure that I would be at the Banhoff in time for the 2:00 AM train. I arrived at ten minutes before 2:00, only to find that there had been a change in the schedule. The train had left at 1:00 A.M. and the next train would not leave until 4:00 AM. The plot was beginning to thicken. I found out that this change had been widely publicized. The information had been sent to all the military bases, and transmitted to the company offices from which it was supposed to have been disseminated to the rank and file soldiers. Apparently, Rambo had forgotten to pass this information on to his troops, and in particular to me.

I began to panic. If I waited for the 4:00 AM train, there would be no way for me to make guard mount on time. I ran out of the Banhoff and hailed the first taxi I could find. I asked the driver how long it would take to drive to Scweinfurt and how much it would cost. He said that for $10 he could get me to the gate of the base by 6:00 AM. I pulled out a $20 bill and said this was his if he could get me there by 5:15 A M. I was lucky that he was adventurous and hungry enough to give it a try.

Fortunately, there was no traffic. The streets through the small hamlets were now barely one lane and my driver barreled through them as if he were driving the Grand Prix. If I had not been so concerned about being court-martialed in my last few weeks as a soldier, I would have been scared out of my wits from the way this guy was driving. I was too scared to look at the speedometer, and I closed my eyes every time he made a ninety-degree or more turn. I used to enjoy the roller coaster ride at Lakewood Park, in Atlanta, but that was nothing compared to this ride. The driver was intent on earning his $20 fare and he did it with time to spare. We pulled up at the gate at 5:13 A.M. I took a deep breath, checked to see if all my body parts were still in tact, gave the driver his $20 and thanked him profusely. I had told him why we were rushing, and he wished me luck on guard mount.

I ran all the way to the barracks. Rambo was surprised to see me so early, but still smiled, because he felt sure that I could not get ready for guard mount in time, unless I was willing to give up competing for Colonel's Orderly. Deep down, I shared that feeling, but I wasn't going to give up. I ran into the barracks and there were Crenshaw, Flanders and Brumbelow standing ready to dress me for the mount. They had polished my brass, pressed my uniform, cleaned my weapon and shined my boots. They had gotten wind of Rambo's plan and made these preparations while I was on pass, in the hope that I would be able to get back in time. I felt like a stage entertainer with a wardrobe crew standing in the wings with a costume change. They got me ready and in less than twenty minutes I was walking tall to guard mount, without a minute to spare.

Rambo took one look at me and shook his head in disbelief. He had already typed "missing guard mount" as the reason on my court martial papers. As I passed him, he tore up the papers, trying to make sure that I saw him in the act. That was his way of saying "the game is over, you win."

I hadn't slept all night, but I was so pumped up that I made Colonel's orderly with flying colors. Not only did I avoid getting court-martialed, but in the process, I broke Strand's record of thirteen straight. That evening, although I had to report bright and early to drive the Colonel around, my faithful wardrobe crew and I celebrated with a few beers. It was a sweet victory for all of us. We all took pleasure in seeing Rambo beaten at a game in which he had set the rules, but for Brumbelow it was very special. It was what he needed to get over the scam that Rambo had pulled on him.

19

SOLDIER OF THE YEAR

I GOT UP BRIGHT AND EARLY THE next morning, a little hung over, but alert enough to do my job as the Colonel's orderly, for the last time. Rambo intercepted me on the way and told me that I was back on the pass list, and would be taken off the guard duty roster in deference to the inordinate amount of times I had been on. He also told me that I had accumulated ten days leave time, and suggested that I take it soon, since time for Operation Gyroscope was getting close. I thanked him and rushed to battalion headquarters, not wanting to be late.

Driving the Colonel around gave me time to think. Rambo's change of attitude toward me was interesting, even amusing. The thought crossed my mind that he might want something from me, then I reasoned that I had nothing to offer him. So I decided to just take it one day at a time. I was a real "short timer" now, and whether he would be friendly or have animosity, I figured I could handle anything in the short period of time left.

The ten-day leave was another matter. I had not anticipated being allowed any leave time. I knew what I wanted to do, but there was no time for preplanning. My idea was to try once again to revisit the places in France that had been the O.S.E. children's homes for Jewish refugees, at which I stayed from 1939 through 1941, before escaping to the United States.

I finished my last day with the Colonel and went straight into Rambo's office to arrange for the ten day leave. Since he was my new friend, I asked him if he could help me find information on Montmorency, Cruese, and Brout Vernet in France. He actually made a few calls for me, but had no luck. The best bet, he thought, would be to go to Frankfurt and go to a reputable travel agency and take it from there. I didn't bother to tell him that I had tried that once before, thinking that as a last resort, I might try it again. I went to see my friends at the service club figuring they would know what information source, through army channels, I could tap to get the directions I needed. The most reliable sources said that to their knowledge, these places did not exist, and suggested that I had my information wrong.

I decided to devote my forty-eight hour pass to preplanning my trip to France, to relive those two and a half years I fared without parents or siblings, before finally reuniting with my brothers and sisters. I went to Frankfurt and started making the rounds of the travel agencies. As before, no one seemed to know anything about the three cities in question, and more importantly, no one cared enough to make an effort to find information for me. Maybe there wasn't enough money in it for them, or maybe they just did not want to be a party to helping a German Jew, who had survived the Holocaust. After two days of meeting with travel agents, who initially were very friendly, but whose demeanor changed dramatically once I explained what I was looking for, I was getting nowhere.

I had become inured to going back to the base in frustration, at least whenever I had tried to accomplish something that required assistance from a German. I knew that the names of the places in France were correct, as I remembered them. According to everyone I had contacted, I was either wrong or these places fell off the face of the earth. I had a couple of days until my leave would start, so I decided to keep trying for the trip to France, and to consider Garmisch, a vacation resort at the foot of the Alps, as an alternative.

Luckily payday was the day before my leave started. This time I actually needed my $90 monthly paycheck, even though I had been saving up a little each month. As I was counting my pay, a squad leader from Baker battery asked if he could borrow twelve dollars, to help him out of a jam. He offered his 35mm camera as collateral, and said I could take it with me on leave. I wasn't used to taking pictures. I generally carried a sketch pad when visiting a place of interest and enjoyed putting my impressions on paper. This was a chance to help somebody in need and at the same time, a new opportunity for me to learn how to document what I see, using photography.

I took off for Frankfurt the next day, not knowing for sure where I was going. It would have been nice to have gone with someone else, but everything happened so fast, and actually everyone I knew had already used up all of their leave time. Once in Frankfurt, I took one last shot at finding out how to get to Montmeroncy, et al, from the Frankfurt tourist office. I had thought that no one could be less helpful than the travel agents had been, I was wrong. I bought train tickets to Garmisch and got on my way to relax without any set goals but to rest and enjoy myself.

GARMISCH WAS LOVELY. MOST OF THE ARCHITECTURE dated back to at least the nineteenth century, and much of it was considerably older. It was not a bustling community. Some of the people dressed in Bavarian outfits. The Zugspitze, Germany's highest mountain in the Bavarian Alps, was a background for the picturesque town. The weather was beautiful, I checked in to a hotel that catered primarily to American soldiers and foreign tourists, put my things away and went for a walk. Walking through Garmisch was like strolling through a theme park. Everywhere I turned, there was a photo or sketch pad opportunity.

I ran back to the hotel to get my sketch pad and pencils. Even though I had a camera with me, documenting my experiences with sketches was something I had been doing since I was a child, and an activity from which I derived great enjoyment. When I was six years old, in Paris, I had made pencil drawings of the Eiffel Tower and the Arc d' Triumph and kept them with me, as treasured possessions, for most of my travels through France. Somewhere along the way they disappeared. Many years later, Mrs. Helen Samuels, with whom I had stayed when I came to Paris in 1938, reminded me that my sister Flo had sent her a drawing from Lisbon, Portugal, in August of 1941. It was a sketch that I had made of the S. S. Mouzzinho, the boat on which my two sisters and I escaped to the United States.

First, I sketched the Zugspitze, then an old stucco building with ornate wood trim and a lovely foot bridge over a stream. I felt relaxed and fulfilled although I had yet to find a person that would sit still long enough for me to compete with the camera.

While I was sketching the bridge, I spotted an elderly man in a Bavarian costume, sitting on a bench smoking a pipe. I had never seen any one sit so still, I figured he was either in a coma or he was posing. I put away the sketch of the bridge, turned the page, and started sketching this example of Bavarian folklore. He had on green velvet short pants and jacket, socks up to his knees, a velvet hat with a long feather in the band, his pipe was bent like a p-trap and with the exception of blowing a little smoke, he barely moved a muscle. He was a classic subject and probably was used to posing, although just as I was finishing the sketch, he looked over at me in disgust, as if I had invaded his privacy, got up and stormed off. I couldn't understand this behavior. I thought he was enjoying posing and I had planned to give him the sketch.

I packed up my material and went back to the hotel to see what sort of night life was in store. The hotel had a large lounge that was sort of a nightclub with German entertainers, who did most of their material and songs in English. I met a few other GIs and spent the evenings with them and the local girls, who used the club as their hangout. During the days I went sight seeing and sketching. Occasionally, some of the people I met at the club would join me for daytime activities. All in all, it was a very relaxing vacation in preparation for our next exercise, which was to be winter training in Waldflecken.

Waldflecken, we were told, was going to be colder than Grafenwöhr, at which there had been several cases of frostbite. Therefore, in preparation for this winter exercise, we were ordered to sit through several films on the dangers of frostbite and the preparations one had to take to avoid it. The films were very graphic and nauseating. They showed mangled feet with toes missing and some cases of entire feet having to be amputated. Then they painstakingly went through the procedure of how to protect your feet in very cold weather to avoid frostbite. After watching these films, I could not imagine any soldier not taking the information seriously.

A new commander had been sent from 7th Army Headquarters to take command of this operation. He was a Lt. Colonel who had been passed over for promotion to Colonel, for lack of field experience. This operation was going to be his first field experience and the officers and non-coms all feared that this experiment was going to be at the foot soldiers' expense. They weren't wrong. The first order that our new commander gave was to remove the tarpaulins from the deuce and a half trucks in which we were to be transported to Waldflecken. He was questioned about the wisdom of that order, considering the well below freezing temperature that would get down to 30 degrees below zero. His response, "My men are prepared to fight the elements," will probably be remembered by every soldier that sat shivering in the back of a truck without a tarpaulin top, almost all the way to Waldflecken.

I was bundled up with two pairs of long johns, a pair of O.D.s, fatigues, a field jacket and a parka. I had on snow boots with liners and two pair of socks. Inside my shirt was an extra set of liners and two extra pairs of socks to rotate with the ones I was wearing. Otherwise, the sweat from my feet would freeze and the rest would be history. With all of that, it felt like I was still freezing to death in that open back truck, and I was not alone. Along the way, pleas went up to the commander who was in the lead Jeep, and who remained undaunted. Our Field Sergeant who was as cold as we were would shrug his shoulders and say "Good training" to anyone who would complain.

Three quarters of the way to our destination, the convoy had to stop to let off over a dozen men that had to be sent back in ambulances, suffering from frost-bite, hypothermia and the like. By this time, the good commander must have realized that he had over estimated the ability of an entire battalion of men to withstand Arctic like elements. He rescinded his order and allowed the tarps to be put on the trucks for the remainder of the trip. For some of us it was too little too late. By the time we arrived at Waldflecken and unloaded, another twenty or so men had to be hospitalized.

The Lt. Colonel was relieved of his command shortly after we arrived. I never found out if he was promoted, but knowing the army, my guess would be that he eventually made general.

Waldflecken was breathtakingly beautiful. It had been untouched by allied bombing raids. We were told that the allied forces did not even know this German military installation existed. It was high up in the mountains and well hidden by evergreen trees. In retrospect, spending a week there made us kind of glad that the place had not been destroyed, even though it had been a German army stronghold. Were it not for all the cases of frostbite and hypothermia, this exercise may have gone down as one of the highlights of our tour in Germany.

SHORTLY AFTER WE RETURNED TO THE BASE, there was a new aura of relaxed tensions throughout the battalion, which probably was evident throughout the 1st Division. Operation Gyroscope was close at hand and you could feel it in the air, sort of like the last week of school without the tension of final exams. The Big Red One, the 1st Division, that had been on the European continent since D-Day, was finally going to leave Europe and be replaced by the Tenth Division, from Fort Riley, Kansas. Almost everyone was excited at the thought of going back to The States. Even the Regular Army guys were somewhat happy at the change of venue to Fort Riley, Kansas. The short timers, like myself, were ecstatic with the prospect of going back stateside to be discharged from the armed services.

A lot of recruiting was going on to get short timers to re-up for a three-year stint, with promises of promotions. A few soldiers without much to go home to in terms of a career, actually took the bait. For most of us, Crenshaw, Flanders, Brumbelow et al, it was time to celebrate the freedom that was just around the corner. Leaves and overnight passes had been suspended, and we were limited to spending our evenings in beautiful downtown Schweinfurt, if we wanted to get off the base.

A few days after we returned from Waldflecken, I was summoned to the office to see Sgt. Rambo and the Captain. At first, I was nervous, thinking that the court martial papers Rambo had torn up may have been just a copy. I shrugged off any thoughts of doom and figured they just wanted to have a little fun at my expense. I wasn't that far off. The unusually warm greeting that I got made me wonder what it was they wanted from me. I wasn't used to being treated like a star athlete by a bunch of alumni. After a few exchanges of pleasantries, they got to the point. The Battalion Commander had suggested, and they whole-heartedly agreed, that I should represent the Battalion in the Division Inspection, Drill and Parade at Kissingen. For the drill portion, each battalion would field their "top soldier" for a competition that would be similar to a guard mount. The winner would be named "Soldier of the Year" and, of course, would bring great honor to his battalion.

I didn't know whether to laugh or cry. I was sure Rambo knew exactly how I felt. These guys made me out to be the biggest eight ball in the battery, and they schedule me for the maximum K.P. and guard duty that army regulations allowed. To cope with this harassment, I worked at becoming proficient at guard mount, and as a result, made Colonel's Orderly fourteen times straight. This in turn made me Rambo's choice to represent Service Battery, and the entire battalion, as candidate for Division Soldier of the Year. I couldn't invent a more ironic situation if I tried. I was able to resist the urge to burst out laughing. The sad part was that I had no choice in the matter, this was a direct order.

I laughed all the way back to the barracks. The situation was absurd enough on the face of it. Neither the colonel, the captain, nor Sgt. Rambo was aware that I had to carry a rock in my left hand at every guard mount in order to be able to respond to rapid fire drill orders, and that I had done this each time I succeeded in making colonel's orderly. Crenshaw, Flanders, and Brumbelow got a real kick out of this fitting closing scene to "Pvt. E2 'Eight- ball'-Hirsch vs. Master Sergeant Rambo."

The big day turned out to be more than a Division inspection and parade. In actuality, these were the farewell ceremonies of the Big Red One, the last hurrah of a division that had served with such distinction in Europe, first as a conqueror and liberator, then as an occupation (peace keeping) force. The inspection was really a competition of the best each battalion had to offer in various categories, which included the gamut from marksmanship with various weapons, to the type of drill exercises we had at every guard mount. The winner of the latter was to receive the coveted "Soldier of the Year" award.

Hardly any spectators ever attended the daily guard mounts at the base, although Crenshaw, Flanders, and Brumbelow had been my cheering squad for my first few. This day was very different. There were a series of drill formations, each with a large crowd of spectators, quietly cheering their favorite on. The winner of each drill exercise then competed against each other in the "Finals." I was the only competitor with a rank less than corporal, but then again, I was the only one who had made Colonel's Orderly fourteen times in a row.

I made the "Finals" to the cheers of my rooting section, which this time was led by none other than Sgt. Rambo, our Captain, and the Colonel, who was C.O. of our Battalion. My left hand was getting very sweaty, but I didn't dare reveal the small rock, which by now was embedded in my palm.

Competition for the final drill exercise was tough. These guys looked so sharp that I felt like walking away to keep from being embarrassed. Apparently, I was no slouch either, and the other guys were as sweaty as I was. It was worth continuing with the competition just to hear Rambo, the Captain, and the Colonel cheering like a bunch of high school football fans. I don't know how I did it, but I made "Soldier of the Year." An "eight-ball," who had been unable to get a promotion to PFC in over twenty months of active duty in the army, had just been awarded the title of best soldier in the Division.

If it wasn't so absurd, it would have blown my mind. There really was no time to sit back and reflect on what had just happened. My rooting section was all over me, jumping in excitement. After all, this was a great honor for our Battalion and for Service Battery. As I was being smothered by well-wishers, I released the rock from my left hand, nonchalantly shaking it loose. For better or for worse, I had redeemed myself with my superiors.

20

P.F.C.

WELL, I HAD MY FIFTEEN SECONDS OF fame. In fact, my fifteen seconds lasted the remainder of the day. I was the unlikely hero to the same group of officers and non-coms that had tried to make my tour of duty in Schweinfurt unbearable. I wasn't quite sure why my winning this drill competition was so important to them. To me, and my friends, it was sort of a victory over the army establishment, but our overt display of joy was tame compared to theirs. In fact, they treated me as if I had scored the winning touchdown of a championship game. I got the congratulatory back slapping, and I almost felt as if I had been part of a team.

That night, the entire battery, with the exception of those on guard duty or K.P., was given passes to go into Schweinfurt. We were cautioned that the word was out in the city regarding the departure of our battalion, and that we should expect local girls to be looking to latch on to G.I.'s for a chance to go to America. About six of us went out in a group, figuring there was safety in numbers. We drank a few beers and caroused around the town, watching as the local girls did their number on soldiers, some of whom had never been in town before. I had learned to take heed when given warnings about the local population or conditions. Some people never learn. At least six G.I.'s came back to the base engaged that night, insisting that they wanted to marry the new found loves of their lives before returning Stateside.

As we stood in formation the next morning, I was told to report to Sgt. Rambo after breakfast. I never knew what to expect when summoned by the first sergeant. Normally the apprehension would have ruined my breakfast, but by this time I had mastered the attitude of a short timer. I felt I could withstand any harassment he could throw my way. As it turned out, I was totally unprepared for what he had for me.

When I arrived at the battery office, the Captain was with Rambo at his desk. They both congratulated me again on making Soldier of the Year. Then Rambo reached in his desk drawer and then put a small packet in my left hand, while shaking my right hand. "This has been long in coming, your promotion to P.F.C. has finally come through. Congratulations!"

As I listened to his words, I looked into the packet and saw a bunch of P.F.C. stripes. I saluted the Captain and thanked both of them and told them that I would be sewing the stripes on my dress uniform. "Oh no," Rambo responded, with the Captain shaking his head in agreement, "you will have to sew the stripes on every uniform you have, including your fatigues."

I thought out loud that it would take at least an evening to sew on all those stripes, and all this for the extra $14.00 I would earn for the last paycheck I would receive from the army. "On second thought," I said nonchalantly, "I don't think it's worth the effort. Thanks for the promotion, but I'll be just as happy keeping my rank of Private E-2 for the month I have remaining in the army."

"You don't seem to understand." Rambo said with a devilish grin. "You will sew on these P.F.C. stripes or you will be court-martialed. For any soldier to refuse his promotion would be an insult to the army, but if you, as Soldier of the Year, would remain a lowly E-2, that would be an embarrassment to your immediate superiors."

Rambo knew that I couldn't care less if my immediate superiors were embarrassed. He also knew that the magic words, "court-martial," could tame the wildest beast. Discretion being the better part of valor, I begrudgingly accepted the promotion and went to the barracks to start sewing.

21

KOREAN VET

THE SHORT TIMERS, THOSE OF US THAT were to be discharged from the army after arrival in the States, were footloose and fancy free, compared to the career soldiers that were preparing for the move to Ft. Riley. That must have been all the more reason for the recruiting to start with full steam. Promotions were offered, special assignments were alluded to. Every possible incentive they could come up with was put on the table. I, who had just made P.F.C. after twenty-one months, was offered an immediate promotion to corporal, along with a selection of administrative type job descriptions. I was amazed at how many of my fellow short timers were considering re-enlisting based on the incentives offered.

The recruiting drive was, from the recruiters' point of view, quite successful. Over a dozen short timers re-upped, some whom I never thought would consider such a step under any conditions. I suppose if I had not been looking forward to certain career goals, I might have been tempted too. As it was, they could have offered me a commission as an officer and I would have turned it down.

Operation Gyroscope was such a vast undertaking that it attracted the major American automobile manufacturers. Each of us were given brochures by both Ford and General Motors which offered "special deals" to soldiers who wanted to buy American cars, without sales tax, and have the cars waiting for them in the United States. The prices seemed reasonable, but even at that, I didn't have the money to pay cash, or a job to guarantee monthly payments.

This must have been, at least in part, related to the recruiting drive, because the soldiers that were remaining in the army were automatically qualified for auto financing. I would have loved to have had a new car, but after my one and only stint of car ownership in Fort Lewis, I figured that a used car would be much more my speed.

My financial status also affected my ability to purchase items that were so much cheaper if bought in Germany. Like German made drafting instruments, German cameras and lenses, and Rosenthal China. I had managed to buy one set of drafting instruments with poker winnings. Cameras and special lenses were out of my league. I had given the squad leader from Baker Battery his camera in return for the twelve dollars he had borrowed. He had insisted on paying 50% interest, but I refused to take it, even though he said that was common practice in the army. That was not the way I wanted to be remembered.

I wrote all of my sisters and brothers telling them that I could buy them a complete service for twelve of the most expensive Rosenthal china, a $3,000 to $4,000 value, for $1,100. I even had a pattern picked out, figuring that at least one of them would want to take advantage of this opportunity. But, alas, none of them felt they had the money to spare. So, I was set to leave Germany a second time. I had not fulfilled any hopes of coming to grips with the loss of my family and the years of my youth. This time I would be leaving with new memories, a set of drafting instruments, and the prospect of being honorably discharged from the army of the United States.

THE SEAS WERE MUCH CALMER FOR THE boat trip back. Only a handful of soldiers became seasick and they probably would have gotten sick riding on a rocking horse. August was a great time to be crossing the Atlantic. If it weren't for all the trappings of army life, it would have felt like an ocean cruise. The most notable part of the trip was the change in attitude of Sgt. Rambo and the Captain. Granted, they had been fawning all over me after the drill competition in Bad Kissingen, but that was expectedly short lived.

Once the ship was out to sea, I started seeing more and more of this duo that had been my nemesis for so many months. It wasn't as if I was seeking them out, au contraire. The rule that forbade officers and non-coms from fraternizing with their subordinates seemed to have gone out the window. From all appearances, they really wanted to be friendly.

On the second day out, I was standing by the side rail of the ship enjoying the view of the never-ending sea, as it disappeared in the horizon, when my two new "buddies" walked up to chat. I wondered if they had thought that I might file cruelty charges against them, and therefore felt that they should make nice. I had no such plans and maybe since their role of instilling army discipline into civilian minded soldiers was no longer in force, they wanted to show me that they were regular guys with interests similar to mine.

We talked about my plans after the army and even the Captain's plans, since he had only two or three years left before retiring. They were fascinated with my plans to become an architect, and even coaxed me into spouting design theories. Finally, there was a lull in the conversation, then the Captain reached into his pocket and pulled out a medal that I was supposed to have received for placing first in the Soldier of the Year drill competition.

The casual presentation took me by surprise. Rambo said that there had not been time to schedule a formal medal presentation, and opined that I probably would not have been comfortable with that kind of pomp and circumstance anyway. I held the impressive looking medal in my hand and gazed at it for a few seconds. The Captain said, "I know you couldn't care less about this kind of thing, but we are proud of you and we think you are very deserving of this award."

Somehow that statement, well meaning as it was, worked as kind of a cue for me to do something bizarre that I would regret later. It was almost as if I had a role to play, one that I felt was expected of me. I looked at the medal and said "this means more to me than making P.F.C." Then I turned and threw it over the rail into the Atlantic. Rambo and the Captain gasped for a moment, then shrugged their shoulders as if to say "what can you expect from an eight ball like that?"

Talk about a conversation stopper! They both patted me on the shoulder and walked away. I tried to tell myself that I had just made a grand gesture, a statement denouncing the system of dehumanization within the army's ranks, and the ridiculous priorities of that system. There was no need, or reasonable explanation however, for me to do such a foolish thing. It was not expected of me, and in reality, I was sorry that I did not keep the medal to show to my family and friends. Maybe, if the presentation had been made somewhere other than by the rail of an ocean liner, I might still have that keepsake.

IT WAS A BEAUTIFUL DAY IN AUGUST when we arrived in the United States. People started saying their good-byes while still on board, since the Ft. Riley bound group would debark and be whisked away as soon as we landed. It was sort of like breaking up camp. Guys who barely ever said hello to each other became emotional at the possible thought of never seeing each other again. Handshakes, hugs and tearful good-byes were the order of the day. For basically being a loner, I was amazed at how many people I felt the need to say goodbye to, and who felt the need to say goodbye to me. I had thought that I would never hear any reference to Kirk Douglas again, since I had been free of any mention of him for almost my entire stay in Europe. I was taken aback when several soldiers came up to me and asked me to give regards to my famous actor brother. A few even asked to take pictures with me for their scrapbooks. Old rumors never die, they just smell that way.

Once we landed, the Ft. Riley bound group was out of sight in no time. The rest of us were sent to Ft. Dix, New Jersey, pending transfer to the bases at which each of us had been inducted into the army. We were split up into squads with the highest ranking soldier in each group becoming the squad leader. To keep us from getting lethargic, we were assigned busy work details throughout the fort. Apparently, a lot of soldiers in transit stopped at Ft. Dix, because they had these detail assignments down to a science. All the crud details were strictly assigned to transits, and while we had our own squad leaders, permanent party sergeants had the job of seeing to it that our assignments were done before any of us were dismissed.

We were only there a few days, but it seemed like weeks. Passes to New York were not available to transits, and available off duty activities were extremely limited compared to what we had been used to. Surprisingly, the squad leaders really flexed their muscles during the daily routine of calisthenics and details. They should have known that this was dangerous among short timers, as our squad leader could later attest to. Henderson had just been promoted to sergeant before we left Germany. We had been together at Camp Chaffee and at Ft. Lewis, where he had always been a little gung ho for an enlisted man. As a corporal in Germany, he had been just one of the guys, though a little more eager to find favor with the brass. Probably, his new sergeant's stripes gave him the feeling of power that he had aspired to for so long. Well, he never saw who hit him or how many they were. He showed up the third day at Dix pretty bruised up, but a whole lot easier on his men. I was glad I didn't know who was involved, although I had my suspicions. He had tried to report the incident, but with no witnesses, and being on a transit part of the base, nothing could be done.

Thievery was a major problem. We had been warned not to leave valuables lying around, but found it hard to believe the thoroughness of the scavengers who preyed on soldiers in the transit section of the Fort. They were like boll weevils in a cotton field. Anything that wasn't attached, and had any modicum of value, was taken. Camp security was aware that this was an on going problem, but their crack investigators could not catch or identify the perpetrators. We came up with the idea of leaving one man behind to guard the squad's personal property, but the permanent party sergeants in charge of our details nixed that idea. We were convinced that these sergeants were involved in the theft ring, but we could not prove a thing.

A couple of guys that had not been stationed in Schweinfurt approached me in the barracks one night, and challenged me on the allegation that I was the brother of Kirk Douglas. I told them

I didn't give a damn what they believed and to please stay out of my private life. If they wanted an argument or a fight, they were not going to get it from me. I had grown weary of that charade long before, and I was not going to let it become an issue again this close to my discharge.

AT LAST, THE ORDERS CAME TO GO to Ft. Jackson, S.C. for final processing and discharge. We had been at Ft. Dix for a week, which threatened to never end. Of the dozen or so guys going to Jackson, Sgt. Henderson was the only one I knew. We sat next to each other on the train and tried to forget that he outranked me. He was a nice guy once his stripes were stripped from his persona. Even though I found it easy to talk to him, I was not anxious to develop a relationship that would continue after discharge from the army. I found it difficult to forget the "chicken s---" orders he had showered on our squad in Ft. Dix, and I told him so in no uncertain terms. He apologized for that behavior, saying that his newly acquired sergeant's stripes made him a little drunk with power, and that he was almost glad that some of the guys put him in his place.

Arriving at Ft. Jackson was like taking a step back in time. Nothing had changed in almost two years. Even the toilets were still being flushed with scalding hot water. So it should have not been a surprise that we were treated like a bunch of recruits, by the officers and non-coms under whose charge we were placed. I was glad that at least we did not have the same compassionate cadre, that introduced me to the rigors and injustice of army life, just twenty-one months earlier.

Our new drill sergeant informed us that he and his superiors had no intention of allowing us to get lethargic and lose our edge, just because we were waiting for the administrative paperwork necessary to finalize our honorary discharge from the U.S. Army. Therefore, we rose at the crack of dawn each morning, marched to every activity to his cadence count, and had daily drill and calisthenics sessions. The saving grace was that it would all be over soon.

Few of us complained. Not only had we become inured to what can only be described as basic army "chicken s---," everyone of us saw all of this as the final act in a pathetic play of power. So we mostly smiled and almost enjoyed this last attempt at letting each soldier, that was leaving the glorious ranks of the army, know how inconsequential he was.

At last the time to muster out came. We turned in everything except our Class A uniforms, which we had paid for. In going through the administrative paperwork, I was given the one and only opportunity to review my files. I was so anxious to put on my civilian clothes and get started home, that I foolishly declined this opportunity. As soon as I picked up my final paycheck, I realized that I had made a big mistake. I had a chance to see how my superiors had written up all the bizarre incidents that made up my army career, and I muffed it. I tried to go back and see if the offer still held, but the window of opportunity had closed, like a steel shutter.

I took my disappointment in stride and started focusing on the rest of my life that lay before me. I was a veteran after serving one year, nine months and twelve days in the U.S. Army. In fact, I found out that I was considered a Korean Vet, since I had served my time during the Korean Conflict.

IT WAS OFFICIAL. WE WERE CIVILIANS AGAIN, and now that we were, our presence at Ft. Jackson was no longer desired. We were given just enough time to pack, change into civvies, and be ready to board a bus that would take us to the central bus station in Columbia, South Carolina, where we would disburse and go our separate ways.

I had never seen Henderson in civilian clothes before. He actually looked human. We swapped addresses and talked about keeping in touch. I had made quite a few friends and met a lot of people that I might have wanted to stay in touch with, but Henderson had been on the other side. He always seemed to be part of the system that I and many of my friends were fighting. Now we were both civilians and he certainly seemed like a nice enough guy, but he was not one that I would have wanted to share army experiences with. He took his bus to North Carolina, I took mine to Atlanta, Georgia.

Going back to civilian life was not a case of taking up where I had left off. I was a different person, not just the same guy two years older. I was very focussed on going back to architectural school, yet I wanted to be sure to explore other interests that I had become aware of while in the service. The G.I. Bill that was going to allow me to go back to college without having to work to support myself, was not what I had anticipated, and certainly less than what my brother-in-law had at the end of World War II. I would receive $110 per month as long as I was taking a full load of subjects in school. This amount was to cover everything, tuition, supplies and living expenses. There was no way I could support myself without working to supplement the G.I. Bill's stipend. At least I was able to work fewer hours, which gave me more time to study.

MY FIRST DAY BACK AT GEORGIA TECH was weird. There was a new architectural building, in lieu of the wooden pre-fabs I had remembered, and the students in all of my classes and design labs were at least two to three years my junior. I had gained quite a few pounds while in the service, so until I could afford to buy some new clothes, my wardrobe was limited to the civilian clothes I had acquired as a soldier, along with the army clothes I had been allowed to take home with me. I didn't own a light jacket, so I wore the top to my class A uniform, more commonly known as an Ike Jacket, named after General Dwight David Eisenhower.

The Army ROTC held all of their formations and drills in the parking lot adjacent to the new Architectural Building, which made my passing by these formations while going back and forth to classes, almost inevitable. Before long, I was reprimanded by a gung ho ROTC lieutenant for improperly mixing army attire with civilian clothes. I couldn't imagine what authority he felt he had over my apparel, but nonetheless, he threatened to have me court-martialed. I had enough of this type of "chicken" behavior in the army, and I certainly did not feel the need to explain that I had no other jacket to wear. Rather, I chose to ignore him and go about my business. Over the first month of the fall quarter, I must have received two dozen such reprimands from him, and other ROTC officers that he got worked up over my apparent disrespect for the holiness of proper army attire. They tried to involve the regular army instructors, but to their credit, they chose not to pursue the matter.

To make matters worse, I had started getting threatening letters from an army reserve outfit, stating that I had been assigned to their unit, and telling me that I must report on a certain date to sign up for the Active Reserve. I had been specifically told, when I was being discharged at Ft. Jackson, that active duty in the reserve was optional. I called the recruiting sergeant and told him what I had been told, and he threatened to have me court-martialed if I did not report as ordered. I began to wonder if the time would ever come when I would not be subject to threats of being court-martialed. I could have used the pay for serving in the Active Reserve, but I did not want to make the commitment of attending periodic meetings and stints of active duty. I had my fill of the army and did not want to have any affiliation with the army mentality. Most of all, I was tired of being bullied around and I resented the recruiters' attempt to scare me into signing up by misrepresenting the facts.

The persistence of the recruiting sergeant, through threatening letters and telephone calls, made me question my rights. At my brother Jack's suggestion, I contacted his attorney. As it turned out, he had a similar experience after his discharge from the army, and he said that the recruiting sergeant did not have a leg to stand on, regarding his threats. Harvey Klein made one telephone call to the recruiting sergeant, telling him that if he did not desist from harassing me, that we would sue him and the army, and that as a result, he would probably be demoted to private. That's all it took. From that moment on I received no more letters, phone calls, or telegrams from the Army Reserve. I finally felt like a civilian.

I had volunteered for the draft with a healthy respect for the Armed forces of the United States, those forces that, along with their allies, defeated Hitler's Germany and liberated the death camps. In spite of the adversarial situations during my tour of duty, I still respected and appreciated the United States Army. It was just, as I have been accused of all my life, that I had been hearing a different drummer, and it was time to get back to civilian life, where that type of behavior is more acceptable.

22

ITS DÉJÀ VU ALL OVER AGAIN

GETTING OUT OF THE ARMY AND RETURNING to my architectural studies at Georgia Tech was a wonderful feeling. I felt like I had just been released from prison. Being a little more mature and a bit older than my fellow students gave me a more serious attitude toward my schoolwork, which in turn made it difficult to make friends. Helmut, an exchange student from Stüttgart, was an exception. For some unexplained reason, he had been placed in the third year design studio although he had already finished four years of design studio in Germany. While most of the younger students were playing around for the first two weeks of our first five-week design project, Helmut and I started to work from the beginning of the assignment.

It took a while for us to take to each other. He was very precise in his approach to everything, and while I believed in working hard, I was more casual, or better put, sloppy, at least in the way I kept my drawing board. The main thing we shared was work ethic and a healthy respect for good design. That was enough to get us going for an occasional beer at Harry's, the favorite hangout for architectural students and professors.

Helmut and I, along with another exchange student from Norway, started taking beer breaks together on a fairly regular basis and the three of us were fast becomes friends. One day, toward the end of our afternoon design lab, Helmut asked if he and I could go to Harry's alone. He said that he had something to discuss with me that was for my ears only. We asked for and got a private booth at Harry's and Helmut sat across the table from me looking a little bit nervous, which was very much out of character for him.

He started off by acknowledging that we were becoming friends and continued that, in light of our friendship, he felt that he must tell me something about his past. He looked down at the table then decided to look me straight in the eye when he informed me that he had been in the Hitler Youth. He had reached the rank equivalent to a sergeant, and as he put it, he was good at what he did. He said that he had never harmed or killed any Jews, but was quick to add that he had never been ordered to either. Knowing his work ethic, he feared that he may have found himself following orders had they been given.

We sat there quietly for about ten minutes but it seemed a whole lot longer. My thoughts went back to those unnamed faces in the streets of Germany that cried on my shoulders. I looked up at Helmut and told him that I respected his courage in coming forth with his past and making no excuses. I did not want to know the circumstances that got him involved in the Hitler Youth. He had joined when he was about six years old and though he may have had choices to do otherwise, I was not aware of any such choices. I told him that I was proud to remain his friend as long as he wanted to remain my friend.

We never spoke of this again and we remained drinking buddies until he returned to Germany after his year was up. We even corresponded for a very short period.

I WAS TOTALLY ENGROSSED IN MY STUDIES at Tech, when my brother-in-law's brother approached me to rekindle my interest in the stage. Bud Shartar had not forgotten that I liked to sing. He was helping cast a play that was being put on by Atlanta Civic Theater, a semi-professional group that he was very active in. He asked me to come over without telling me what he had in mind. When I arrived he asked me to sing one of the songs I had sung at the semi-finals in Würzburg. In response to my inquiry, he told me that they were casting for a play with a singing part and he wanted to consider me for the part. I wasn't sure if I would have the time, since I was now in my fourth year at Tech, but the ham in me wanted to see if I could get the part before tackling the time issue. I sang "Lost in Loveliness" and felt good about it even though it was without accompaniment. If I had known he was taping it, I probably would have choked. He said he liked the song very much and would play the tape for the casting committee, but as far as he was concerned, the part was mine.

I expressed concern over the time required for rehearsals, since I was carrying a full school load and working. I also mentioned that I had no acting experience. He told me that the part had very few lines other than the song and that they would be flexible with me on rehearsals if I got the part. I had mixed emotions on finding out what their decision would be. As it turned out, I was able to make almost every rehearsal.

The play was "Time of Your Life" by William Saroyan and my part was the singing newsboy, whose main part was to sing "When Irish Eyes Are Smiling." I figured the part was mine by default since they could not find an Irish tenor.

A professional photographer was hired to take individual theatrical poses of each cast member to put in the marquee outside of the Women's Club, which was located on Peachtree Street and was where the play would be performed. Bud had a major part in the play, so he was there to bolster me up when I didn't rise to the task. The rehearsals were kind of fun, even though some of the actors were certifiable emotional cases. Bud said that these neuroses were par for the course for actors.

The Women's Club was across the street from a Movie theater at the corner of Peachtree and 13th Street. As fate would have it, during the week that our play was on, the 13th Street Theater was playing "Lust for Life," the movie about Vincent Van Gogh, starring Kirk Douglas. I was told that several people had come to the Women's Club to see "Lust For Life," ostensibly because they said they had seen Kirk Douglas's picture in our marquee. Some of them even decided to see the play after they realized their mistake.

Had I thought about it beforehand, I would have invited Hobgood to the play.

23

My Only Eye Witness

I HAVE DEVOTED A GREAT PART OF my adult life to being a student
of the Holocaust. I have lectured, taught classes, written articles
and letters to newspapers and magazines, designed Holocaust
memorials, created museum exhibitions and been a leader in the
survivor community. Through these endeavors, which some
members of my family have called obsessive, I have reaped many
rewards as well as frustrations. Aside from my need to be in
touch with my past and to honor my martyred family, the raison
d'etre for all of these efforts is to not allow the Holocaust to be
forgotten through the passage of time. To loosely quote Jean
Baudrillard, "Forgetting the Holocaust is part of the Holocaust
itself."

Of the many frustrations in promoting Holocaust education,
the assault on memory goes to the head of the class. The most
obvious culprits are the Holocaust deniers, who I am convinced,
don't believe any of their own propaganda. Theirs is an attempt
to put the finishing touches to Hitler's carnage. He murdered
millions of Jews and they are trying to destroy the memory of
Hitler's victims. I take them for what they are, lying haters of
Jews who would stop at nothing to further their agenda. They are
not however, the main focus of my frustration regarding the
assault on memory.

I have often vented my frustration at the zealots who have
built a Capuchine monastery/chapel on the grounds of Sobibor,
the Nazi death camp in Poland that was erected solely to murder
Jews, and at which One quarter of a million Jews were
murdered, before an uprising closed the camp. Equally as
disturbing are the continuing attempts to build a Carmelite

chapel & convent at Auschwitz, since it is obvious to me that both of these offenses to the souls of Jewish victims and to the surviving Jewish people, are to posthumously proselytize the over one and a half million Jews that were murdered at those sites. While this is another assault on memory, I consider the source and expect to have to continue to speak out against this outrage.

One of my greatest disappointments has been what I consider to be an assault on the memory of survivors from Jewish academia. These are people whom I would expect to be more sensitive to survivors' need to bear witness and to the pain that discounting their memories would subject them. I can understand a scholar not accepting as fact a particular aspect of the memory of survivors of the camps for the lack of what they call sufficient proof in the face of technological improbability. I can only assume that this is what Raul Hillberg, one of the most respected Holocaust historians, had in mind in his definitive study *Destruction of European Jews* when he concluded that "the use of human fat for soap cannot be established as a fact from available documentary evidence and eye witness reports." Hillberg's conclusion does not state that soap being made from the fat of Jewish or other victims is unequivocally untrue, as some of the next generation of "Holocaust scholars" do, ostensibly because they fear that allowing such unproven claims from survivors to circulate unchallenged could play into the hands of Holocaust deniers or "revisionists."

I was first confronted with the insane notion that soap was made from Jewish bodies in 1970. It was Friday, February 27, I received an unusual telephone call from my rabbi. Rabbi Emanuel Feldman always seemed to have a handle on resolving the problems of his congregants, without losing his composure. This time however, his voice betrayed that he was truly shaken by the situation that he was about to share with me. A member of our synagogue— Congregation Beth Jacob—had been a soldier in the United States army, serving in Europe at the end of World War II. He had gone into one of the Concentration Camps a few days after liberation where he found four bars of soap, marked RJF. He was told that the marking stood for "Rein Juden Fett," (pure Jewish fat). He had heard that Nazis made soap from the remains of Jews and decided it would be better to take the bars of soap with him than to leave them for someone else to wash with.

He never could figure out what to do with these mementos of the horrors perpetrated by the Nazis, so he wrapped them up in a bundle and kept them with him as he moved from place to place. He never told anyone about them. As fate would have it, the woman he married was a survivor of the concentration camps. When their three children were teenagers they moved into a house near the synagogue, where he stashed his Mysterious package on a shelf in the basement and forgot about it.

In the wee hours of the morning, the day before Rabbi Feldman called me, he had received a frantic call from this WWII veteran. Earlier that evening his wife had gone down to the basement to do some laundry and she ran out of detergent. She started searching around the basement for any kind of soap to complete the washing, and fortuitously, she thought, found a package with the four bars of soap. As she was scrubbing away with one of the bars, he came walking down the stairs and let out a scream of horror as he realized what she was doing. She in turn got startled and started crying. To calm her down, he felt that he had to explain his reaction and tell her the origin of the soap. This made matters even worse for her. It took hours for her to get her emotions under some semblance of control, and that was when he called the Rabbi, about three in the morning.

Before he called me, Rabbi Feldman had been on the phone all day consulting Rabbinical authorities in Israel and in New York, to establish, within Halacha (Jewish Law), a procedure for what to do with these bars of soap that apparently contained remains of Jewish victims of the Nazis. It was finally decided that they should be treated as if they were dead bodies and be buried in a cemetery, and that a funeral should be held as soon as possible. The Rabbi was familiar with the *Memorial to the Six Million* that I had designed, and that was built in the Jewish section of Greenwood Cemetery, in 1965. We both agreed that it would be proper that the burial be on the grounds of the Memorial.

It was getting close to the Sabbath so there was not enough time to go to Greenwood to decide on a burial spot, and the cemetery office was already closed. The funeral was scheduled for Sunday afternoon and the cemetery gates did not open until 9:00 A M, which did not give us time for the necessary arrangements. We made plans to go there at 5:00 AM on Sunday and climb over the fence, if necessary, to work within our timetable. In the meantime, I contacted Abe Besser, the contractor who built the Memorial, and who was a survivor of the Nazi camps. I asked him to make a small wooden casket for the bars of soap and have it ready by Sunday morning.

I had a lot to think about that Shabbat. It was difficult to maintain the spirit of the Sabbath with thoughts of the Holocaust racing through my mind. Rabbi Feldman picked me up at 4:30 A.M. Sunday morning, and as we rode to the cemetery we started contemplating the possibilities of getting caught climbing over the fence. All the humorous scenarios, of rabbi and lay leader getting caught stealthily breaking into a cemetery, were just that. We climbed the fence, made our way to the Memorial and I selected the spot for the burial.

The funeral went as planned, and was well attended. I took my seven-and-one-half-year old daughter, Shoshanah, to give me strength. I then designed and ordered a stone that now sits on the grave. The inscription is in Hebrew and English, "Here rest four bars of soap, the last earthly remains of Jewish Victims of the Nazi Holocaust." I may have heard talk about the Nazis making soap out of Jewish bodies before, but this was the first time that I was personally involved in dealing with the issue, and I was totally blown away. This event had such a dramatic effect on me, that like a swift kick to the head, it pushed me back into my quest for answers about my past.

I was greatly disturbed, years later, when I read a quote from a Holocaust scholar regarding the four bars of soap buried next to the Holocaust Memorial in Greenwood Cemetery. This academician stated that it was an established fact among "Holocaust scholars" that no soap was made from human fat by the Nazis, notwithstanding the testimony of survivors of the death camps.

Some time later, I poured out my frustration to my brother Asher in one of our conversations, and he told me that our Uncle, Philipp Auerbach, had been a chemist in Auschwitz, among other camps, and that he had admitted to him that he had made soap from human fat, under orders from the Nazis. I received a letter from Asher, dated March 3, 1997, going into more detail about his conversations with Uncle Philipp. In his letter, Asher tells of first meeting with Uncle Philipp in 1946, while Asher was serving with the U.S. Army in Germany. It was then that he told Asher that he had seen our mother, from some distance, with Werner and Roselene, standing in line to the gas showers in Auschwitz. Asher's letter elaborates,

> In view of the fact that Uncle Philip was doing such a good job in the British Zone, the Americans offered him the job of Reichskommisar for the Religious, Racist, and Political persecuted in Munich. I made it my business to get papers to go to Munich to further obtain information in person from Uncle Philip, substantiating what he had told me on the telephone. During this conversation he explained to me that having been a chemist, he saved his life by producing soap from the bodies of those killed by the Nazies." He continued on in his letter, "I do not recall if I ever told you that Uncle Philip, as the closest relative, brought me under the Chuppa when I was married in Switzerland in 1949. In view of the fact that even then people questioned the fact that soap was produced from human bodies, I asked him once again about it. He was not very proud of how he saved his life, yet he reluctantly assured me that production of soap from human bodies was a fact in Auschwitz, and, that he and others produced such soap from human bodies.

After reading Asher's letter, I called my cousin Helen, Uncle Philipp's daughter, to hear if she had any direct knowledge of her father's activities to save his life. She was not surprised by the revelations in Asher's letter, though she had nothing further to add from her recollections of her brief conversions with her father. She then reminded me of Uncle Philipp's unpublished memoirs that I had once scanned several years before, and suggested that I may want to take a more careful look at the manuscript. She sent me a copy and I perused it as if I had never laid eyes on it before.

In his memoirs, Uncle Philipp recounts that after he was moved to Auschwitz in March 1943 and had been beaten unmercifully by a Capo,

> A physician and friend of mine helped me to cure my wounds and some days later on, after having used all imaginable pretext to avoid labour, I was presented to Sturmbannfuhrer Pflaum in order to work as a chemist.
>
> By this office also the soap for the personal use of Herr Hitler and SS Reichsfuhrer Himmler had to be produced. This production has given to me as chief chemist and to my collaborators a good source of income.
>
> The good soap had a good market in the women camps where we changed it against underwear, pullovers, and gloves. I am of the opinion that Hitler would resurrect from his tomb when knowing how much of his good soap had been exchanged. Mr. Pflaum was an intimate friend of the Reichsfuhrer SS Himmler, and to this man I was called as chief chemist. The first thing he did was that he forced me to accede him all my recipes and inventions.
>
> The offices and laboratories were under the command of the staff of high SS-leaders. Obersturmfuhrer Haugg, a man of awful anti-semitic attitude, has been tamed by me. I taught him that he had to refrain from his anti-semitic attack in my presence (I worked in his office). He is an accomplice of this crime, still not expiated up to the present. Chief of the office Obersturmfuhrer Verbruggen, an upright,

coarse, uncouth, and stupid Bavarian. During the air-attacks on Auschwitz he remained all the time over in the "shelter of heroes," and therefore, by a proposal of his superior, he was decorated with D S C. of war. — A noble man who, active SS-man, was the scientist of the office, former Oberregierungsrat Dr. Kunicke, had nothing to do with the cruelties of the SS. He always treated us very friendly, did what he could for the prisoners and I am unable to conceive how a man of such a high education and kindness of heart could wear the uniform of an officer of the SS. The still crowds of Unterscharfuhrer and Rottenfuhrer (corporals and lance-corporals) and similar rabble, all desirous to get a shirking job in this department, where many hundred prisoners were employed from which, unfortunately, only very few are alive.

As chief of the soap-production I had to take care of the production of fat and to make controls in the Slughter-house. Nearly every week I have been three or four times there in order to get the waste of fat and of the bowels for the soap-manufacutre, which was always profitable to me. A German proverb ways: "The wheels of a man who has greased well are going well." And our soap was not only good for washing but also for "greasing. Finally it was the soap made for exclusive use of Reichsfuhrer SS Himmler and the Fuhrer of all Germans, Adolf Hitler.

While reading Uncle Philipp's memoirs, I also became aware of something that I had never heard of or read about before, the making of coal from human bones in the camps. It was a startling revelation, but the fact that it was used as a remedy for an epidemic among the imprisoned masses, makes it much easier to comprehend.

Uncle Philipp was among those who evacuated Auschwitz in January 1945 and was forced to march towards Germany. He arrived in Buchenwald after a short stay in Gross-Rosen about two and a half months before the camp was liberated by the

Americans. It was in Buchenwald that Uncle Philipp was ordered to devise this macabre method of saving the lives of his many ailing "comrades," as he explains in his memoirs,

> The hygienic conditions were miserable. Every barrack took in 1,500 men and the small latrine could not do, especially considering the great diarrhrae epidemic which caused hundreds of victims. For weeks we had no water, the pipeline being destroyed by air-attacks on Weimar. There was scarcely enough water to supply the kitchen. In view of the enormous crowd of people it was hard to maintain a medical service and many a good comrade became a victim of the neglect in this respect. Everyday the corpses lay in front of the barracks and the hearses drove round to fetch the naked bodies like cattle. 200 casualties a day was the average in the small camp. The official list stated for the month of February 4,900 men died from "regular" diseases, 5,600 in March and much more were assassinated. The sick-room of Buchenwald, managed by our comrade, Ernst Busse, did the best. Amongst the doctors and nurses all nations were represented. Professor Fischer, Lt. Colonel the well-known French physician Dr. Horn, and Matschuk the able Czech comrade. Dr. Sowis the doctor of the Poles, and Dr. Weissbecker a young German physician were some of those who worked day and by night for the welfare of their comrades.
>
> It was exceedingly difficult to give real and efficient help in view of the lack of medicine, of the insufficient food and of the overcrowding of the camp. On you, comrades of the sick-rooms of Buchenwald having worked self-sacrificing by day and by night for the patients, our gratitude and appreciation be bestowed.
>
> Here one could see what real comradeship can perform. Typical was the way in which the Dutch under Dr. Kas have taken care of their comrades. They had to work hard but they did their voluntary service and with such a devotion which one could not find in any other

camp. Later when the liberating Stars and Stripes streamed above us we saw what these men were really able to do as soon as they had the necessary support and supply of medicine. After a few days I was appointed to manufacture bone-coal as a remedy against the diarrhea-epidemic, and I am proud that I could manage to produce the medicament with which hundreds and thousands of comrades could be healed in spite of the more that primitive means at my disposal. The "bone-burner of Buchenwald" was my nickname of which I pleasantly remind myself, because I not only had to work hard and was dirty all the time but I could help very many comrades. Thus I was transferred to the sick room as a member of the cooperative group. It was a grand feeling to see the spirit of comrade-like cooperation at Buchenwald and we must be ashamed how wrong we had organized our sick-room at Auschwitz.

There is no way to rate the unspeakable atrocities committed by the Nazis. If there were, I am sure that forcing prisoners to participate in repugnant acts in order to survive would be among the most cruel. I do know that my only eye witness to the fate of my dear mother, brother, and sister was one of those unfortunate souls.

After all the years Uncle Philipp had survived the death camps, and after the years of working to secure reparations for survivors while trying to keep ex-SS members out of civil service and political office, he could not overcome the lies and false accusations of embezzling reparations funds of survivors, that were leveled against him by the Bavarian government. After receiving the guilty verdict, in despair, he committed suicide, and was laid to rest in the Jewish cemetery of Munich on August 18, 1952, only to be totally exonerated four years later by the Bavarian parliament.

I feel it would be appropriate for Holocaust scholars to re-evaluate their conclusions on the use of human fat, primarily of Jews, for soap during the Holocaust years in light of Dr. Philipp Auerbach's testimony and in his memory.

Reading, from his memoirs, of all that Uncle Philipp went through to survive, it is difficult to imagine him taking his own life. In spite of a very personal and emotional suicide note, I have often wondered if he had not been murdered by the Nazi German patriots that he had been monitoring. Regardless, the fact is that he was wrongly imprisoned and that he did not leave the prison alive. Controversial a person as he was, he was one of the last people to see my mother, Werner, and Roselene alive and I deeply regret that I never had a chance to speak with him.

24

"BENNY, BENNY"

IN LOOKING BACK ON MY TOUR OF duty in the army of the United States, there were countless reasons for me to feel relieved when it was finally over. For starters, I finally got my identity back. I was no longer being taken for the brother of a famous movie star. I didn't have to concern myself with the consequences of the truth coming out that it had all been an unfortunate extension of a prank, that turned into a rumor, and eventually reached a point of no return. Anyone in Atlanta who knew me would only have laughed at any hint of such a rumor, and just consider it a silly joke. Part of my incentive for volunteering for the draft, came from being a child survivor of the Holocaust and the dreams I had of making everything better by finding my younger brother and sister, Werner and Roselene. In my compartmentalized mind, that was all that was needed to right the wrongs of my world. Even before I was transferred to Europe, I began to realize that the experiences of my youth, even those I can't remember, were such an integral part of me. Virtually every decision I made in life was in someway affected by the fact that I survived the attempt to murder all of Europe's Jews while my dear mother, father, brother, and sister did not.

By the time it became apparent to me that Werner and Roselene were indeed murdered by the Nazis, I was so immersed in my past, that nothing, short of finding them alive, could have made the world right again. That one year, nine months and twelve days of my life in the army, as bizarre as that may have been, somehow gave me much needed guidance and direction on how to and how not to approach the rest of my life.

One of the main reasons I had volunteered for the U.S. Army during the Korean War was to try to maneuver myself, through the army, back over to Germany to find my brother and sister and to also try to put the pieces of the puzzle together with regard to the fate of my parents, as well as my two years and eight months in hiding from December 1938 to August 1941.

Even though my covert plans were successful in getting me back to what once was my homeland, when my tour of duty was over and I returned to my new homeland, the U.S.A., I was very frustrated that I had not achieved enough of my objectives. I did not give up however, and I never allowed my quest to end.

After graduating from Georgia Tech in June 1958, I started focusing on getting my life in order. I was working late hours at a small architectural firm in Macon, Georgia, and came back to Atlanta on weekends to supervise the construction of my brother Jack's house, the first house I had designed out of school. I married Jacqueline Robkin in March 1959 and, after moving back to Atlanta in 1960, we focused on starting a family. In October 1962, while Shoshanah was still an infant, I started my own business. I basically had taken a sabbatical from my search for facts and meaning relating to the Holocaust from the time I graduated Tech until 1964, when I heard that Eternal Life-Hemshech, a newly formed group of survivors of the Holocaust, was planning to build a memorial to the six million victims of the Holocaust. I decided to attend their meeting, which was open to the public and in which they presented the design of an oversized white marble tombstone with the number 6,000,000 on the front and back and white marble candelabra on top. I waited patiently for the meeting to end and approached Dr. Leon Rozen and Mrs. Lola Lansky, who were running the meeting. I explained to them that I was a survivor and an architect, and that I had something to offer for this project. I asked for the opportunity to present a different design for the memorial and, to counter any suspicions regarding my motivation, I said that my efforts would be *pro bono*. They were reluctant since the tombstone design had been approved that evening, but they finally gave in to my insistence that my design would be from the heart. They gave me two weeks to come up with a design and cautioned that it would have be in the same budget as the white tombstone, which was slightly over $6,000.

I laid awake that night and got up around 3:00 A.M. to sketch on paper what I had been thinking of. I got up the next morning, rushed to the office to draw out the design and build a model out of cardboard and clay. I presented the sketches and model within three days, and with help of Lola Lansky's persistent championing of my design concept, the committee agreed to the design with the provision that I would go along with them to major donors to help sell the idea. Abe Besser, a survivor from Poland and a contractor, built the memorial and it was dedicated on the first Sunday after Passover in 1965. Every year since, on the first Sunday after Passover, the Atlanta Jewish Community has held Yom Hashoa, Holocaust Memorial Day services at this memorial.

EARLY IN 1973, MY WIFE AND I started making plans for a trip to the Holy Land which would coincide with an International Conference for Architects and Engineers that was co-sponsored by the Guild for Religious Architecture, an organization in which I was active and from which I had received two national design awards, including one for design of the Memorial to the Six Million. This conference was to take place in Jerusalem, starting on the first of September. As we were discussing our plans with Albert Kaddosh, a friend and native of Paris, he started coming up with reasons that we should visit France on our way back from Israel. I had earlier mentioned the frustrations I had, during my army stint in Europe, in trying to find the places that had been children's homes in which I was sheltered as a young boy. In response to his prodding, I told him that if I thought I could find the family that had taken me in when I first arrived in Paris, in December, 1938, I would definitely go to Paris and visit with them. "However," I added, "I don't remember their names," which was the reason I couldn't look them up as a soldier in Europe.

Albert was not deterred. He really wanted us to visit his homeland. He started pumping me to see if I could think of anyone that would remember the name of this family that took in a total stranger, a six year old boy who was fleeing the Nazis. None of my brothers or sisters remembered, but my sister Flo suggested that I call my cousin Margo, in whose parents house I was supposed to have stayed, since they were the ones who ostensibly made the arrangements with this family. Margo didn't know but she thought her elderly mother might remember. I called my aunt and she apologized for only being able to remember their last name, which was Samuels. I thanked her profusely and excitedly turned to Albert with the information.

"Samuels in France is as common as Smith in the States" he said dejectedly, as if we had reached another dead end. All of a sudden his face lit up. "Wait a minute!" he shouted "the man who runs the kosher hostel for college students in Paris is Nathan Samuels, and he would be just the kind of man to take in a child in time of need."

This was beginning to sound like it had possibilities. I called Loretta, my travel agent, and asked her to set us up in the kosher hostel in Paris for three nights in early September, on our way back from Israel. Albert had told me that the hostel takes in non-student guests when school is not in session. Loretta was able to make reservations for us. I would hopefully find the right Samuels family and would at least try to find the children's home in Montmorency, outside of Paris.

While the conference and our stay in Israel was eventful and exciting, I was anxious to leave so we could go on to Paris and possibly reunite with the Samuels. As soon as we arrived at Orly Airport, I rushed to a telephone to call the hostel to confirm that we were on our way. The man who answered spoke English and curtly told me that there must be a mistake, that he had no knowledge of our reservations and that non-student guests were not allowed. He hung up so abruptly that I had to call back to ask to speak to Mr. Samuels. He curtly told me that Mr. Samuels had just retired and responded in the negative when I asked if he knew how I could get in touch with Mr. Samuels, before abruptly hanging up once more.

Talk about a letdown. I was ready to cry. I tried to gather my thoughts and after a few sad moments, I turned to my wife and suggested that we make the best of our three days in Paris, and try to get over the disappointment. We hailed a taxi and asked him to take us to a hotel that was near a kosher restaurant. The hotel was two doors away from the Sabrina Restaurant where we had a relaxing meal while we tried to plan out the next two days. Loretta had given me the name of a colleague at Mazel Tours, in case we ran into any problems, so we decided to call her in the morning to see if she could arrange for us to go to Montmorency and maybe even to Creuse, or Vichy. I had no feel for the distance of these places from Paris.

I got up bright and early the next morning and called Mazel Tours as soon as they opened. Marlene answered the phone and I explained who we were and gave regards from Loretta. She proceeded to make recommendations for an itinerary for the rest of our stay. I told her where we were staying to get directions to where she was. As it turned out, we were around the corner from Mazel Tours. We walked there in five minutes and as we were finalizing the itinerary, I mentioned my disappointment with the hostel and the missed chance of finding out if Nathan Samuels was the man in whose house I had taken refuge in 1938.

She was moved by the story and incensed at the rudeness of the hostel personnel. Figuring they would not be so rude to a French speaking person, she called them to ask of Mr. Samuels whereabouts. The same jerk answered the phone, told her Mr. Samuels has retired and hung up in her face. She was startled and angry at being treated in this manner. She called again and started to give the jerk a piece of her mind. She demanded that he not hang up on her and that he listen to what she had to say. After she told him who I was and why I wanted to speak to Mr. Samuels, he said "oh, why didn't you say so in the first place, Mr. Samuels is standing right here," and proceeded to hand him the telephone.

Marlene handed me the phone and the voice on the other end said "Benny, is that you?," as if we had not spoken in weeks instead of thirty-five years. I was in total awe, speaking to this man, who only a few minutes before, was another part of my past that I felt sure I would never be in touch with. We made plans to come to his apartment for coffee that evening and meet with his wife and daughter. I was reeling with excitement. Jacquie, my wife, was skeptical. She said that this had to be some kind of scam, because "things just don't happen this way." I tried to assure her she was wrong and finally told her to wait and see. In the meantime, we made plans to go to Montmorency the next day and on a tour of night clubs for our last evening in Paris. Creuse and Vichy were out of the question because of distance and lack of public transportation to these out of the way places.

Evening couldn't come quick enough for me. I knocked on the apartment door and a man about 5'-3" tall, with a small mustache, answered the door. We embraced and I looked at him, "you seemed so much taller then," I said naively. He responded, "you were much shorter then." We laughed, his wife, Helen Samuels, came up and embraced me, and patted my shoulders. "Benny, Benny," is all she said, while tears were running down her cheeks. She could not speak English and I had forgotten French over thirty years before. Nathan's English was far from fluent, but at least we could communicate.

We all sat at the table and Mrs. Samuels served coffee and pastries. My wife was still skeptical. Helen had Nathan ask if I spoke Hebrew. I told them that I did not but that Jacquie did. The door was now open for communication. She asked if we had any pictures of our children. Looking through the photos from my wallet, she stopped at the picture of our second daughter, Adina, pointed and said "Zot Benny," (this is Benny). That was all it took to make Jacquie a believer, and she started conversing with Mrs. Samuels like they were long lost friends.

Moments later there was a knock at the door. It was Fannie, their daughter, who lived several floors up with her family and whom I had last seen when she was three years old. She took one look at me and screamed, "you exist! I thought you were a legend." She proceeded to tell stories that she either remembered or had been told to her, particularly about the time I had fed her goldfish. I had told most of these stories to my family as well, over the years. I asked about the one story that was not told, about the time I found an open can of black paint with a brush, in the toilet room, and I proceeded to paint the room black. I was standing on my toes on the toilet seat, painting as high as I could reach when Mr. Samuels saw what I was doing and had a fit. They didn't even remember the incident, while all this time I had thought that this was the reason that I had been sent away to the children's home in Montmorency. Mr. Samuels set the record straight. I had been sent away because the German army was coming to Paris and it was not safe for Jews to stay there. The Samuels' had also left Paris, shortly thereafter, and went into hiding.

In our conversation, it came out that Nathan and Helen Samuels had plans to move to Israel within six months. That made the chance meeting at this time that much more incredible. Had we not made contact with each other as we did, we probably never would have met each other again. We parted with promises to keep in touch.

The next morning, still on a high from having met the Samuels, we boarded a train to Montmorency, a small city north of Paris. The train ride was less than an hour. At the station we found a taxi driver who, though he spoke no English, seemed to understand what I, with my very limited French, was looking for. The main problem was that my memory was not totally correct. Maybe because all of the other children's homes I had stayed at were chateaus, I had thought the home in Montmorency was Chateau de Montmorency, where the driver dutifully took us. I immediately realized that this was not the place. At least my trip to France was partially successful.

IN THE SUMMER OF 1974, MY WIFE and I went to Upstate New York to visit our three daughters at Camp Hedva, in Liberty. When we arrived at the camp, Michal the youngest, who was eight then, met us at the gate and told me that Mrs. Ebstein, the head nurse, wanted to see me the moment that I arrived. I ran to her thinking that something was wrong with either Shoshanah or Adina. She greeted me and asked which of Rev. Asher Hirsch's brothers I was. After I told her I was Ben, she said, "ah, you're the one who had appendicitis in Marseilles in 1941 and had to stay behind while your two brothers left."

I was duly impressed. "How did you know that?" I asked. She replied that she would tell me anything I wanted after I answered one question for her. "I understand that you left on the second and last escape train," she asked, "exactly when did you leave France?" I thought for a moment and told her it was early August in 1941.

She took a deep breath and blurted out, "you saved my life."

I looked at her as if I thought she had lost her mind. "I don't even know you," I protested, "How can you say I saved your life?"

She said that when I came down with appendicitis, she took my place in the escape transport and that if she would have had to wait for the second escape group she would have turned sixteen, which meant that she would have automatically been turned over to the Nazis by the quisling "Free French Government." I told her that my appendicitis turned out to be a stomach ache that went away shortly after the train left. Another piece of memory verified.

MY OLDEST SISTER, FLORA, SENT ME A book entitled *Out of the Fire* which she inscribed "3/21/76, Ben, Lest you forget whence you came. Flora." The book was written by Ernst Papanek who had been the man hired by OSE to organize and run the children's homes in France for Jewish children orphaned by the Nazis. The book tells how in 1938 an organization called OSE began buying up castles in Southern France to serve as shelters for refugee children, and that the same year they invited Papanek to be the director of these homes. Finally, it was all in writing. All the homes I had been in, the OSE home in Montmorency, Chateau de Magillier in Creuse, Chateau de Morrell in Brut Vernet near Vichy, as well as the four or so other ones, were written about along with selected stories of children that lived there. Some that survived and some that did not. There was even a group picture on the back of the book sleeve that included my brothers Asher and Jack. If only this book had been available in 1954, I might have been able to convince those German travel agents that these places did exist.

On page 235 of *Out of the Fire* a quote from Ernst Koppstein briefly describes his odyssey from Chateau de Magillier to Marseilles, and finally to Lisbon by way of Madrid. Although the name meant nothing to me, he and I were on the same bus from Magillier to Marseilles and he stayed with the first escape group, with my two brothers, from there, all the way to New York. Finally, I found someone who had been in Magillier and I wanted to get in touch with him. Through the publisher, I got in touch with Dr. Papanek's widow and she told me that she was in frequent contact with a few of the OSE children, including Dr. Ernst Koppstein. She gave me his phone number in Baltimore and invited me to visit her in New York where she offered to take me to the New York Public Library that had Dr. Papanek's papers. Ernie was about seven years older than I and did not remember me, but we enjoyed meeting and keeping in touch.

I took my brother Asher with me when I met Mrs. Papanek at the library. I asked her about Chateau de Montmorency and she straightened me out. The OSE home in Montmorency was actually in a villa called Helvetzia, which was a fraction the size of the Chateau. She showed me pictures of it and of correspondence from my parents to the Papaneks. Yet another piece of the puzzle.

The first international gathering of Holocaust survivors was held in Jerusalem in June of 1981. Over ten thousand survivors came from all over the globe to share in this reunion. Many attempts were made to reunite survivors with members of their family whose survival they had no knowledge of. The Hall of Survivors was an incredible scene. It was a large hall broken up into sections of various European countries of origin, each with bulletin boards at which survivors would leave messages regarding who they were looking for and survivors milling around with posters or T-shirts delineating who they were hoping to find. The few survivors who found family members, thirty-six years after the War's end, made a lasting impression on everyone there and those who watched the proceedings on world wide television.

Unfortunately, I had no one to look for. By this time, I was certain about those in my family who had perished and those who survived. I was, however, looking for child survivors who had been in the OSE homes with me. I wrote a note to that effect, listing the OSE homes, and pinned it to the bulletin board in the French section. After two days of checking every few hours for responses, I finally retrieved a note from a lady that had been at Magillier. She asked that I "please call her" at a local phone number. I excitedly called the number. A man answered, speaking fluent English, saying he and his wife had been waiting for my call. His wife spoke no English, but he was an American and offered to translate for us in the hope that I could get her to open up and talk about her experiences. I was as anxious to talk to her as she was to talk to me. I took my daughter Shoshanah, who was living in Jerusalem, to share the experience and to help with the translation.

The lady's story was very sad. She was three or four years old when her parents entrusted her to an OSE home, right before they were arrested. She never saw them again. She had been in Chateau de Magillier until the Nazis, with the help of the Vichy government, shut it down in early 1942. All the children tried to escape, going in different directions on their own, trying to find farmers who would put them up. In response to my question, she said that at least 60% of the children who had been at Magillier and the other OSE homes that were attacked in January 1942 were murdered either by the Nazis or their collaborators.

She survived by hiding out in open fields and eating whatever she could find in farmers' fields. She was turned in by a farmer and sent to a labor camp just weeks before liberation. She had nowhere to go after liberation and was taken in by a very organized group called Shomer Hatzaeer, an actively anti-religious Zionist group that was traveling all over France looking for young survivors to recruit. Although she had come from a religious family, this group indoctrinated her to follow their anti-religious ways and sent her to a Shomer Hatzaeer Kibbutz in Israel. She was miserable and at her first opportunity, she escaped the kibbutz and found her way to Jerusalem, where she eventually came back to her religious roots.

The two things I learned from this encounter was the fate of the OSE homes after my siblings and I had escaped and the possible identity of the group that tried to make me eat ham and tore up my four cornered fringed undergarment when I was a vulnerable seven year old skinny boy in France.

The last night of the reunion, ten thousand people gathered at the Western Wall for the closing ceremonies. Chairs were set up on the plaza outside of the prayer area. Shoshanah and I arrived early in order to get a good seat and I asked her to save my seat while I went to pray Mincha, the afternoon service. I came back twenty minutes later and found Shosh running at me excitedly. While I was gone, she had taken a piece of note pad paper, and using a magic marker, wrote the words "Frankfurt am Main," then proceeded to walk up and down the aisle displaying her little sign.

Within minutes, a lady called her over and said she had been in Frankfurt from 1939 to 1941. Shosh suggested that she might have heard of her grandfather, Dr. Hirsch. She responded that she had lived with a Hirsch family, but that he was a dentist. When my daughter said her grandfather was in fact a dentist and his name was Dr. Hermann Hirsch, the lady almost fainted.

Her name was Claire Heyman and she was anxious to relate her story to me. Her parents lived in a small town outside of Frankfurt. After Kristallnacht, she was no longer allowed to attend public school and her parents were looking for a way to continue her education. My father had returned from Buchenwald in early 1939 and Claire's father contacted him for help with his daughter's education. Claire was taken into our house, to board, so she could go to the Jewish Day School in Frankfurt. She slept in the room with Werner and Roselene for about two years, until she was arrested by the Nazis and sent to work in a munitions factory in Berlin. She said my father came to visit her in Berlin, as late as 1941, so now I know that his final incarceration in Sachsenhausen and Auschwitz was for about a year. His death is recorded as being November 5, 1942, in Auschwitz. She had wonderful things to say about my parents and my little brother and sister. She told me that she was not the only child that my parents looked after, or helped out, and that my father ran a kosher soup kitchen for the elderly from the house next door, where my grandparents used to live. It was a wonderful chance meeting for both of us. She got to meet the son of the family who had sheltered her and cared for her for two years and I got to hear about my parents and younger siblings during those two years, of which I had no knowledge. The next year—1982—she came to Atlanta for my son Raphael's Bar Mitzvah and got to meet the rest of my family, including my surviving brothers and sisters.

IN JUNE OF 1994, I ATTENDED A convention in Nashville, Tennessee, sponsored by the Association of Holocaust Organizations. The first evening we were presented a program done by Ann Weiss, called *Eyes from the Ashes*. She started the program by telling us about the guided tour of Auschwitz that she had been on some eight years earlier. As the group passed a locked door, she asked the guide what was behind the door. He replied that it was just a storage room, and she then requested to see what was stored in the storage room. The guide unlocked the door, and in the room was one table with a crude photograph album containing about 2,500 photographs. These photos had been taken from the clothes of Jews after they were ordered to undress, as they got out of the train cattle cars just before they were taken to the "showers," (gas chambers). This particular batch of pictures was confiscated over a period of about one-week in the fall of 1943 and, for some reason, were the only ones not burned.

Being a photographer, Ms. Weiss asked for permission to photograph them and permission was granted. She later selected 200 representative photos from the group to make a short video of stills and this was the video that she was showing us that evening in Nashville.

The lights went out and she narrated, in her soft voice, as each image came to the big screen. About half way through her presentation an image of a young boy and girl playing on a tree was flashed on the screen, and I let out a gasp. Even though I was startled and anxious, I waited until the lights went back on before I said anything. I asked if it was possible to see the actual photos, because I was sure I had recognized someone. The whole room began to buzz with side conversations. Ann Weiss suggested that I stay around after the program to look into this further.

After everyone left, Ms. Weiss started to rerun the video for me. Over a hundred images flashed on the screen and nothing looked familiar. I was beginning to think that I had been dreaming when the image flashed and I yelled for her to put it on pause. I stared at the image and started to cry convulsively. I tried to compose myself and explain that I was as positive as I could be, under the circumstances, that this was a snapshot of my brother Werner and sister Roselene. The setting was in woods and I was not familiar with the surroundings. It appeared to be autumn time and they looked like they were about five and four years old respectively. I took out a picture that was taken when they were 2 1/2 and 1 1/2 years old, that was given to me by my cousin Arno a couple of years before, and used it for comparison. Then I took out a photo of my oldest grandson, Nachaliel, who appeared to be a clone of the older child on the screen.

A few months later I got permission to review the entire collection of 2,500 photos at the Wiesenthal Center library in Los Angeles. I had a very difficult time reviewing the photos and the library even allowed me to stay after closing hours, but I found no additional photos that related to my family. As I sat in the plane flying back to Atlanta, I felt like I had been on an emotional roller coaster, but this was something I had to do.

January 31st, 1995 was a happy day for my wife and me. We had gone to New York for the wedding of our youngest child, our son Raphael. Among the invited guests was Claire Heyman, the boarder my mother and father had taken into their house, in 1939, for two years. Premeditatedly, during a break in the festivities, I pulled Claire aside and asked if she would like to look at a photo that I had been carrying around in the breast pocket of my coat. It was a copy of the photo Ann Weiss had sent me after the convention in Nashville. She took a discerning look at the photo and said that there was no doubt in her mind that this is a picture of Werner and Roselene.

IN NOVEMBER, 1995, I WAS INVITED TO Germany by the Federal Republic, as part of an informational tour for key personnel in Holocaust museums. At that time, I was in the process of designing the Holocaust museum portion of the William Breman Jewish Heritage Museum of the Atlanta Jewish Federation, and thereby invited to go on the tour. Frankfurt am Main was not on the itinerary except for arrival from and departure back to the United States. I extended for a few days so that I could be in Frankfurt for the 9th of November commemoration of Kristallnacht, spend a Shabbat in Frankfurt and to go to Poland to visit Auschwitz/ Birkenau.

On Friday, November 10th, after having attended the Kristallnacht commemorative services the night before, at the West End Synagogue, and at Paulskirche, a civic building that had been a cathedral, and after realizing that this was not a "home" to come back to, I made plans to visit memorable sites from my youth. I took a cab to the site of the Friedberger Anlage Synagogue to see the bunker that was built there, after the ruins of the synagogue had been totally dismantled, and the memorial that had been put up on the remaining part of the site. Even though this was not a part of the government sponsored informational tour— which was officially over—they provided me with an English speaking guide for my stay in Frankfurt.

I tried to find the exact spot at the curb of the Anlage (park) across the street, at which I stood with my twelve year old cousin Arno Horenczyk, fifty-seven years before while the Synagogue was being destroyed. It really didn't matter whether or not I was standing in the same spot. I shut my eyes and tried to recreate the scene in my mind. It didn't work. It was not only a different time, it felt like a different place.

We got back into the cab and traveled to Grünestrasse, which actually was in walking distance from the Synagogue site. I did not recognize the street. It looked so different from the bombed out street I remembered seeing in 1955. Both sides of the street had been rebuilt, apparently many years before, from the appearance of the buildings. I got out of the car and started looking for number 30. The houses were all attached, as they had been before the war, and they were all the same height, three stories from exterior appearance. The guide pointed to one of the houses across the street from where we had parked, where a woman was working in the front garden. It was number 30.

He approached the lady and asked her if she lived there. She told him that she had recently bought the house from her mother, for an investment, and that the house was currently empty while undergoing renovations to meet the changes in zoning that had been enacted by the city. The house, which had been divided into six apartment units, was now in the process of being changed to four units, by city mandate.

He turned to me to translate what the lady had told him and proceeded to introduce me and explain my connection to her house. She asked if I spoke German. When I answered in the negative, she offered that she spoke English. She was a spry lady of about fifty. This was her day off, so she decided to work on the landscaping of her new investment. I asked if I could see any part of the inside of the house and particularly the back yard. I explained that I wanted to see the window that Sarah and Jack had jumped out of when they tried to teach me how to swim in the playroom, when I was three. I was still a toddler at the time. I couldn't remember that much about the house, but she let me see any part that was not a construction area. We spoke for about thirty minutes. I shared some memories of the house and later thanked her for showing me around and for being so gracious.

For some reason I felt good about the encounter. As I was getting back into the car, the guide looked at me and said, "I thought you said you couldn't speak German."

"Of course I can't," I responded, somewhat incredulous that he was even making such a statement. "What are you talking about?"

"Don't you realize that you have just been speaking fluent German to that lady for the last half hour?" He saw that I didn't believe him and turned to the cab driver who shook his head in agreement.

We waved to the nice lady as we drove off, although I was in a daze. Were they pulling my leg? They convinced me they were not. I had to wonder what else was hidden in that spongy mass in my head.

I then tried to find out why the *Gedenkbuch* (Memorial Book, an official publication of the Federal Republic of Germany)—which is a list of all the Jewish German citizens that were deported to the death camps by Nazi Germany—stated that our father was killed in Auschwitz on the same date that International Red Cross had reported his demise in Oranienburg, November 5, 1942. I contacted the archives at Sachsenhausen, the concentration camp in Oranienburg outside of Berlin, and found out that Himmler had sent a memo in October, 1942 to rid Sachsenhausen of all Jews. As a result, all Jews, except for a skeleton crew to finalize the records, were deported to Auschwitz. They had a list of the small crew that remained and my fathers name was not among them. Though the archives in Auschwitz was not able to verify that my father died there, they readily admitted that they only have records of a fraction of those who perished there. I have to assume that, in this case, the *Gedenkbuch* is correct.

IN DECEMBER 1995, I HAD THE OPPORTUNITY to read through my files, and those of my siblings, from the Jewish Children's Service, that previously had been unavailable to me, at least in their entirety. According to these files, my brothers Asher and Jack had been sent to Chicago to one of the three temporary shelters for the further distribution of children, a short time after their arrival in New York in June 1941. Correspondence from these files refers to an address book that Asher had in his possession that contained names and addresses of relatives in the United States.

There was an Uncle Eli, a brother to our mother who, when released from a concentration camp in 1938, found his way to

San Francisco. When contacted, he declined to take my brothers in, stating that he knew that the boys were religious and that they should be in a religious environment. He also mentioned that he needed to get his own life in order, having recently arrived as an immigrant himself.

Then there was our mother's first cousin, Rabbi Selig Auerbach, who lived in Rome, Georgia, about eighty miles north of Atlanta. According to correspondence between Mrs. Lotte Marcuse, director of placements for the German-Jewish Children's Aid, Inc., in New York City, and Mrs. Armand Wyle, director of the Children's Service Bureau in Atlanta, dated between July 10 and July 17, 1941, Mrs. Wyle was asked to communicate with Rabbi Auerbach to see if he could take the two boys. The correspondence reveals that Rabbi Auerbach, to his regret, was unable to take the boys into his small home, in which he lived with his wife and baby, or to offer financial support on his meager compensation as a congregational Rabbi. He was, however, willing to give moral support and occasionally visit them, if homes could be found in Atlanta. In the letter of July 17th, Mrs. Wyle said she was sure that the committee would agree to accept responsibility for the two Hirsch boys.

In August 1941, further correspondence from Mrs. Marcuse indicates that the German-Jewish Children's Aid, Inc. had just become aware that three more Hirsch children, using the same escape route, had left Lisbon, Portugal on the same boat, and were heading for the United States. She wrote that while she realized that it might have been too much to ask that the Atlanta Jewish community take responsibility for the three additional Hirsch children, it would be optimum for the five children to at least live in the same city. Apparently the Atlanta community agreed to take responsibility for us too. It is no wonder that I have a very warm feeling toward the Atlanta Jewish community, and have tried, in my own limited way, to pay back the community for their kindness to my family.

I AM NOT THE ONLY PARENTLESS BOY nor the only foreign boy who grew up in Atlanta. Like most parentless boys, I learned to adapt to my new environment. With all the social, religious and physical changes going on in my life, long before I was made aware that I was an orphan, I secretly awaited the opportunity to be a part of the armed forces that would ultimately defeat Hitler's Germany.

The opportunity came, but it was after the fact. So instead of fighting Nazis, I ended up fighting the system of a peacetime army that was involved in fighting on the Korean front and a cold war in Europe. In spite of my bizarre experiences in the army of the United States, I feel sure that if I had been given the opportunity to contribute to a combat situation in defense of the United States and its ideals, that I would not have hesitated to give my all.

Reflecting back on my time in the armed services, it was an experience that I would not exchange for anything in the world. At the same time, I would never volunteer to go through it again. I feel like I learned so much about people and the ways people interact. Many decisions I make today are based on experiences I had in that period of time. More importantly, I learned a great deal about myself. I learned how important my Judaism is to me and what an important role it has played and continues to play in every aspect of my life. I think back at the cadre in Camp Gordon, who forced me to go to Chapel on Friday night and assured me there would be no repercussions from my barracks mates. I can't forget those religious soldiers in Ft. Lewis, Washington, whose interest in and questioning about Judaism made me realize that I had been turning my back on the religion and way of life for which many members of my family were murdered. I remember Chaplain Goodblatt, who coaxed me into leading the Friday night services at the Palace of Justice and tried to keep me on the straight and narrow when my hormones were flowing. All of these are a part of me.

LIKE EVERYONE ELSE, I AM THE PRODUCT of the sum total of my experiences. I have often wondered to what extent my life would have been different if the world of my family had not been destroyed? No one can answer that question. Much of what I am today was shaped by the events in the first nine years of my life in Europe, along with growing up in America in the 1940s and 1950s.

The lessons I learned my first twenty-one years, both in Europe and in America, were of survival. I came to this country as a forty-three pound, nine-year-old foreigner and a Jew, without any parental support. These were the three most powerful and formative influences on my life in America, where I found that my survival skills would be put to the test more often than in the previous nine years in Europe. But, that is another story for another time, perhaps even another book.

I continue to live with the realization that I am not the master of my destiny. I try, however, to make the best of the cards that are dealt to me and I thank God for having the opportunity to play them my way.